MW00359049

From Miracle to Mirage

From Miracle to Mirage

The Making and Unmaking of the Korean Middle Class, 1960–2015

Myungji Yang

Cornell University Press
Ithaca and London

Cornell University Press gratefully acknowledges support from the First
Book Subvention Program of the Association of Asian Studies, which
aided in the publication of this book.

First published 2018 by Cornell University Press

Printed in the United States of America

Library of Congress Cataloging-in-Publication Data

Names: Yang, Myungji, 1978– author.
Title: From miracle to mirage : the making and unmaking of the Korean
    middle class, 1960–2015 / Myungji Yang.
Description: Ithaca : Cornell University Press, 2018. | Includes bibliographical
    references and index.
Identifiers: LCCN 2017028420 (print) | LCCN 2017029565 (ebook) |
    ISBN 9781501710742 (pdf) | ISBN 9781501710759 (epub/mobi) |
    ISBN 9781501710735 (cloth : alk. paper)
Subjects: LCSH: Middle class—Korea (South) | Social status—
    Korea (South) | Korea (South)—Social conditions.
Classification: LCC HT690.K8 (ebook) | LCC HT690.K8 Y36 2018 (print) |
    DDC 305.5095195—dc23
LC record available at https://lccn.loc.gov/2017028420

Cornell University Press strives to use environmentally responsible suppliers
and materials to the fullest extent possible in the publishing of its books.
Such materials include vegetable-based, low-VOC inks and acid-free papers
that are recycled, totally chlorine-free, or partly composed of nonwood fibers.
For further information, visit our website at www.cornellpress.cornell.edu.

To my parents

CONTENTS

Illustrations

Tables

Figures

Map

ACKNOWLEDGMENTS

It feels unreal to finally finish a book and to write the acknowledgments. While I spent numerous solitary hours reading through archival materials at libraries and writing in front of the computer screen, this book would have not been completed without much guidance, support, and advice from my mentors, colleagues, and friends. During this process, I have accumulated numerous debts to many people.

This book started at Brown University, an extraordinary intellectual community where I learned comparative thinking, careful research design, and respect for theory and practice. First of all, I am deeply indebted to my mentor Patrick Heller, whose enthusiasm for democracy and social justice, intellectual rigor, and critical thinking greatly influenced my intellectual growth. I could not ask for a more patient, generous, and supportive advisor. He read every chapter of the original draft with care and interest and always encouraged me to draw a big picture. I am also grateful to other mentors who helped to sharpen my ideas and gave unfailing support over time: Jose Itzigsohn, Melani Cammett, Jim Mahoney, John Logan, and Richard

Snyder. I have been fortunate to have amazing peers and friends who read my work, discussed it over coffee, and shared insights, as well as provided moral support, including Sinem Adar, Erin Beck, Julia Drew, Chris Gibson, Esther Hernandez-Medina, Adriana Lopez, Shruti Mamjudar, Holly Reed, Gabriela Sanchez-Soto, and Laura Senier. Special thanks to Jen Costanza, Sukriti Issar, and Celso Villegas, who have provided both intellectual and moral support over the years when needed.

A new intellectual home, the University of Hawaiʻi, Mānoa, has been a great place to be an Asianist/Koreanist. I am extremely lucky to have great colleagues and friends in this intellectual community. I would like to thank Hoku Aikau, Petrice Flowers, Vernadette Gonzalez, Hagen Koo, Nevi Soguk, Manfred Steger, and Sankaran Krishna, who read parts of my manuscript and provided constructive feedback. I am also grateful to Manfred Henningsen and Ehito Kimura for their encouragement and generosity. A writing group for the first two years at UH was a great source of inspiration, both in the early stages of the manuscript and afterward. I thank Jennifer Darrah, Joyce Mariano, and Colin Moore for their timely comments and comradeship.

I had the luxury of spending a year working on my manuscript at the Korean Studies Institute, University of Southern California, in 2015–16. Thanks to a generous postdoctoral fellowship through the Academy of Korean Studies, I could commit myself to revising my manuscript without the burden of teaching and administrative work. I would like to express my sincere gratitude to David Kang for his intellectual and professional guidance. KSI also hosted a book workshop for me, which gave me the opportunity to clarify my argument and to refine the entire manuscript. I owe a great deal to Stephan Haggard and Laura Nelson, who served as reviewers at the workshop, carefully read the entire manuscript, and gave valuable suggestions. Daisy Kim and Hannah Lim, two other postdoctoral fellows at KSI, were great company, and not only provided constructive feedback on the manuscript but also made a year in LA less lonely. Our writing retreat to Palm Springs was memorable. I also thank Linda Kim, Gloria Koo, and Sarah Shear, who provided institutional support and made the Ahn House more enjoyable.

Numerous individuals helped me to make this book better along the way. For thoughtful comments and critical insights, I thank the late Nancy Abelmann, Nicole Constable, Nicholas Harkness, Junhee Kwon, Yoonkyung

Lee, Eileen Otis, Saeyoung Park, Jaeyoun Won, and Sharon Yoon. Two anonymous reviewers for Cornell University Press gave incredibly detailed and sharp comments. Juyoung Lee, Haewon Moon, and Seungwoo Chin helped me present professional-looking maps and gave important advice on reading quantitative data. Jiyeon Lee and Miyoung Lee were always reliable friends whom I could ask to scan and send primary sources that I needed urgently. Jaehoon Bae also helped compile the references. I am deeply grateful for their time and critical input. I am also indebted to my mentor back in Korea, Dongno Kim, who taught me the importance of time and history in the social sciences and shaped my perspectives on Korean society.

This book would not have been possible without generous institutional support from the UH Center for Korean Studies, the UH College of Social Sciences, the Core University Program for Korean Studies through the Academy of Korean Studies at both UH and USC, Brown University, and the Watson Institute for Public and International Affairs for funding for research trips and editorial assistance. My appreciation also goes to the Institute for Social Development at Yonsei University, which allowed me to affiliate with it and to use its library resources. I also benefited greatly from participating in workshops and conferences, which helped to crystallize key ideas in the book. I would especially like to thank the participants in the 2009 SSRC Korean Studies Dissertation Workshop, the 2014 SSRC Korean Studies Junior Faculty Workshop, and a 2016 workshop on the middle classes at the Hebrew University of Jerusalem. An early version of chapter 1 appeared in *Sociological Inquiry*'s August 2012 issue under the title "The Making of the Urban Middle Class in South Korea (1961–1979): Nation-Building, Discipline, and the Birth of the Ideal National Subjects." The book benefited from the input of the journal's anonymous reviewers.

Roger Haydon at Cornell University Press has patiently nurtured this project with great faith in my work. I could not ask for a better editor to work with; his prompt responses and strong support made the process of completing the book much smoother. Gary Ashwill and Colin Ong-Dean, two fabulous professional editors, read multiple drafts of the manuscript and made the best out of my writing.

Thanks to incredible groups of friends in both Korea and the United States, the long writing process was less burdensome. The conversations over coffee, dinners, and drinks were always lively, delightful, and encouraging. Deep gratitude goes to the Aikaus (my three angels, Sanoe, Imai, and Tita),

Eunjin Cho, Minhyo Cho, Gru Han, Manfred Henningsen, Yangsook Jeon, Hyosun Kim, Jiyeon Lee, Miyoung Lee, Colin Moore, Sunmi Park, Hyera Shin, and Eunhye Yoo. Thank you for your friendship and your faith in me. Special thanks to Eunhye Yoo for helping me recruit interviewees during my fieldwork. I would also like to extend my gratitude to Korean hiking group members in Hawai'i, Kyungim Baik, Taeung Baik, KyungHee Cheon, Hojong Do, Seunghye Hong, Jiyoung Kim, Yangsun Kim, Sang-hyop Lee, and Young-A Park.

This book would not have been completed without the openness and generosity of many individuals who shared their personal stories with a stranger. Although I cannot name all of them because they appear in the book under pseudonyms, their contributions are enormous. I deeply appreciate their time and insights.

Lastly, my family helped me get through this arduous process. To my only and younger sister Hyunjung, thank you for your unwavering faith and confidence in me. This book was also inspired by my parents, who experienced struggles similar to those of the downwardly mobile middle class who are the protagonists of this book. As middle-class Koreans, they made sacrifices for their children's success, endured difficult times with hope and optimism, and taught us how to maintain our integrity. I dedicate this book to my parents as a small tribute to their hopes and dreams.

Notes on Romanization and Translation

All Korean words have been romanized according to the McCune-Reischauer system; exceptions are proper nouns, such as Korean people's names and geographical names such as Gangnam. For Korean names, I generally put the given name first. The exceptions are famous political figures such as Park Chung Hee and Kim Dae Jung. But I use Syngman Rhee instead of Rhee Syngman because the former is more familiar in English and much of the West. All translations from Korean to English are mine.

From Miracle to Mirage

Introduction

The State, Development, and the (Un)Making of the Middle Class

After working for two decades as a midlevel manager for a big corporation, Mr. Kim was suddenly forced to retire in 2008. In his early fifties and casting about for options, he found himself unexpectedly embarking on a new career: he opened a small fried chicken restaurant in his neighborhood. Investing all his money, including his retirement and savings, and using his home as collateral for loans, he hoped that this small business would help him to retire comfortably. Contrary to his expectations, he now finds he has to scramble just to make ends meet. A sudden proliferation of fried chicken restaurants near his own significantly lowered the sales of his restaurant. Even though he and his wife work sixteen hours a day and take only one day off a month, after paying the rent and other bills they make barely two thousand dollars a month. Extremely concerned and stressed about their decreasing income, he has thought about closing the restaurant a number of times, but he does not have any alternatives. Twenty years ago, when he first got the corporate job that seemed to promise him everything, he never imagined he would face such a challenge at this point in his life. Instead of looking forward to a secure retirement, he now worries about his increasing debts.

Mr. Kim's story is not an uncommon one these days in South Korea (hereafter Korea, unless specified). After the economic crisis of the late 1990s, opening a small business such as a restaurant, convenience store, or coffee shop became a popular solution for baby boomers in their fifties or sixties who had been forced to retire from big corporations. Yet due to extreme competition and low sales, more than half of these small businesses fail within three years, and 70 percent go out of business within five (KB Research Institute 2012). Small business owners in Korea are almost forced to stake everything they have in starting a business, a bet that can lead to dangerous outcomes for themselves and others.

Currently, many Korean citizens are experiencing downward mobility, and the gap between haves and have-nots is growing. Since the economic crisis in 1997, the socioeconomic landscape in Korea has been completely overturned; the virtual lifetime employment and ever-increasing wages, based on seniority, that had supported stable middle-class lifestyles for many years are no longer widely available. Instead, many corporate employees are forced to retire in their forties or fifties, while younger generations have a hard time finding decent jobs and are forced to make do with irregular employment, low pay, and no benefits. Because Korea has an almost nonexistent social safety net and a severely constricted job market, young Koreans have limited chances for upward social mobility, while middle-aged citizens like Mr. Kim are thrust into working for themselves after forced early retirement. Membership in the middle class, a symbol of social and economic possibility and confidence in the 1970s and 1980s, is now a challenging status to maintain and is increasingly characterized by heightened anxiety and frustration. Many Koreans perceive their standard of living as having deteriorated, and belief in the chances of upward mobility is declining. Indeed, fewer and fewer identify themselves as members of the middle class (Korean National Statistics Office 2011), and those who believe that they belong to the middle class are anxious about their future financial situation. "Class polarization" (*yanggŭk'wa*) and "the collapse of the middle class" (*chungsanch'ŭng mollak*) have become media buzzwords in Korea. The decline of the middle class as a major social force has emerged as a serious concern among news media, politicians, and academics.

Economic indicators illustrate the growth of the squeezed middle class and rising social inequality. Official statistics show that the size of the Korean middle class as an income-based group (defined as those earning 50–150 percent of the median income) has declined by almost 10 percent, from 75.4 percent of the population in 1990 to 67.5 percent in 2010 (Korean National Statistics Office 2011).[1] As the size of the middle class wanes, the overall picture of inequality becomes worse: the relative income of the middle class has declined, and the income disparity between the upper and middle classes has increased since the late 1990s (J. Lee 2015). At the same time, social inequality indices such as the Gini coefficient, relative income poverty statistics, and measurements of the top 10 percent versus the bottom 10 percent have all shown inequality significantly increasing over time.[2] Yet changes in the economic landscape are not limited to statistics; the deteriorating economic conditions have translated into negative and pessimistic views and belief systems among ordinary citizens. For example, in 2009, 90.2 percent of surveyed Koreans agreed that income disparities in Korea are substantial (T. Lee 2015, 96). Furthermore, the majority of citizens are pessimistic about the prospect of upward mobility. More than 80 percent of people between the ages of twenty and fifty believe that it will be impossible to achieve upward mobility no matter how hard they try. And Koreans are more pessimistic about the future of their children's generation than citizens of China or Southeast Asian countries: 68 percent of Koreans believe that their children will have more difficulty becoming successful than they did, whereas only 38 percent of Chinese agree with the same statement ("An toel kŏya ama, ibŏn saengae nŭn" 2015, 46–47).

Korean society is certainly not alone in witnessing a shrinking of the middle class and increasing social inequality. This phenomenon has become more common and widespread on a global scale. The global economic crisis has worsened ordinary citizens' standards of living by accelerating unemployment, poverty, and social inequality. The model of middle-class society and social inclusion in North America and Europe during the post–World War II period is in crisis. The US media have told us a story of the disappearing middle class: with the 2008 financial crisis, many middle-class families lost their jobs and homes, and increasing costs for housing, medical care, and college tuition have made the lives of many more challenging. Politicians have wooed their constituencies with a promise of the recovery of the middle class, yet it seems that for many the comfortable middle-class lifestyle is long gone, due in part to a shortage of good job opportunities. Despite the economic recovery after the crisis, US society is experiencing ever-increasing income disparity between the rich and the rest of the population. European countries are facing similar challenges to varying degrees across countries. While the European welfare state model has been believed to be stronger than the US model, income inequality in Europe has been rising, and stagnant wages and curtailed welfare provision threaten the well-being of the middle class. The growing popularity of the radical right and their winning of elections in Europe, including but not limited to France, Hungary, and Austria, while complicated, can be seen as a social backlash against immigrants and supporters of the European Union by those who have experienced economic deterioration and felt deprived of opportunities. Korea's neighbor Japan is not much better off. After the economic bubble burst in the early 1990s, Japanese society saw the decline of the middle class and a similar pattern of socioeconomic polarization. As Japanese corporations began to downsize and restructure their businesses in response to economic recession, lifetime employment was no longer the norm, and the flexible labor regime created low-paid, part-time workforce. Beginning in the 1990s, many Japanese youth entering employment as contract or temporary workers have subsequently been labeled "the lost generation"—a generation that is trapped in a bad economy and suffers from economic hardship and a sense of insecurity. Prevailing economic precarity and lack of social protection caused new social problems such as declining marriage, low birthrates, and increasing poverty and crime. In the midst of economic recession, the struggles of ordinary citizens to make ends meet are a familiar story.

It is common everywhere that many middle-class families experience a stagnant standard of living, while their children have a hard time maintaining the lifestyle and social status their parents had. The decline or collapse of the middle class in developed countries has often been explained by globalization and neoliberal economic restructuring (Frank 2007; Newman [1988] 1999; Sullivan, Warren, and Westbrook 2000; Zunz, Schoppa, and Hiwatari 2002). The movement of white-collar jobs from developed countries to places like China and India, corporate restructuring, retrenchment of welfare benefits, and rising costs of living all combine to increase the economic burdens on the shoulders of middle-class citizens and to increase their suffering. While it is important to understand how these changes after the economic crisis have led to the economic deterioration of the middle class in Korea, this perspective misses how particular domestic factors, such as housing and education, have affected the lived experience and collective identity of the middle class.

The waning and suffering of the Korean middle class are more striking and dramatic because of the prevalence of images depicting its dazzling economic success and achievements. As one of the Four Asian Tigers, Korea has been taken as the most exemplary case for other developing countries, having transformed itself from a poor, war-shattered nation into one of the world's most successful economies within a mere generation. Explosive growth for three consecutive decades lifted the majority of the population out of absolute poverty, and it was not uncommon in the 1970s and 1980s to see the children of poor peasants attain comfortable middle-class lifestyles. In 1987 the country's authoritarian regime was overthrown by popular protests, and Korea became a democracy. Now a member of the Organization for Economic Cooperation and Development (OECD), Korea has joined the ranks of high-income, developed nations, as Korean corporations such as Samsung and Hyundai produce some of the best-selling cell phones and cars in the global economy. In addition, the entertainment industry in Korea, with the rise of the Korean Wave (*hallyu*), now makes huge profits by exporting K-pop (Korean popular music), soap operas, and movies to neighboring China and Southeast Asia and throughout the world. As of 2012, K-pop was a US$235 million industry (*Korea Times* 11/4/2013). In 1960, GDP per capita was US$156 (current US dollars), whereas it was US$27,222 in 2015.[3] Korea's GDP per capita in 1960 was similar to that of Ghana or the Congo and much below that of the Philippines, but five decades later Korea had become the thirteenth largest economy in the world. For many scholars and commentators, Korea has seemed to be an ideal case of achieving both economic development and democracy.

This perception of Korea's miraculous transformation has shaped academic discourse on the nation's development. Many scholars have focused on explaining how Korea achieved this unprecedented economic development, overcoming adverse conditions such as its lack of natural resources and its unstable geopolitical situation. They argue that exceptionally successful, large-scale economic transformations in Korea (and also in East Asia) were made possible by the well-organized, efficient developmental state with a capable bureaucracy and effective policy implementation (Amsden 1989; Chibber 2003; Evans 1995; Kohli 2004; Woo-Cumings 1999). Korea's high economic growth and material prosperity, in turn, enabled the growth of the Korean middle class as a social backbone. Comprising massive armies of white-collar workers, corporate managers, and engineers in large conglomerates, the Korean middle class was provided with high wages, job security, and consumer lifestyles. By the late 1980s, the Korean middle class had become the dominant social force and played a crucial role in the democratic transition (Koo 1991; Villegas and Yang 2013). Many members of the Korean middle class were born to unprivileged backgrounds, but hard work and education enabled them to get decent jobs and to climb the economic ladder. The tale of the Korean middle class and its upward mobility is paralleled by the tale of the Korean nation as a whole—a change from a backward, agricultural, completely undeveloped country smothered by Japanese colonialism and torn by the Korean War to a strong player in the global economy. This inspiring story of the "miracle on the Han River" told by most scholars becomes quite puzzling, however, when one hears about the daily struggles that the current Korean middle class faces. This book tackles the puzzle of why the celebrated middle class of developed Korea has entered a period of decline. Why, in this age of prosperity, is Korean society experiencing a large-scale decline of the middle class? Why is household debt growing rapidly, and why are ordinary middle-class citizens losing their grip on the comfortable lifestyle they thought they had earned? What are the political economic dynamics that have exacerbated the lives of the middle class? Why does it *feel* more difficult to achieve and sustain a middle-class lifestyle now? And what are the broader social and political implications of the shrinking of the middle class?

The goal of this book is to explain why the Korean middle class is where it is now: first, by describing historical processes that triggered the current conditions faced by the Korean middle class; second, by offering a new account of the practices that constituted urban middle-class life; and third, by demonstrating how the notion of the middle class has changed over time. Throughout this book, I examine the origin, process, and outcome of middle-class formation along with Korean capitalist development—from ideological construct to mainstream actuality, and from the rise of comfortable lifestyles to a decline into a precarious existence. I look at the rapid, large-scale social transformations resulting in the making and unmaking of the middle class that took place in Korea within just a couple of generations, from the 1960s to the end of the 1990s and beyond. By demonstrating *who* has become the middle class and *how*, and how the rules of the game have changed over the past five decades, I seek to explain why the seemingly successful and progressive state project of building a middle-class society resulted in such an unexpected and unintended outcome. This book argues that the current conditions that the Korean middle class faces—its overall economic deterioration and its heightened level of status anxiety—can be understood only by looking at the historical trajectory of the middle class: the particular ways in which the Korean middle class was formed, both *speculative and exclusive*, have shaped the condition of the middle class and the pattern of social inequality in the long run.

Many of the first generation of the Korean middle class acquired their wealth by purchasing homes and gaining hefty benefits from skyrocketing real estate prices. In the midst of an overheated property market, those who invested in real estate were able to climb the social class ladder, leaving others behind. The success of profit making and upward mobility through real estate investment had a lot to do with simple luck. Some entrepreneurial people knew where to invest, which would bring them substantial income, but many families bought homes in booming areas by pure chance. Those who *happened* to own real estate in booming areas could get further ahead of others with similar household incomes and occupations who bought property somewhere else—sometimes acquiring three or four times more wealth due to differential increases in real estate prices.

This book also views the process of middle-class formation as exclusive in two different ways. First, only certain groups of people could be the beneficiaries of state policies, and in particular the housing system. In a tight housing market, income-eligible people, mostly white-collar families, could apply for new, affordable apartment units in newly developing areas. Second, upwardly mobile social groups tried to nurture their own distinctive communities and culture and to prevent outsiders from gaining access to their networks and rationed benefits. By forming closed social networks and sharing information exclusively among themselves about schooling or investment opportunities, the upwardly mobile could perpetuate their privilege.

The speculative and exclusive process of middle-class formation contradicts a widely accepted depiction of the middle class as based on open membership and class mobility through merit and hard work during periods of high economic growth. This exclusionary process of selecting economic winners produced a corresponding sense of unfairness and frustration among those who did not benefit from the system—a feeling that the actual rules of the game were unfair and defective. By looking at the process by which economic winners were selected and, in turn, perpetuated their privilege over the long term, this book offers a story of the reality behind the myth of middle-class formation and the economic miracle in Korea and reveals the contradictory and contested nature of Korean development.

Why the Korean Middle Class?

As far back as Aristotle, scholars have paid attention to the critical role of the middle class in social and political changes. The middle class has been considered variously as a carrier of economic and political modernization (Huntington 1968; Lipset 1959) or as a coalitional actor for political trans-formations (Luebbert 1991; Rueschemeyer, Stephens, and Stephens 1992). As countries industrialize and urbanize, the middle class emerges, expands, and becomes the social and cultural mainstream. For the government and politicians, the growth of the middle class is the basis of social and political stability, mitigating class tensions and promoting social cohesion. The expansion of the middle class exemplifies the material improvement of overall living standards for ordinary citizens. Thus, the growth and welfare of the middle class are linked to political legitimacy in important ways. For the business and corporate sectors, the rise of the middle class represents enhanced spending power and consumerism. Appealing to the middle class determines the success of their businesses. For these reasons, the middle class has often been the central topic in market research and political discussions in the public sphere as well as in scholarly debates.

For example, addressing the welfare of the American middle class has become a concern of US politicians and policymakers, and the agenda of rebuilding the middle class has been critical to winning elections. For emerging economies like those of China and India, creating a robust middle class is essential to attracting foreign direct investment and to achieving successful economic reforms by strengthening national development. In most societies, building the middle class has been an important political project: the social contract that promises the aspirational middle-class lifestyle as an outcome of hard work and frugal living becomes a source of political legitimacy, and the presence of the middle class in turn reinforces national identity and social unity (Fernandes 2006; Yang 2012). While the specific characteristics of a middle-class lifestyle might differ across time and place—from owning a home in the suburbs, to owning a car, to sending one's children to college, to having enough retirement savings in the bank—the term "middle class" has long evoked material comfort and optimism. However, when this "norm" or "social contract" shared by ordinary citizens is challenged or no longer applies, it can lead to frustration or social conflict. As the living conditions of the middle class strongly affect the overall social and economic conditions of a particular society, the middle class shapes contemporary political dynamics that influence political identity and public opinions.

Despite the importance of the middle class in the general literature, it has received relatively little attention in scholarship on Korea. Mainstream development scholars focus on state elites or state-business relations, whereas critical scholarship examines socially excluded or marginalized groups. Scholars of "developmental states" focus on explaining how rapid economic development was possible in East Asia. In this field, scholars provide state-centered, elitist explanations, emphasizing in particular how state bureaucrats promoted industrial transformations by collaborating with capitalists—mainly, big businesses, or chaebol (*chaebŏl*)[4] in the Korean context (for example, Amsden 1989; Chibber 2003; Evans 1995; Waldner 1999; Woo-Cumings 1999). According to this line of thinking, particular geopolitical conditions in East Asia during the cold war were important, as economic failure could potentially jeopardize national sovereignty and interests (Campos and Root 1996; Doner, Ritchie, and Slater 2005). Under the pressure of economic growth, East Asian leaders built incentives for good performance into the system. Scholars argue that East Asia's "equitable" and "shared" growth strategies have allowed the wider population to reap long-term benefits, as indicated by relatively low rates of income inequality (Campos and Root 1996, 2). This approach contributes to understanding how the autonomous, efficient state bureaucracy promoted economic development in Korea (and East Asia). Yet its focus on strong economic growth emphasizes only the positive side of development and discounts the tremendous socioeconomic costs inherent in "compressed modernity" (Abelmann 2003; K.-S. Chang 1999), such as a lack of labor and welfare rights, chaebol's monopolistic business practices, and a growing rural-urban gap. Its elite-based, state-centric view also excludes the subordinated, popular classes from its explanations.[5]

A more critical perspective, running counter to the vast celebratory developmental state literature, examines how the socially excluded and marginalized undergirded the so-called economic miracle in East Asia. This approach takes account of political and economic costs as well as the human costs of growth-oriented development. These critics have identified a variety of social subjects who have had to make immense sacrifices for the glory of development—be they workers, the urban poor, farmers, or women (Abelmann 1996; K.-S. Chang 1999; Deyo 1989; S.-K. Kim 1997; Koo 2001; N. Lee 2007; Seungsook Moon 2005). By examining the politically or economically dispossessed, these scholars highlight tensions, conflicts, and struggles between the authoritarian state that tried to impose its own modernization project and the disempowered who challenged this project. Yet the emphasis on a dichotomous relationship between the state and the populace leaves unexplained the situation of the majority of people who were neither exploited nor politically active.

Unlike the socially disadvantaged, the middle class was placed in a better position and benefited greatly from state-directed development. It was a social group that was neither economically deprived nor politically active, made up of individuals who were able to improve their lives by negotiating with, adapting to, and riding the wave of a rapidly changing society. Taking advantage of the chances provided by the state to the fullest, and following (but sometimes bending) the rules of the game to attain economic success, many middle-class citizens ascended the social ladder during Korea's socioeconomic transformation. Analyzing *who gets what* in the midst of social and economic transformations and how those who climbed the economic ladder have deployed diverse strategies to maintain their status enables us to illuminate the process of class formation. Through an examination of dramatic shifts in middle-class conceptualizations, identities, and boundaries over time, this book tries to contribute to the understanding of the nexus of development, social mobility, and class politics.

The Middle Class as a Contested Concept

Before moving on to explain how the Korean middle class was created and what changes this social group experienced over time, we need first to consider who the middle class is. Conceptualizing and defining social class, including the middle class, have long been controversial and challenging tasks in the social sciences. Not only is the concept of the middle class ambiguous—

people use the phrase in different ways and mean quite different things by it—but the heterogeneity within the middle class itself also makes it difficult to classify this group of people as one social class. This task of conceptualizing the middle class is particularly daunting in the context of developing countries, because their socioeconomic structures and degrees of development are very different from those of their Western counterparts. Moreover, the notion of the middle class becomes more ambiguous in societies where there is sociopolitical diversity that creates different layers of social inequality. As William Mazzarella writes, "Even if we accept the validity of the middle class descriptor for India, we are still left [with] a sense that the term is being stretched to cover a staggering diversity of socio-economic cultural situations. An income that in smaller towns or rural areas might qualify a family as middle class will, in the major Indian cities, only be barely enough to sustain life outside the slums" (2004, 2–3). No matter how challenging it is to attempt to conceive of the reality of the middle class, the category itself has been an important symbol of identification, aspiration, and public discussion.

Many scholars of social stratification and mobility have defined the middle class by *objective* socioeconomic characteristics, including income, occupation, wealth, and educational level (for example, Goldthorpe 2008; Weeden and Grusky 2005). Using one of, or clusters of, these attributes, these scholars have measured the size of the middle class and focused on how people are *objectively* located in distributions of material inequality. Official statistics adopt this approach by defining the middle class as an income-based group due to the methodological convenience and plausibility of these factors. Yet this definition, mainly focusing on individual attributes, does not account for power relations and various mechanisms of exclusion and closure built into certain class positions (Wright 2008). By contrast, neo-Marxist scholars understand class as a *relational* concept (for example, Abercrombie and Urry 1983; Burris 1992; Wright 1985). From this perspective, the middle class occupies a unique, "contradictory class location," because it belongs to neither the bourgeoisie nor the proletariat (the working class) (Wright 1985). This middle class is distinct from the bourgeoisie since it does not own any means of production. Yet, unlike the working class, it is endowed with a certain level of power and privilege, as it derives its economic opportunities from organizational authority or possession of scarce occupational skills (Fernandes and Heller 2006). Human capital, the stock of skills and credentials a person possesses, generally commands higher wages in the labor market (Becker 1971; England and McLaughlin 1979; England 1992). The higher wages and occupational prestige of the middle class can be seen as the "natural" market outcome—in other words, higher returns on years of schooling and/or job expertise. Yet the differences in pay scale and prestige between the middle and working classes are also maintained by the gate-keeping practices employed by the middle class to exclude others from access to resources (Wright 2008). Through the mechanisms of "opportunity hoarding" and "social closure" (Giddens 1973; Tilly 1998), the middle class reproduces its relatively privileged position with autonomy and capability. For example, people with higher education and professional expertise effectively control access to certain jobs through institutional sanctions such as legal recognition of credentials or higher returns on certain skills. Furthermore, social networks and gatekeeping confer advantages by granting monopolized access to information and other resources. According to this definition, the middle class has three broad strata. The first includes professionals and technical elites with professional credentials or advanced skills. Because their skills and expertise are not easily replaced, they can enjoy a higher level of income and authority. The second category includes salaried employees in both the private and public sector, who are mostly white-collar workers. The last group is the old middle class or petty bourgeoisie, including self-employed small-business owners, merchants, and shopkeepers. This book focuses on people in the second and third categories, who are more vulnerable to downward mobility during economic crises. Many displaced workers in the second category also become self-employed, given the lack of options after an early forced retirement.

Previous scholarship on the middle class in Asia has adopted this approach, based on objective socioeconomic characteristics, by investigating the economic status and political perceptions of the middle class (Goodman 2008; Hong 2005; Hsiao 1993; Li 2010). Using quantitative or survey data, scholars in this school measure the size of the middle class or portray particular characteristics of the middle class, including lifestyles, political orientations, and consumption patterns. The essential assumption here has been that class behaviors and actions are derived from class interests based on actors' structural positions (Marx 1978). This approach helps to draw a broad picture of social inequality and stratification, placing the middle class within the larger class structure. However, because of the narrow definition of class as a static category that this approach adopts, it is difficult to see the *process* of class formation—how class identity is produced.

By contrast, anthropologists adopt a practice-oriented approach focusing on daily cultural or consumption practices of the middle class (Heiman, Freeman and Liechty 2012; Lett 1998; Liechty 2003; O. Moon 1992; Sukjae Moon 2000; Nelson 2000; Vogel 1963; Zhang 2010). Following Pierre Bourdieu (1984), who emphasizes class as performed and reproduced through daily interactions between objective conditions and subjective experiences, scholars in this tradition examine various aspects of middle-class lifestyles, including housing, family life, marriage strategies, education, and consumption patterns. Though this approach does not deny the fact that similar socioeconomic conditions produce class, it emphasizes everyday practices through which class is made and remade. In this approach, social class is not a fixed entity simply grounded in structural conditions. Instead, class boundaries and identities are constructed and reconstructed on a daily basis, as people perform symbolic cultural strategies. Ethnographic studies help us to understand how class is practiced and performed in everyday life. This scholarship makes it possible to grasp class as it is practiced daily rather than as a static structural category. However, it tends to overlook larger political and economic dynamics and historical processes that shape the patterns and structures of social cleavages and inequality over the long term.

Scholars of working-class formation, who were inspired by E. P. Thompson's *The Making of the English Working Class* (1966a), have emphasized lived experience and historical contingency. Class is *made*, not given, in an active process, which arises in human relationships. Class is also a historical phenomenon, as it occurs in the experiences and relationships of real people in specific contexts. As Thompson powerfully puts it, "We cannot understand class unless we see it as a social and cultural formation, arising from processes which can only be studied as they work themselves out over a considerable historical period" (1966a, 11).

This Thompsonian view offers some insights for scholars of the middle class. First, the middle class is not a fixed, structural category; it should be understood as a *process* "when some men, as a result of common experiences (inherited or shared), feel and articulate the identity of their interests as between themselves, and as against others whose interests are different from (and usually opposed to) theirs" (Thompson 1966a, 9). As Loïc Wacquant has noted, "The epistemic ambition of defining the real boundaries of the middle class is doomed to failure because it rests on a fundamentally mistaken conception of the ontological status of classes: The middle class, like any other social group, does not exist ready-made in reality" (1991, 57). Second, the Thompsonian view asks us to conceive of class as an emergent historical property, situated in certain historical moments, rather than as timeless. Class consciousness, dispositions, and languages are outcomes shaped by past historical experiences and struggles over a long time. Thus, this view helps to explain how members of the middle class *came to* articulate their particular identities, ideas, and dispositions.

Emphasizing historical dynamics that shaped the making of the middle class in Korea, I conceptualize the Korean middle class as three different but related levels: social narratives, structural existences, and cultural practices. First, I attempt to analyze competing narratives about the middle class—the ways in which concepts of the middle class in Korea were expressed, discussed, represented, and imagined in public discourses, through political speeches, newspapers, magazines, and advertisements. This dimension of the middle class is not so much the objective reality as a discursive construct containing a series of normative positions and ideas. Middle-class narratives invoked social desires, aspirations, and national imaginaries and established cultural norms by projecting particular aspects of middle-class culture and lifestyles. By looking at how the social narratives of the middle class have changed in Korea, I identify the middle class as an ideological arena in which different social groups have championed particular visions of and values for Korean society and the Korean nation.

The middle class is constructed and represented in social narratives, yet it has a corporeal and material reality as well, existing both in structural forms and through being practiced on a daily basis. Structural formation of the middle class takes place based on the clustering of people with similar incomes, occupations, and educational levels. But, at the same time, the middle class is articulated and takes actions together in a particular space in which people share common experiences, build social networks, and engage in collective actions. Through ongoing processes, they share similar dispositions, states of mind, and values and develop a sense of belonging. Class identity becomes more clearly articulated as it promotes solidarity and unity among members of certain groups, forging struggles against others with conflicting interests. Thus, in addition to looking at the macro-level conditions that structurally form particular occupational groups, I closely examine the everyday process of class making in which individuals engage in inclusionary and exclusionary practices.

In this book, I analyze the *urban* middle class, particularly in the Seoul metropolitan area.[6] The middle-class citizens who appear in this book are mainly white-collar workers and midlevel corporate managers employed in large conglomerates and the public sector, professionals and small-scale entrepreneurs who live (or once lived) middle-class lifestyles. Occupation is one of the most important criteria used to delineate the middle class, as other scholars have previously noted, for this structural condition provides material circumstances under which certain groups of people can pursue particular kinds of lifestyles. Income can be another important criterion for structurally defining the middle class, yet it is not the best indicator, as living costs vary across different locations, and income levels change over time. Thus, occupation is a more stable basis of material conditions. In addition to structurally defined characteristics, this book considers various markers of middle-class status particular to Korean society. As some scholars have pointed out, high-rise apartment living is an important feature of middle-class culture and identity in Korea (Gelézeau 2007; Lett 1998; H.-C. Park 2013). Such features broadly delineate who the middle class is (and was) in Korea. I map out how apartment living was promoted as a middle-class norm, how individuals strived to become apartment owners, and how homeownership status in turn affected people's state of mind and sense of security. Capturing different moments in the emergence, reproduction, and fragmentation of the Korean middle class, this book highlights how the boundaries and identities of the middle class have been continually contested and transformed over time.

The Making and Unmaking of the Middle Class in Korea

Throughout this book, I analyze a dynamic process of the making and unmaking of the Korean middle class over the past five decades. To do so, I adopt a dialectical approach that bridges the gap between economic and cultural approaches, macro and micro levels, and class structure and practices. First, I reconcile the gap between economic and cultural conceptions of social class. A social class is not simply a group of people who are located in a similar position in the social hierarchy and have similar occupations and incomes. It involves individuals engaging in similar cultural activities and sharing similar tastes (Bourdieu 1984). This book shares a basic understanding of social class as derivative of capitalist production and state policies, that is, a material entity with certain objective conditions; but studying ideologies, cultural norms, and meanings associated with the middle class helps to provide more-nuanced analysis and to revise economically oriented explanations.

Second, I link political economic factors such as development and economic restructuring at the macro level with individual strategies at the micro level. Socioeconomic transformations broadly influence individual lives, yet different choices and strategies made by individuals in turn shape different life trajectories and outcomes. By highlighting how individuals strive to improve their standard of living during times of transformation, I try to portray divergent pathways of social mobility and various sensibilities about social change and development.

Third, this book focuses on the process of "becoming" middle class: how ordinary citizens become class subjects, engage in consumption and spatial practices in their everyday lives, and make sense of their positions in relation to other groups of people. This class practice and subjectivity are not universal but rather are embedded in particular social and cultural contexts. Looking at the lived reality that ordinary citizens have experienced and its changes over time, I demonstrate how middle-class identity was formed and articulated.

While adopting a dialectical approach to studying the middle class by overcoming dichotomous perceptions, this book foregrounds the middle class as a historical phenomenon: the constituency, concept, and experiences of the middle class are specific to a particular time period, and they change across time periods. I capture three differentiated historical moments of Korean middle-class formation: emergence, expansion, and contraction. The first moment is a period of social mobility, witnessing the emergence of the middle class in the course of industrialization. With rapid economic growth promoted by state-directed developmental plans in the 1960s and 1970s, a nascent middle class appeared. Mainly comprising salaried white-collar employees, teachers, and government employees, the middle class started to gain in numbers over time. The middle class did not simply grow in the material sense. The idea of the middle class as a vanguard of national modernization—

the embodiment of national desires and qualities, including hard work, frugal living, and a balanced political orientation—was promoted by the state to evoke hope and optimism and to garner the legitimacy of nation building and modernization.

The second moment is the expansion of the middle class between the late 1970s and the early 1990s. Rapid industrialization and increasing real wages provided material conditions through which white-collar workers and mid-level managers could enjoy comfortable lifestyles. Moreover, state-sponsored programs helped white-collar families with stable incomes to become homeowners and to benefit from skyrocketing real estate prices—especially those who purchased homes in the Gangnam district. Not only did the middle class expand to include more people, but distinctive middle-class culture, lifestyles, and space were also developed. Members of the middle class engaged in "classificatory practices" to reproduce their relatively privileged positions (Bourdieu 1984). In particular, apartment living provided a space where particular middle-class norms and culture were being cultivated and where collective actions and living experiences of residents created clear boundaries against "others."

The third moment is the contraction and fragmentation of the middle class since the economic crisis in the late 1990s. Many members of the middle class saw the deterioration of their standard of living, and the chances of class mobility started to narrow because of increasingly precarious work arrangements, wage stagnation, and lack of economic opportunities. Along with the overall contraction of the middle class, there is an increasing polarization within the middle class. There has been a growing gap between those who had accumulated wealth in addition to their salaries—primarily through real estate investment—and those who had not, and this gap has shaped different trajectories for their children. I argue that while this growing inequality resulted partly from globalization and neoliberalism, it is necessary to look at domestic policy dynamics in which some people could take advantage of particular opportunities for making windfall incomes more than others.

In what follows I elaborate on the important factors that have affected the rise and fall of the middle class in Korea over the past five decades, including geopolitical contexts, state economic policies, urban space and the housing market, and globalization. The interplay of these factors has shaped three distinct periods: the emergence, expansion, and contraction of the middle class.

The Language of Social Class in the Context
of a Divided Nation (1948–)

It is necessary to understand the historical and geopolitical backdrop that shaped the subsequent language and meanings of social class (*sahoe kyegŭp*) in South Korea. Although class hierarchy and social inequality have existed throughout Korean history, as in other places, using the term and the concept of "social classes" had long been a taboo. Cold war politics in the Korean Peninsula produced a repressive anticommunist South Korean state that stifled the language of class and labor.

The birth of a right-wing regime in South Korea after the national partition and the Korean War was directly related to the repression of class language and discourse. Using hostility toward communism and North Korea as a fundamental ideological pillar, the authoritarian regimes repressed any radical and leftist language outright. On this extremely narrow ideological and political terrain, any critical thought or discourse could be cast as a threat to the national security of South Korea and condemned by association with North Korea. Merely using terms such as "social class" (*sahoe kyegŭp*), "revolution" (*hyŏgmyŏng*), "labor" (*nodong*), and "radicalism" (*kŭpchinjuŭi*) was enough to brand someone a "radical" or "commie" (*ppalgaengi*). Discussing class and inequality was immediately condemned as communist and connected to North Korea. In this particular context, South Korea was a "classless" society not because social classes were abolished but because nobody dared to utter the word "class" or publicly discuss social inequality. Any talk of class, whether moderate or radical, was completely suppressed, and class identity based on material conditions was never developed in South Korea. Not until the 1980s, when *minjung*[7] movements and social activism developed fully and radical discourse was popularized, did class discourse emerge. It was even rare to study social class and inequality in academic circles.

Against this backdrop, the term "middle class" played a role in depoliticizing and sanitizing class language in South Korea. The Korean term *chungsanch'ŭng* refers literally to the middle propertied stratum, as opposed to *sŏmin*, which refers to nonprivileged, unpropertied, or impoverished people.[8] Though social scientists and academics used the more academically exact terms *chungsan kyegŭp* (propertied middle class) and *chunggan kyegŭp* (middle class) to refer to the middle class, *chungsanch'ŭng* was used more widely. Use of the term *kyegŭp* (class) was linked to Marxist or leftist thought, which assumed a confrontational relationship between the exploiter and the exploited. Even though *chungsanch'ŭng* indicated a social stratum, the avoidance of the Marxist term "class" in *chungsanch'ŭng* made it more moderate. In this sense, *chungsanch'ŭng* was a more sanitized term that did not imply class conflict or class tensions.[9] Unlike *nodongja* (workers) or any other class terms, the usage of *chungsanch'ŭng* was thought to be free from any ideological taint. As a vague term, it could effectively and conveniently replace more explicit class language by celebrating equal opportunity and upward mobility. Given that class language was otherwise largely banned, it is noteworthy that the majority of the population identified themselves as middle class over several decades.

Middle-Class Formation as a State Project (1961–1979)

The state plays a vital role in the making of the middle class (Davis 2010; Fernandes 2006; Heiman, Freeman, and Liechty 2012; Savage, Barlow, Dickens, and Fielding 1992; Yang 2012). As a main provider of education, a source of employment, a propagator of ideology, and a regulator of social and economic policies, the state allocates and redistributes resources, selects economic winners, and shapes class structure. The state bureaucracy makes decisions about particular industrial, labor, welfare, and tax policies, which in turn affect the pattern of income distribution and social inequality. While the middle class is often treated as an outgrowth of capitalist development and industrialization, especially in the case of the earlier middle class in Europe, the expansion of the middle classes in western Europe, the United States, and Japan was an outcome of state efforts to build "mass society" and of proactive social policies providing extensive safety nets during the postwar era (Zunz, Schoppa, and Hiwatari 2002). In the context of developing countries, particularly in East Asia, the role of the (developmental) state becomes even more direct and proactive in making and unmaking the middle class. I emphasize the *political* nature of middle-class formation as a *deliberate* state policy, in both material and ideological senses.

First, the state formulates specific industrial and social policies that shape the overall welfare of citizens. The export-oriented, big-business model that the Korean state pursued to promote heavy industry beginning in the 1970s produced white-collar workers, engineers, midlevel managers, and technicians who could take advantage of rising wages and extensive welfare benefits provided by employers—mainly big businesses. This developmental model, emphasizing trickle-down effects, focused on rapid economic growth and produced distorted economic outcomes over the long run by ignoring the welfare of the majority of workers. Unlike in Europe and the United States, where extensive welfare benefits and social security programs created broad middle-class social contracts—embracing blue-collar workers—during the postwar period, the middle class in Korea was more limited to salaried white-collar employees in big corporations, though it is true that the living standards of the majority of the population improved somewhat. More notably, an apartment lottery program adopted in the mid-1970s promoted homeownership among white-collar families who had stable incomes and employment by allowing them to purchase homes below market prices. Those who bought homes (mostly apartment units) in booming areas greatly benefited from housing price inflation and climbed the economic ladder much faster than others.

Here it is worth noting how different state policies produced divergent outcomes in the welfare of ordinary citizens. Hong Kong and Singapore, two other Asian Tigers that experienced industrialization and urbanization in roughly the same time frame as Korea, provide illuminating comparative cases in which strong states controlled the real estate market and provided more inclusive state-sponsored homeownership (Castells et al. 1988; B. Park 1998; Shatkin 2014; Yuen 2009). Like Korea, both Hong Kong and Singapore have high population densities and have historically promoted high-rise housing for efficient living, yet their paths diverged sharply from Korea's: they built high-rise public housing stock on a massive scale and housed the majority of the population there. The strong coalition between the state and private developers (notably chaebol) in Korea led to less equitable housing distribution than in Hong Kong and Singapore. Government housing policies and privatized high-rise building projects promoted homeownership primarily for middle-income families, not for the less privileged, and less regulated speculative activities escalated housing prices and worsened housing inequality over the years.

In addition to shaping material conditions such as homeownership, wages, and welfare benefits, the state also propagates particular ideologies and ideas about the middle class. By doing so, the state attempts to shape a particular class subjectivity that helps to shore up its political legitimacy and strengthen national identity. For example, the official discourse of middle-class society and mass consumption in Japan in the 1950s evoked a sense of prosperity, national confidence, and social peace (Neitzel 2016; Young 1999). Similarly, the postsocialist Chinese state's promotion of middle-classness and a vision of *xiaokang* (moderately prosperous) society was an effort to dispel the intense class struggle and conflict of the Cultural Revolution, to legitimize increasing social inequality brought about by economic reform, and to disseminate specific conceptualizations of model citizens embodied in the entrepreneurial, self-responsible, and educated middle class (Anagnost 2004; Ren 2013; Tomba 2009). The middle class in official discourse in Korea was often associated with the ideal Korean nation, one that was economically productive and had a politically docile citizenry. Economically, a middle class consisting of hard-working, savvy consumers was seen as vital for growth. And politically, an educated middle class with rational, moderate, balanced worldviews was believed to contribute to social stability without the taint of any oppositional ideologies, particularly communism. The state projected the idea of the middle class as model citizens who would contribute to social homogenization and harmony.

The middle class, in this sense, was an aspirational category (Heiman, Freeman, and Liechty 2012, 19) rather than a reflection of the current class structure. By promoting the images of consumerism and comfortable lifestyles associated with the middle class in commercial and social rhetoric, the state and elites could contain discontent and prevent social disruptions—though this strategy was not always successful. The authoritarian state promised ordinary people prosperity and national progress, and many bought into the notion of the ascendant middle class. The ideals of the middle class—a new social group manifesting an ethos of opportunity and upward social mobility—helped the state strengthen its vision of development.

Speculative Urbanism and the Pathways to Becoming Middle Class (1978–1996)

Housing issues are critical to understanding the welfare of citizens, social rights, and social inequality as the site of social reproduction. Housing is more than the physical built environment or shelter; it is a source of personal safety and security. Rampant eviction and displacement, as well as the lack of affordable housing, which are increasingly common everywhere—including, but not limited to, New York, London, Shanghai, Mumbai, and Lagos—deprive ordinary citizens of a universal necessity and threaten their lives. Thus, as David Madden and Peter Marcuse argue, housing should be understood as the "political-economic" problem that reveals the existing class structure and power relationships (2016, 12).

Gentrification and lack of affordable housing have often been understood in the context of neoliberalism, financialization, and the flow of transnational capital (Smith 2002). Henri Lefebvre described real estate as a means of capital accumulation: "As the principal circuit—current industrial production and the movable property that results—begins to slow down, capital shifts to the second sector, real estate. It can even happen that real-estate speculation becomes the principal source for the formation of capital, that is, the realization of surplus value. As the percentage of overall surplus value formed and realized by industry begins to decline, the percentage created and realized by real-estate speculation and construction increases" (2003, 160).

Deregulation, financialization, and globalization have contributed to hyper-commodification of housing, subordinating it to the logic of the market and making it an investment for private companies (Madden and Marcuse 2016, chap. 1). The amount of public and rent-stabilized housing has decreased, and gentrification has become the dominant strategy to transform "underutilized" buildings into more valuable, profitable "commodities." Justifying development projects and construction as boosting local economies by creating jobs and tourism and generating tax revenue, local governments often promote development projects and gentrification in partnership with private developers. These processes usually create starkly unequal, distorted outcomes: private developers and investors make tremendous fortunes in the real estate market, whereas low-income households lose their homes and are forced into uninhabitable dwelling spaces.

In a similar way, housing and real estate properties are a major source of capital accumulation and class inequality in Korea. But it is difficult to argue that globalization and neoliberalism are the main causes of this phenomenon. Rather, it should be seen as an outcome of domestic political-economic dynamics. Real estate speculation was pervasive among domestic actors, not among foreign investors or multinational corporations, and was the outcome of state-directed industrialization and urbanization. The state promoted rapid urbanization and changes to the built environment, and the strong alliance between the state and private developers carried out massive construction projects. Rapid industrialization and urbanization stimulated the real estate market, and the surplus capital was channeled to the real estate market. Seeing the opportunities presented by rapidly increasing real estate values, chaebol and construction companies alike engaged heavily in real estate speculation (J.-M. Son 2003; N.-G. Son 2008). Many individuals also participated in speculative activities, expecting windfall profits from real estate investment. Widespread speculative activities among both corporations and individuals, coupled with lack of state regulation, resulted in skyrocketing real estate prices. Since the late 1960s, land prices have risen sharply, and real estate speculation in land and housing (especially newly built apartment units) has exacerbated the situation. Between 1974 and 1996, land prices in Seoul increased by 32.9 times, and in the six largest cities by 28.9 times (H. Jung 1998, 136). Increases between 1963 and 2007 were even more stunning: land prices in Seoul increased by 1,176 times, and in six major cities by 923 times (N.-G. Son 2008, 25). Given the rise of this overheated real estate market over several decades, it is unsurprising that many organizations and individuals who invested in real estate made huge profits and quickly became rich. In the process, land and housing have become *commodities* that are sold and bought for profit, as well as a *means* of capital accumulation.

Homeownership and ownership of other real estate properties greatly shaped individual paths of social mobility and social inequality in Korea. Since real estate prices increased more rapidly than wages, real estate investment provided a better channel for making fortunes and enhancing one's economic position than education and occupations such as corporate manager, government bureaucrat, or white-collar worker. It is true that the more highly educated and those who were corporate employees or bureaucrats had better access to information and resources about real estate investment than the rest of the population, and the entrepreneurial path through real estate investment was not mutually exclusive with other paths through education or occupation. Yet different real estate property values produced divergent financial and economic standings even among people with similar incomes and jobs, as real estate values in booming areas rose much more sharply than others. For example, apartment buyers in Gangnam in the late 1970s eventually improved their financial standing far more than those who bought houses elsewhere in Seoul around the same time. The value of a Gangnam resident's property ended up being three or four times greater than that of a resident of another district with a similar job and income.

While decision making about buying a home in particular areas or investing in real estate properties might have been rational, based on financial savvy, entrepreneurial spirit, and access to information, it was also often based simply on chance. But decision making greatly affected one's material conditions and class status. This particular path to the middle class through real estate investment ran counter to the notion of the middle class as a symbol of open opportunity and merit and produced a growing sense of social injustice and unfairness among those who did not seize the opportunity (Abelmann 2003, 32). In the long term, the ever-increasing real estate property values resulting from speculative activities made it more difficult for non-homeowners to purchase homes in big cities. Moreover, those who were lucky enough to own multiple apartment units in booming areas could pass on their real estate to their children, which reproduced (or increased) housing inequality in the next generation.

Apartment Communities and Cultivating Middle-Class Culture (1978–)

Urban sociologists and geographers have explored the spatial dimensions of class power, paying attention to the role of residential location in shaping class difference (Castells 1996; Harvey 1985; Savage et al. 1992). Different locations bring different social, economic, cultural, and even political returns to residents. Where one lives determines differential access to social and cultural networks and to private and public services such as libraries, roads, schools, and other facilities (Massey and Denton 1993). Additionally, because of differential increases in real estate prices, the location of one's home determines property values and future financial conditions. Thus, residential locations affect residents' economic, social, and cultural capital and shape the formation and reproduction of social classes.

The process of class making is intertwined with the making of distinctive space where residents fashion a particular lifestyle and create cultural norms. Thus, it is necessary to look at how the class is *spatially* formed around particular neighborhoods and how members of the class engage in cultural practices, which in turn produce clear class boundaries and territories. A bourgeoning literature on Asia addresses economic and spatial transformation and the emergence of middle-class residential communities (Fernandes 2006; Pow 2007; Tomba 2004; Zhang 2010). These studies help us grasp how the middle class engages in spatial exclusion and how middle-classness is performed through gatekeeping practices at the micro level. The urban middle class in Korea materialized in a very particular space: high-rise apartment complexes (*ap'at'ŭ tanji*). While in many other places in the world, apartment buildings represent public housing for lower-income families, in Korea apartment construction was promoted by the state on a large scale to house salaried white-collar families. As the prototypical style of modern housing, high-rise apartment buildings in Korean cities both exemplify and signify affluent and cultured lifestyles.

The production of a particular urban space constitutes the central mechanisms by which the new class reinforces and reproduces its class identity. The new middle-class identity becomes visible in and is articulated through a distinct middle-class "cultural milieu." The nuclear family's members—the "salary man" husband, the stay-at-home housewife, and the children—were the core residents of apartment complexes, and the standard physical space—the same size and interior layout—within the apartment complex led residents to pursue similar cultural activities and consumption practices to keep up with their neighbors. As places where more Westernized and modern lifestyles could be fashioned, apartment complexes suggested a model of prototypical middle-class living and enhanced the feeling of privilege among apartment residents.

New apartment complexes in newly developing areas in Korea demarcated both physical and symbolic class boundaries between middle-class apartment residents and "others." Gates, walls, and barricades marked clear boundaries between insiders and outsiders and prevented "strangers" from invading the communities. At the same time, living in a certain apartment complex symbolized middle-class status and privilege, making its residents distinct from non-apartment residents and producing symbolic and psychological boundaries between them. Urban space becomes the ground of class struggles, in which different interests of social classes clash, yet the marginalized and less privileged are often excluded and displaced from the space, and an unequal, stratified spatial order is created.

Interactions between Global Forces and Domestic Policies
(the Post-1997 Period)

As many scholars have pointed out, the middle class is by its nature not a homogeneous social group (Fernandes 2006; Koo 2007; Zhang 2010). We often encounter contradictory images of the middle class: one of a middle class that enjoys material comforts and a cosmopolitan lifestyle symbolized by traveling abroad, speaking fluent English, and consuming global high-end brands, the other of a precarious middle class that suffers from unstable employment, stagnant wages, and rising living costs. The former group usually consists of the uppermost tier of the new middle class, benefiting from globalization, whose status is derived from capital, credentials, and expertise. The latter group is the rest of the new middle class, largely without these kinds of advantages. This internal split and fragmentation characterize the changing dynamics of the current middle class. Many studies maintain that globalization and neoliberal economic restructuring contributed to social differentiation and disparities within the middle class (Fernandes 2006; Koo 2007; Robison and Goodman 1996). While this recent trend may be seen everywhere, the patterns of social inequality and class structure in different societies are shaped by different social contracts and welfare policies. Thus, it is national politics and domestic policies coupled with globalization that produce the increasing internal differentiation within the middle class.

In the Korean context, we need to understand how the housing market produced fragmentation within the middle class and deepened it over the long run. As astronomical incomes from real estate price appreciation dwarfed other sources of income, there was a growing disparity in wealth between those who invested in real estate and those who did not, between those who purchased homes in booming areas and those who did so somewhere else, and between homeowners and non-homeowners. Those who managed to accumulate wealth by purchasing extra homes (mostly apartment units) or real estate properties in booming areas comprise the upper segment of the middle class. With an entrepreneurial and adventurous spirit and some luck, they were able to mobilize finances through personal or family connections, buy land or houses in lucrative areas, and boost their wealth considerably. Exploiting the given opportunities to the fullest, they were able to ride the waves of their times and get far ahead of their contemporaries. Their stable sources of income, derived from real estate properties, now allow them to engage in advanced consumption and to lead a comfortable middle-class lifestyle. By contrast, the rest of the middle class consists of white-collar salaried employees who did not buy homes in profitable districts and did not own any extra properties. In terms of jobs and education, this group of people may not be significantly different from the former group, yet they were neither entrepreneurial nor interested in informal economic activities, and relied mostly on their salaries. Without any buffer, they were more vulnerable during economic downturns to wage reductions, layoffs, or forced retirement.

This split within the middle class has grown over time and is largely reproduced in the next generation. The children of the first group directly benefit from their parents' wealth when getting married or purchasing homes. Because of the high cost of living—in particular, housing costs—it is almost impossible for the younger generation to build their own lives from scratch. Thus, the children of the former group start their adult lives at a better point than those of the latter group. But parents' economic capital also shapes children's life trajectories in an *indirect* way. The children of the former group tend to be more advantaged than those of the latter group in getting into more competitive colleges and getting better jobs, as they are able to benefit from their parents' wealth by taking part in extracurricular activities, getting private tutoring, and cultivating language skills through trips abroad. As Bourdieu (1984) notes, economic capital is often converted to cultural and social capital, or vice versa, and this mechanism helps class reproduction and reinforces social inequality.

While one can observe class inequality and class reproduction in any country, the ways in which social inequality is created and aggravated affect the collective perception of class identity and social mobility. In Korea, interpretations differ by generation: older generations share the perception that economic winners often accumulated their wealth through illegitimate and unfair means—mainly real estate speculation—during times of high economic growth; and younger generations have a collective sense that the relatively open mobility that existed in the times of high growth does not exist any longer and that they cannot make their lives better than those of their parents' generation. The opportunity structure of a generation ago, in which many people could pursue economic gain encountering almost no barriers, is now gone, destroyed by socioeconomic changes. This perception is translated into a sense of relative deprivation and frustration.

Methodology

This book is a study of ordinary middle-class citizens in Korea over the past five decades, a familiar story of my parents' generation as well as my own: how each individual strived to make her or his life better in the midst of socioeconomic transformation. It is a story of both success and failure, of confidence and insecurity, and of hope and frustration. Many people of my parents' generation emerged from nothing to become prosperous and comfortable. Yet even with more competitive qualifications than their parents, the younger generation has far fewer opportunities to match the achievements of the older one. Furthermore, many of those in the older generation who did not take part in the speculation craze could not enjoy the level of wealth their more aggressive cohorts did. Sketching diverse individual trajectories of both upward and downward mobility—paths shaped by the significant historical events of the past five decades—this book tries to reconcile structure and agency, history and biography, and economy and culture.

This book draws from fieldwork I conducted in Seoul, the capital city, where I was raised, went to school, and have maintained social networks. The most intensive part of the research was conducted during 2008 and 2009 and in the summers between 2006 and 2015. I draw on three different sets of data. First, I use quantitative data, including official statistics and survey results, to identify the numerical trends of the middle class. These data show the changing patterns of income and employment, consumption, Korean citizens' class self-identification, and social inequality. Such data are useful for seeing the overall pattern of class structure and social stratification over the long term, from a macro perspective.

Second, I collected a wide range of archival data, including government documents, newspapers, academic and popular magazines, political speeches, advertisements, and films and fictional works. These sources enable me to examine the top-down process of middle-class formation as a state project. Newspapers and magazines help illuminate political and cultural representations of the middle class—the various images of the middle class in mass media and the official and popular discourses on the middle class that were created and appropriated. Furthermore, many stories in newspapers and magazines deliver a relatively accurate picture of how ordinary citizens tried to improve their living standards and engaged in informal economic activities through real estate investment and homeownership.[10] Discourse analysis helps us to understand the ways in which the middle class was constituted: how the middle class was defined by different groups, including the state, political parties, intellectuals, and mass media; what meanings, symbols, and implications the middle class carried; and how middle-class citizens recognized their own lives.

Third, I conducted thirty in-depth interviews with a varied group of informants, including white-collar workers, professionals, government employees, corporate managers, and self-employed small-business owners, as well as informal conversations with academics and acquaintances. I recruited these interviewees, typically categorized as middle class, through snowball sampling.[11] Each interview took around one to three hours, and, if necessary, I conducted follow-up interviews. The interviewees' life stories, in addition to their objective socioeconomic conditions and political orientations, allowed me to map out their multiple life trajectories—the processes and life experiences through which they came to achieve their current wealth and social status. These stories included when and how they got jobs and bought homes; what strategies they adopted to improve their standard of living; how they maintain their social status and economic wealth; what their life goals and challenges are; how they cope with and negotiate these challenges; and how they envision their future lives.

Through analyses of these data, the book aims to demonstrate the tensions and gaps between the middle class as discourse and as lived reality. The disjuncture between the hegemonic representation of the middle class and the lived realities and experience of the middle class helps us to understand the ways in which people reconcile their lived realities with their own life expectations. By closely observing people's coping strategies on a daily basis, this book analyzes how middle-class identities are contested and practiced and how collective sensibilities and shared understanding then affect the prospect of sociopolitical stability.

A Look Ahead

Chapter 1 sheds light on the discursive and ideological dimensions of the middle class. It examines the process by which the Korean state promoted the urban middle class as a social imaginary during the Park Chung Hee regime (1961–1979) as part of a political-ideological project to reconstruct the nation and strengthen the regime's political legitimacy. General Park Chung Hee, who came to power through a military coup in 1961 in the midst of political crisis and economic destitution, believed that a new nation-building project was urgently needed to overcome the devastating experiences of the Korean War and national partition. Through the portrayal of a middle-class subjectivity as frugal, patriotic, and politically moderate, state elites and mass media tried to project the ideal citizen. In addition, comfortable and modern middle-class lifestyles mediated by consumption of modern household goods and new apartment living suggested a model for the future nation and produced a widespread aspiration for upward mobility, thereby strengthening the state's vision of development.

Through the case of the Gangnam district in Seoul, chapter 2 explores how the urban middle class actually materialized through popularized apartment living in the 1980s and how becoming middle class in Korea became associated with living in apartment complexes. This chapter highlights a speculative and exclusive process by which some white-collar salaried families were able to buy homes and benefit from housing price inflation. Throughout the chapter, I emphasize the role of the state in the housing market, which allowed certain social groups—mainly white-collar workers and government employees who had stable incomes and jobs—to purchase homes below the market price and to climb the economic ladder through real estate investment. New apartment complexes also provided a space where apartment residents with similar socioeconomic conditions fashioned a Westernized and cultured lifestyle by making distinctions between themselves and "others." The development of Gangnam created middle-class identity based on apartment living and stratified residential space over the years.

Coming to present-day Korea, chapter 3 examines the unintended consequences of state-sponsored building of the middle class, namely, the collapse of the social contract that had raised many citizens' living standards to those of the middle class. This chapter discusses contradictory, fractured images of the current middle class—a celebratory, comfortable middle class on the one hand, and a precarious middle class on the other hand—and argues that the interactions between external globalization forces and internal domestic policies brought about the internal split and fragmentation within the middle class. By documenting the pattern of increasing divides within the middle class and social inequality over time, this chapter suggests that the anxieties and frustrations shared by the majority of the middle class are

the long-term outcome of the Korean development project's failure to promote social equality.

Finally, the conclusion analyzes current Korean social phenomena as a
result of lack of opportunities that thwarted social mobility. Then I summa-
rize the book's main arguments and theoretical contributions to the broader
field. I also outline some comparative implications that this book has for a
more general understanding of the relationship among class, the state, and
economic development in developing countries, and discuss possible futures
for the middle-class politics in the context of the globalized and increasingly
unequal world.

Chapter 1

An Imagined Middle Class

The Birth of the Ideal National Subject, 1961–1979

> By the end of the 1970s when the Third Economic Development Five Year Plan is completed, we will have built an affluent society of mass production and mass consumption, with a new motto: "Consumption is a virtue."
>
> —Park Chung Hee, the President's annual address to the National Assembly (1/18/1966), 1973A, p.584.

In 1966 *chungsanch'ŭng* (middle class) was a keyword[1] in Korea, the centerpiece of social agendas in both politics and academic circles. Beginning with an address by an opposition party leader, the government, politicians, state officials, and intellectuals talked about the middle class. The term "middle class" appeared everywhere—in newspaper columns and op-eds, popular magazines, academic journal articles, and political speeches. The issues related to the middle class were diverse: how to define and conceptualize the Korean middle class, what the political orientations of the middle class were, what lifestyles the middle class pursued, and what roles the middle class should play in Korean national modernization. Ironically, in 1966, when the *idea* of the middle class—as opposed to the working or lower classes—was prevalent in the political arena, the middle class had not yet arisen as a visible mainstream social force in Korean society; in post–Korean War society, the majority of the population was destitute and could barely make ends meet on a day-to-day basis. One might ask, then, why was the idea of the middle class so popular among political elites? Why was it so urgent to address the issues of the middle class? How did the state create the idea of the middle class even *prior* to its existence? And who was actually considered part of the middle class?

This chapter explores how the authoritarian Park Chung Hee regime (1961–1979) promoted social imaginaries of the urban middle class and cultivated the urban middle class as the foundation of its hegemonic nation-building project during the very early stages of industrialization in Korea, when the making of the middle class was equated with the making of a modern nation. I argue that urban middle class formation in Korea was a political-ideological project of the authoritarian Park regime to reconstruct the nation and strengthen its political legitimacy. While according to conventional wisdom the middle class was a subsequent outcome of economic development and modernization (for example, Huntington 1968; Lipset 1959), I pay attention to the discursive construction of the middle class by the state, politicians, and intellectuals. The ideal middle class comprised disciplined, responsible citizens who practiced frugal living and worked hard, but it also symbolized comfortable lifestyles and mass consumption. By embodying economic success and upward social mobility, the middle class could represent a prosperous and modern nation—one that had successfully overcome a "backward and humiliated" national past haunted by colonialism, partition, and civil war (B. S. Shin 1970, 287).

In this chapter, I illuminate the process through which a specific category of the "middle class" was formulated by the state; how the middle class was framed by different groups, including the state, political parties, intellectuals, and mass media; what kinds of discourse the state formed around the middle class; what meanings and implications this class category held; and how middle-class discourse served to promote national modernization. By disseminating particular cultural norms, embodied in the middle class, throughout society, the authoritarian state attempted to strengthen national identity and its vision of development. In doing so, the state could legitimize the developmental process and mobilize the entire population as part of the developmental project.

Building a New State, Constructing a New Nation

The three years of the Korean War (1950–1953) were a traumatic experience for all Koreans. Most families lost members and had to leave their homes behind to escape the atrocities of the war. The tragic experiences and suffering of ordinary citizens during the war left deep, indelible scars on Korean people's minds and hearts. The war also caused enormous economic damage to both North and South Korea, with most economic infrastructures and facilities completely demolished. Amid the ruins of the war, the most important tasks for both North and South Korea were consolidating their own political systems and rebuilding the economy.

It was an extremely challenging situation. Shortages were ubiquitous, and the South Korean economy was completely dependent on aid from the United States and the United Nations. Many people were displaced—approximately 450,000 citizens escaped from the North to the South (Gong 1989, 233). Most refugees had no economic means; they frequently went hungry and struggled to survive. During the 1950s, the number of the unemployed was estimated at between 500,000 and 600,000 out of the total population of 20 million (Gong 1989, 261). Because of the extreme shortage of jobs, many people worked as day laborers or peddlers. The historian Bruce Cumings vividly describes what everyday life was like during the postwar era: "South Korea in the 1950s was a terribly depressing place, where extreme privation and degradation touched everyone. Cadres of orphans ran through the streets, forming little protective and predatory bands of ten or fifteen; beggars with every affliction or war injury importuned anyone with a wallet, often traveling in bunches of maimed or starved adults holding children or babies; half-ton trucks full of pathetic women careened onto military bases for the weekend, so they could sell whatever service they had" (Cumings 1997, 303). South Korea also experienced dramatic population change and rapid urbanization in the 1950s (S.-G. Cho and Oh 2003). Cities, particularly big cities such as Seoul, Busan, and Daegu, experienced explosive growth as they absorbed refugees from the North and migrants from rural areas. As a result of this growth, the already damaged cities acquired even more problems. In particular, housing became a life-or-death issue for many people. City-dwellers were crammed together in tiny houses, and many migrants clustered in new, disordered neighborhoods, haphazard collections of temporary wooden shacks that blossomed on the cities' hillsides.

Amid social chaos and extreme poverty, almost no one imagined that the South Korean economy would recover. On the eve of General Park Chung Hee's military coup in 1961, socioeconomic conditions were dismal. Although the extremely corrupt and incompetent Syngman Rhee regime

(1948–1960) was overthrown by student protests, and the new, democratic Chang Myun regime came to power, ordinary citizens' lives did not improve. In 1960 and 1961, inflation became serious: the price of rice increased by 60 percent from December 1960 to April 1961, and the price of oil and coal rose by 23 percent over the same period; the GDP growth rate decreased by 12 percent from November to February; and the unemployment rate reached 23.7 percent in 1960 (*Hankook Ilbo* 4/23/1961). Despite this urgent economic situation, political leaders focused on factional strife and did not effectively address the social demands from below.

In the midst of economic crisis and political disorder, Park Chung Hee justified the coup as necessary to save the Korean nation; he claimed that the coup would eradicate corruption and social evils and establish new and sound social morals (Supreme Council for National Reconstruction 1961, title page). Park identified Korea as "historically dependent on and exploited by other countries, and always vulnerable to military attacks and political interventions" (C. H. Park [1962] 1970, 166). Thirty-six years of Japanese colonialism, the Korean War, and the division into two Koreas had brought national humiliation.[2] Park Chung Hee believed that his military revolution was like surgery to remove diseased flesh. His ultimate goal was to build a strong and modernized nation-state that would be on equal terms with world powers such as Japan, China, the United States, and the Soviet Union. In his view, only strong leadership could fix the prevailing problems, rebuild the state, and lead to national unification. Though Park came to power through an illegitimate military coup, his urgent call for extensive and thorough social reforms appealed to the entire population, including liberal progressive students and intellectuals (B. Kim 2006; H.-A. Kim 2004).[3]

For Park Chung Hee, the building of a new nation-state, represented by economic development and national modernization, meant two different but complementary projects: institutional reform and "spiritual revolution" (*chŏngsin hyŏngmyŏng*). First, Park maintained that the most important task was to build a new social system, resistant to corruption and inefficiency, that would lead to political stability, a new social order, and ultimately victory against communism (C. H. Park [1962] 1970, 164). As soon as he came to power, Park attempted to implement political reforms and anticorruption campaigns. He imprisoned corrupt politicians, army officers, and businessmen and reined in smuggling, the black market, dance clubs, and prostitution (ibid., 92–95). In doing so, he reinforced his image as a reformer, differentiating his administration from that of the corrupt Rhee regime and the incompetent Chang regime. Prioritizing economic development above all, the Park regime began to spearhead export-oriented industrialization in the early 1960s. The government bureaucracy was streamlined to promote rapid economic growth. Park instituted the Economic Planning Board (Kyŏngje Kihoegwŏn), which centralized economic information and produced economic policies. The regime also nationalized banks and centralized the financial system (Amsden 1989; Chibber 2003; Evans 1995; Kohli 2004; Waldner 1999; Woo-Cumings 1999). The regime's "reformist" actions were intended to compensate for its lack of political legitimacy and to draw societal support: after its "original sin" of overthrowing the previous democratic government, improving people's livelihoods became the key to maintaining stability.

Along with this institutional reform, the Park regime also encouraged people to change their mind-sets and attitudes, which Park called a "spiritual revolution." He accused Koreans of being lethargic and feeling inferior to Western countries (B. S. Shin 1970, 287). Park thought that in order to overcome Korea's "backward" and "shameful" past, it was necessary to improve the "quality" of the population (*ch'ejil kaesŏn*). In this logic, the ups and downs of the nation depended completely on the mentality and willingness of the citizens to change the existing system and to improve current living standards. National wealth could be produced only after transforming both society's value system and the thinking of individuals (B. Kim 2006, 130). The Park regime argued that the biggest obstacles to realizing the goal of reaching an advanced industrialized country were indolence, inertia, resignation, and a lack of determination (B. S. Shin 1970, 127). Unless these "old" mentalities and dispositions changed, Park warned, prosperity would be impossible. He maintained that "modernization of the mind" and "rationalization of social life" were necessary to accelerate economic development, and he called for eliminating traditional habits and advocated living diligently and frugally (ibid., 127–28). Through slogans such as "Founding an advanced Korea [*sŏnjin Han'guk ŭi kit'ŭl*]," "Creating Korea in the world [*segye sok ŭi Han'guk ch'angjo*]," "Pioneers who create tomorrow [*naeil ŭl ch'angjohanŭn sŏn'guja*]," and "New vigor for modernization of the fatherland [*choguk kŭndaehwa rŭl wihan saeroun hwallyŏkso*]," the Park regime tried to disseminate a message of optimism and confidence (Baek 2004, 215–16). When the majority of Korean society became enthusiastic about building a new nation-state, Park claimed, it would be possible to break the vicious cycles of poverty and backwardness.

The Park regime promoted discipline in everyday life. Frequently citing the case of German rehabilitation as an exemplar for Koreans, Park maintained in his speeches that Koreans should endure the long years of reconstruction with diligence and patience, as the Germans had done: "They [the Germans] refused to eat or dress well, solemnly determined only to rebuild Germany again. Housewives saved cloth by cutting one more inch from their skirts. To save matches, only when three met together did they strike a match. Workers resolved not to strike until the day the German economy was rehabilitated, and not to raise their own salaries until their factories were healthy. Germans ate very frugally even after the economic recovery, and invested their savings in production and construction" (B. S. Shin 1970, 25). As reflected in this speech, Park believed that the entire population should tolerate the current difficulties and sacrifice themselves for the nation's glory. While encouraging savings and frugal living in domestic life was an essential component in making the state's development project successful, the state also justified repressive labor practices by adopting nationalist language— workers had to tolerate low wages and long work hours to participate in the modernization project. These were the "patriotic" actions that ordinary people could undertake in daily life. Conversely, demanding higher wages or shorter work hours would delay modernization. Therefore, labor activism and political demonstrations were branded as unpatriotic and even pro-communist, as those actions could lead to social instability and thus vulnerability to military attack from North Korea.

In this sense, Park's national development project was a "disciplinary revolution":[4] just as the Protestant ethic shaped the rise of capitalism in western Europe (Weber [1930] 2001), the Korean state's emphasis on savings and frugality crucially affected the effort to build a new nation. The state tried to impose new societal values and create new social subjects to overcome what it perceived as the traditional and backward past. While promoting economic growth and sustaining specific political regimes are political and administrative processes, they equally involve disseminating social discipline and knowledge (Gorski 1993, 266). As Philip Gorski notes: "States are not only administrative, policing and military organizations. They are also pedagogical, corrective, and ideological organizations" (2003, 165–66).

The state could manage its population with less coercion and violence by imposing social discipline throughout society and creating more obedient and industrious subjects (Foucault 1977; Gorski 1993). This is not to say that the state was not repressive. Rather, it tried to achieve its goals by employing specific discourses so as to avoid cruder methods. The problem was how the state could effectively impose discipline on a whole society. The solution was to focus on a particular "carrier" group that would help extend the new forms of discipline more efficiently and deeply into the population (Gorski 1993, 270–71). In Korea's case, the state and intellectuals emphasized the role of the middle class in the development of a disciplined and productive citizenry, whose education and hard work earned them enhanced living standards and modern lifestyles—an alternative to the way of life of "backward and traditional" peasants.

Discovery of the Middle Class as Model Citizens

In the early 1960s, Korea was a largely agricultural country, with more than half of its population living as peasants in rural areas. The rural space—bucolic and idyllic—often symbolized traditional Korean society, yet it was also seen as "left behind" or in need of modernization. In the eyes of the state, which saw industrialization as the path to national modernization, this largely agrarian economic structure had to be transformed. Small-scale farmers, therefore, could not be the future of the industrial Korean nation. The state needed a new and progressive social body to represent a new, modern nation-state. Many intellectuals participated in this modernization project by producing discourses on development. Though some liberal intellectuals were critical of the Park regime's authoritarianism, they did not necessarily disagree with its overall picture of national modernization (B. Kim 2006). Instead, a number of intellectuals, including university professors and journalists, actively engaged in discourse about national modernization and modern citizenship in the new Korea.[5] In the mid-1960s, many intellectuals were concerned that Koreans' own culture was subordinated to the strong influence of Japanese culture (Cha [1965] 1998; "Saenghwalmunhwa ŏmnŭn Han'guk" 1965). Both the state and intellectual circles agreed that the colonial mentality had to be overcome through modernization and economic development. Intellectuals believed that the rise of the middle class would enlighten the rest of society and develop Korea's own culture in opposition to commercial and foreign infiltration (Cha [1965] 1998, 275).

In 1966 middle-class issues emerged as an important political and social agenda. In a New Year's keynote address in 1966, the opposition party leader, Park Soon Chun, first brought them up: she argued that the growth of the middle class was an urgent issue. She asserted that because the middle class was the driving force for democracy and national unification, "protecting and serving the economic interests of the middle class as a state policy should be of primary concern" (*JoongAng Ilbo* 1/21/1966). The party's spokesman, Kim Dae Jung, who became president of Korea in 1998, articulated the party's agenda, emphasizing the welfare of the middle class: "Under current situations, where we witness the collapse of midlevel merchants, farmers with midsized farms [*chungnong*], salaried men, and intellectuals, we cannot expect democracy to endure forever. Nor can we expect social stability and national unification to triumph over communism. We will focus on revival and reconstruction of the middle class [*chungsan kyech'ŭng*] by returning all economic benefits to them" (*Kyunghyang Shinmun* 1/19/1966). In response to the opposition party, the ruling Democratic Republican Party (Minju Konghwadang) also emphasized support for the middle class, along with industrialization and national modernization (*Chosun Ilbo* 1/28/1966). While both parties used the term "middle class" (*chungsanch'ŭng*), what they meant by it was quite different: the opposition party identified middle-level peasants, salaried men, and shopkeepers as the core of the middle class and focused on promoting a form of popular capitalism (*taejung chabonjuŭi*)[6] that emphasized equitable redistribution; in contrast, the ruling party thought only of small and medium-sized enterprises and businessmen as middle class and advocated industrialization and economic growth over redistribution.

The so-called middle-class debate between the ruling and opposition parties expanded into arguments among social scientists, politicians, and journalists over such issues as how to restructure industries to foster middle-class growth, the role of the middle class in modernization, and the definition and categorization of the middle class itself.[7] Yet it was not simply a debate over the middle class. Rather, it was a debate over the future path of Korean national modernization and development. The definition of the middle class proposed by intellectuals varied, as did the strategies put forward for its development. Definitions of who belonged in the middle class, and corresponding policy recommendations about economic development, could differ greatly. Despite disagreements about the conceptualization of the middle class and particular policies for expanding it, one thing was clear: the middle class—whatever that meant—was the key to national development and represented the future of the Korean nation. The terms of the heated debate about the Korean middle class in intellectual circles in the mid-1960s epitomized how Korean elites tried to promote the idea of the middle class while moving forward with the modernization project. This view of the role of the middle class, widely shared in intellectual circles, was influenced by the modernization theory of Seymour Lipset (1959) and Walt Rostow (1960), a universalistic and evolutionary perspective proposed as a model for Third World countries.

Yet Korean intellectuals also emphasized a nationalistic character of the Korean middle class—one that could nurture a new "Korean" culture that would strengthen national identity *against* Westernization and foreign powers as well as communism. Both the upper and lower classes were believed unsuitable, and perhaps even too dangerous, to be carriers of nationalism and national identity: the upper class could potentially ally with foreign powers in promoting market expansion to serve its self-interest, while the uneducated and poor lower classes might easily be agitated by communist rhetoric (*Chosun Ilbo* 10/27/1966; Go 1966). Only the middle class was perceived as capable of unwavering nationalism, able to avoid both communism and economic colonialism. According to these scholars, the middle class was the ideal social nucleus around which a nation with a moderate political orientation and rational intellectual culture could be built. The sociologist Young-bok Go wrote an article arguing that the middle class was a moderate social force, balanced between extremes:

In our society, which social group is the one that can promote national independence and unification, pursue both freedom and equality, and strike a balance between tradition and reform? The upper class would prefer freedom to equality, whereas the lower class would appreciate equality more than freedom. Given that the upper class in Korea depends on or is allied with foreign powers, nationalism supported by the upper class might easily lead to toadyism. On the other hand, nationalism supported by the lower classes might be too radical: since they are ignorant and not socially mature, they might sympathize with communism. From these facts, we can conclude that the carrier of Korean nationalism should be the middle class. (Go 1966, 131–32)

Given that South Korea was in constant confrontation with communist North Korea, anticommunism was an important ideological pillar supporting South Korea's political legitimacy and superiority. Because of its nature as an intermediate, relatively well-off group, the middle class was believed to contribute to the strengthening of national identity and anticommunism. Furthermore, some believed that the middle class could promote a "quiet revolution," which would reduce social inequality and build a wealthy nation by strengthening social stability. The sociologist Chaeyoon Kim wrote in an op-ed piece in a major newspaper: "The middle class has the potential to be hard-working and high-quality citizens. They are not bound by short-term self-interest, like the ruling elites, and they can address given situations more rationally than does the working class. We should disseminate these characteristics of good citizenship throughout our entire society. Through the nurture and growth of middle-class values and the improvement of middle-class socioeconomic conditions, we will reach national modernization" (C. Kim 1966). As depicted in such writings, the middle class was ideologically and politically sound. Intellectuals and other commentators believed that its moderate and balanced perspectives would help strengthen public morals and national security—in this sense, intellectuals and commentators were projecting their own political and ideological values onto the middle class. This normative thinking about the middle class as a good and desirable citizenry also served the interests of the authoritarian state. The middle class, it was thought, would further the state's aims of national modernization through its everyday industriousness. More importantly, it was seen as politically docile, willing to endure sacrifice and hardship for the sake of national gain without challenging the authoritarian order. Intellectuals and the state believed that middle-class citizens would have little incentive to advocate communism or radical social reform because of their relatively comfortable lifestyle and that they could be relied on to support the existing social order. The middle class was interpellated[8] by the state and intellectuals as a new social body that would contribute to the nation-building project. Socially responsible and politically compliant, the middle class was an ideal partner for the authoritarian state, which wanted to promote rapid economic growth without disrupting social stability. By defining the middle class as possessing such characteristics as self-discipline and civility, political elites and academics alike attempted to facilitate the state's national vision of development and modernization through its middle-class subjects.

Yet this narrative of the middle class as a mainstream social force was a discursive construct rather than an existing entity. Not only was the creation of occupational groups such as professionals, managers, and white-collar workers in its infancy, but the overwhelming majority of the Korean population was still struggling to obtain the basic necessities of daily life. The number of those who could be categorized as middle class in 1960s Korea was quite small.[9] United Nations reports classified South Korea as among the world's poorest countries, and the average per capita annual income was less than US$150 (United Nations 1962). In this sense, discussions of the values and lifestyles of the middle class can be seen as mere wishful thinking. However, as scholars came to discuss and use the term "middle class," concepts of the middle class became more visible and important. As Ann Anagnost noted, these studies of the middle class were *proleptic*: "They represented something that had not yet come into view as if it already existed in fact" (1997, 8). Though the middle class was still small in the 1960s, it was believed to be an important and growing social force for economic development and modernization. The term "middle class," carrying images of affluence and modernity, suggested a new model for development and national identity.

The Making of Modern Middle-Class Housewives

The middle class did not exist merely as an abstract concept or as the subject of academic discourse; it also exemplified particular social values—through very specific images of hard-working families saving their money and living frugally—that were emphasized by the Korean government. Throughout the period of state-directed economic development, frugality was held up as the proper manner of living, essential to the welfare of the nation as well as the individual household (Seungsook Moon 2005, 89; Nelson 2000, 150). Austerity and prudence in everyday life were portrayed as precious values that would lead to rapid economic development; extravagance and luxury were regarded as social evils to be abolished. Excessive consumption was consistently linked with moral decay and lack of patriotism and became in itself an object of blame. The state encouraged citizens to pinch pennies and spend wisely. Because of their perceived role in performing these duties, middle-class housewives were seen as critically important national subjects (*kungmin*).

Through political campaigns and propaganda, the state extolled the values of thrift, austerity, and discipline. From the very beginning, the Park regime emphasized the "rationalization of daily life" (*saenghwal ŭi hamnihwa*) as a new way of promoting modernization. Rationalization meant frugality based on systematic budgeting, so that there would be no waste of money or resources. Presenting advanced countries as exemplary cases, Park and other political leaders maintained that it was because Korea's citizens squandered money on unnecessary expenses that it had fallen behind other countries economically (B. S. Shin 1970). Park and political elites encouraged citizens to simplify their daily lifestyle, including their dietary and dress habits. Specifically, this included reducing the number of dishes in each meal, avoiding the frequent purchase of new clothes, buying recycled products, reducing the consumption of alcohol and cigarettes, and buying products made in Korea (*Dong-A Ilbo* 7/23/1968; *Kyunghyang Shinmun* 6/8/1968). Major mass media also followed the government and launched national campaigns for the rationalization and scientification of lives: "The rationalization of life should not be limited to merely simplifying traditional customs. Broadly speaking, we have to think scientifically and rationally, corresponding to the age of science, and have to reduce unnecessary waste and practice frugal living. For example, we should eliminate, as soon as possible, such widespread evil customs as going to see fortune-tellers before big life events, performing exorcisms, and preparing too much food for parties. For both our country and our own lives, it is urgent to achieve the rationalization of life" (*Dong-A Ilbo* 12/1/1972).These national campaigns were strongly gender-based, chiefly targeting women in charge of household finances. The state mobilized images of middle-class housewives as strong advocates of domestic saving and rational consumption. Middle-class housewives were depicted as proponents of national modernization in their practice of diligence and thrift at home. By contrast, extravagant upper-class women and traditional rural women were the targets of state discipline. According to the state's logic, these two social groups, which had not undergone "spiritual revolution," were delaying the modernization of Korea.

Upper-class women, the consumers of foreign cosmetics, luxurious furniture, and high-end clothing, were criticized by the state and intellectuals (both conservative and liberal) as damaging the Korean economy with their self-indulgence and extravagance. Consumption of foreign cosmetics was considered an especially immoral and unpatriotic act that would make the

Korean economy vulnerable to Japanese or Western infiltration. Yet extravagance was viewed as not merely an upper-class problem; the Park regime also portrayed consumption habits in rural areas as unnecessarily lavish, claiming that most rural households wasted money on expensive traditional customs such as wedding ceremonies, funerals, and ancestor worship. The government actively suppressed what it viewed as excessive consumption by implementing in 1969 the Family and Ritual Code (*kajŏng ŭirye chunch'ik*) (Nelson 2000, 132), which banned wedding invitation cards (*ch'ŏngch'ŏpchang*) and encouraged the simplification of other ceremonies. Moreover, large families were regarded as a barrier to sustaining economic growth. Through fertility control and family planning programs, "undisciplined and uncivilized" women with many children were a prime target for the disciplinary apparatus. Only when these unproductive and inefficient behaviors were eradicated, Park believed, would economic development finally be achieved.

The state and mass media alike identified middle-class housewives as the agents who would introduce a disciplined lifestyle into their households and society as a whole. Wise and frugal middle-class housewives, in contrast to extravagant upper-class women and unenlightened rural women, were believed capable of rational household management, which was presented as the key to national economic development. The role of a wise and rational housewife in managing her household to save money and accumulate wealth was considered critical in constructing a self-sustaining national economy. By leading this exacting economic life, housewives became avatars of state-sponsored economic development. Popular women's magazines such as *Yŏsŏng Dong-A* and *Yŏwŏn* often featured articles describing smart and economical middle-class housewives as desirable modern women. Leading magazines published housewives' stories about how they achieved "frugal lifestyles." By paying attention to small, almost negligible matters such as electricity and water costs, they could cut unnecessary expenses.

Many articles in these magazines also described how ordinary housewives could purchase their own homes by living plainly and saving money. A number of articles in popular women's magazines wrote of thrifty middle-class housewives who became homeowners after pinching pennies for a few years. After taking care of basic living expenses, the young wives of white-collar workers or engineers usually put aside most of the rest of their husbands' income in savings accounts or *kye* (rotating credit associations).[10] Step by step, they approached their long-held goal of homeownership. The ability of women to run a household on a meager income was considered vital in the creation of family wealth.

The most common money-saving strategy that exemplary housewives adopted was to keep a daily written record in a household account book (*kagyebu*). In 1967 state officials formed the Women's Central Council for Savings Life (Yŏsŏng Chŏch'uksaenghwal Chunganghoe), incorporating some twenty women's associations (Garon 2006, 174), and launched a campaign encouraging housewives to keep a household account book on a regular basis. By fastidiously tracking all household expenses, a housewife could carefully analyze her family's consumption patterns and trim unnecessary expenses. With government support, some women's magazines held an annual competition for women's household account books and even published the best examples. These officially recognized "good housewives" not only meticulously recorded everything they spent but also put aside almost 30 percent of their monthly income in savings. Printing and publicizing private household account books made "good housewives" into leading examples for other women. As a result of political campaigns urging Koreans to save money and live simply, the savings rate in Korea became extremely high compared with other developing countries (Kohli 2009). Personal savings rates steadily increased in the 1960s and by 1979 reached 22.2 percent (Korean National Statistics Office 1998), demonstrating the considerable success of the state's campaign to normalize the practice of saving.

Middle-class housewives were also supposed to epitomize "moral" modern women. When the husband worked abroad as an engineer or a technician to earn foreign currency, a middle-class homemaker had to manage the household without wasting money or cheating on her husband (Yerim Kim 2007, 361–62). In doing this, the middle-class housewife could practice patriotism: her domestic commitment allowed her husband to dedicate himself to work without any worries. As the crucial ingredient in so-called sweet homes, the middle-class housewife was distinguished from "debauched" women who abandoned their families. As divorce rates increased, particularly among couples whose male partners worked abroad, praise was showered on "normal" middle-class housewives who sacrificed themselves in order to maintain happy families. Poor, uneducated factory or domestic workers, on the other hand, were seen as ignorant and sexually depraved. Housemaids (*hanyŏ* or *singmo*) were often portrayed in films as dangerous and wicked home wreckers who seduced their landlords.[11] By contrast, the middle-class landlady was represented as a good homemaker and wise mother trying to protect her family; suffering the loss of her husband, she was an innocent victim of the wicked housemaid.

In sum, the state and mass media created images of middle-class housewives as wise consumers and avid savers and spread the gospel of the disciplined lifestyle throughout the country. Keeping household account books, living economically, and saving money, educated, middle-class housewives were described as "waging a war" in the domestic sphere. However, they were still expected to be traditional women in their domestic lives—loyal wives and wise mothers who did not disrupt family life. By circulating images of middle-class women as frugal and moral housewives, the state successfully turned middle-class women into ideal social subjects embodying the virtues of discipline and austerity that would lead to national wealth and prosperity. This was a national vision of the middle class distinctive to Korea; contrary to the US or western European models, in which the purchasing power of the middle classes stimulated the domestic market and sustained economic growth (Cohen 2006), the Korean government tightly controlled the consumer market and promoted saving.

The Heavy and Chemical Industrialization Drive and the Rise of Salary Men

The concept of the middle class promoted by the state thrived in official discourse by suggesting a model of national development and modernization. In reality, however, only a small segment of the population could be categorized as middle class. Most middle-class citizens were part of the old middle class—which included small-scale farmers, agricultural producers, and shopkeepers—which was not a product of modern capitalism. Few were members of the new urban middle class, such as office workers and government employees. As the heavy and chemical industrialization (HCI) drive was launched and chaebol were expanded by policies of the Park regime in the early 1970s, the class structure was transformed, and the urban middle class emerged. The shift in emphasis from light to heavy industry produced an alliance between the state and chaebol that led to the employment of a large number of white-collar workers with high incomes and extensive benefits.

Korea's economic strategy in the 1960s was based on the labor-intensive nondurable consumer goods industry, creating products such as textiles, toys, and shoes. Though this strategy promoted rapid economic growth, Park Chung Hee, who feared a political and security crisis in the late 1960s, decided to implement a new political economic strategy: the installation of the Yushin regime based on martial law and the "big push" toward heavy industrialization. The Yushin Constitution, launched in 1972, eliminated outright formal democratic institutions, guaranteeing Park a lifetime tenure in office through the introduction of indirect presidential elections and granting the president nearly unlimited authority (J.-J. Choi 1986).[12] Under the Yushin regime, oppositional forces were severely suppressed, the ruling party became a mere appendage of the executive, and the National Assembly was completely marginalized (Haggard and Moon 1993, 76). The promotion of heavy and chemical industries was a new economic strategy to support the Yushin system. It would provide an "engine of rapid economic growth and export expansion to counter eroding international competitiveness and growing protectionism among light, labor-intensive manufacturers in the United States" (ibid.). It would also realize military self-reliance. In exchange for the denial of political rights and freedom, the Yushin regime promised stability, security, order, and efficiency, simultaneously pursuing high growth and prosperity (J.-J. Choi 1993, 32).

For Park, the promotion of heavy industry was synonymous with building a self-sufficient economy, modernization of the fatherland, and national revival, and this led to his emphasis on HCI as a development model. His vision of national development, which underscored the importance of science and technology and viewed engineers and technicians as the keys to modernization, was often featured in his speeches: "In the late twentieth century, the nation that develops a high level of science and technology will dominate the world. It is common sense that economic development and technological innovation are indivisible. In particular, high-skilled workers are the driving force of economic development. Without technological development, we cannot defend our country. Engineers and technicians are the arms and the shields of the country. From this perspective, we should support science and technology development" (Oh 1999, 90). With the declaration of heavy chemical industrialization (*chunghwahak kongŏphwa*) and "scientification of all citizens" (*chŏn kungmin ŭi kwahakhwa*)[13] in 1973, the Park regime accelerated the state project of heavy industrialization. The development of

HCI in the early 1970s brought about dramatic changes in the Korean economy. First, the industrial structure changed rapidly: the traditional agrarian
economy was industrialized quickly. For example, 63 percent of the Korean
population worked in agriculture and fishing in 1963, but this fell to
50.4 percent in 1970 and to 34 percent by 1980 (Korean National Statistics
Office 1998, 99). By contrast, the percentage of the workforce in the mining
and manufacturing industries increased quickly, from 8.7 percent of all
workers in 1963 to 22.5 percent in 1980 (manufacturing taking up 21.6 percent)
(Korean National Statistics Office 1998, 99). This transformation was much
rapider than in other industrial countries: while England took almost two
centuries and Japan a century to make the transition from an agricultural
economy to an industrial one, Korea accomplished it in three to four decades
(K. Shin 2004, 32).

Second, the acceleration of heavy industrialization resulted in the rapid
growth of big businesses (chaebol) in the 1970s. The Park regime implemented policies favorable toward big business groups, particularly Hyundai
and Daewoo, because of their willingness to invest in heavy industry (Clifford 1998; E. Kim 1997; Lie 1998). Since heavy industry was capital-intensive
by nature, small or medium-sized firms found it difficult to compete against
larger chaebol. In exchange for their plunge into heavy industry, chaebol
were awarded with aggressive, pro-corporate state policies, especially granting of the "investment license," which gave corporations monopolies over
particular commodities (Lie 1998, 92). Furthermore, chaebol enjoyed better
access to capital at subsidized interest rates and benefited from tax incentives,
protective trade measures, and tariff exemptions for importing capital goods.
Between 1972 and 1979 more than 60 percent of policy loans and 50 percent
of general bank loans went to one hundred business groups (Haggard and
Moon 1993, 77–79). These chaebol-favoring state policies boosted big
businesses' share of the national economy. In 1974 sales of the ten biggest
business groups were equivalent to 15 percent of the GNP. By 1980 this
share had increased to nearly half, and by 1984 it had grown to more than
two-thirds (Lie 1998, 91). The ten largest chaebol grew rapidly in the 1970s,
at a rate five to nine times faster than the economy as a whole (E. Kim 1997,
152). Daewoo, the fastest-growing among the ten largest chaebol during
this period, recorded a stunning 53.7 percent average annual growth rate in
total assets, followed by Hyundai's 38 percent (ibid., 155). This economic
strategy focusing on heavy industry created distorted outcomes. The high

concentration of chaebol in the Korean economy made it challenging for small and medium-sized firms to survive; many either went bankrupt or became subcontractors for big businesses. In addition, the rural sector was completely excluded from industrialization, and the income gap between the urban and rural sectors widened over time (Koo 2001, 72).[14]

Last, HCI and the rapid growth of chaebol also affected the Korean labor market as corporations launched massive recruiting drives. In the 1960s, educational elites tended to enter government service, but by the 1970s business was attracting increasing numbers of top-flight graduates (Clifford 1998, 124). As large numbers of skilled and semiskilled workers on the shop floor were hired in the automobile, shipbuilding, and machine industries, the number of managers, engineers, and technicians who supervised workers at the upper level also expanded (D.-M. Cho 1994; Hong 1983; K. Suh 1987). In order to supply skilled labor for heavy industry, the state promoted higher education in science and engineering and established a number of technical high schools, which nurtured and produced a huge group of technical experts (Oh 1999). During the two decades between 1963 and 1983, there was a rapid increase in the number of professionals and managerial and clerical workers (not including sales employees), from 6.8 percent to 16.6 percent of the entire workforce (see table 1.1). During the same period, the number of engineers increased tenfold and that of managers doubled (Amsden 1989, 172).

Those who acquired more education and technical skills, particularly in the sciences and engineering sectors, could easily get decent jobs in big firms, which guaranteed job security, good salaries, and excellent perks. As table 1.2

Table 1.1. Employees by occupation, 1963–1983 (%)

	Technical/ administrative/ professional/ managerial	White-collar workers	Sales workers	Service workers	Production workers
1963	3.3	3.5	10.1	5.2	15.0
1968	3.9	4.5	13.5	5.9	19.9
1973	3.1	6.2	12.2	6.7	21.9
1978	4.7	8.2	12.7	6.9	29.2
1983	6.1	10.5	15.5	10.1	28.4

Source: Korean National Statistics Office 1998, 100.

Table 1.2. Average monthly earnings by occupation, 1971–1981

	Earnings (in thousand won/month)					
Year	Technical experts	Administrative/ managers	White-collar workers	Sales representatives	Service workers	Production workers
1971	40.4	60.8	34.0	20.2	15.5	17.5
1972	44.3	67.8	32.5	24.1	16.6	18.4
1973	51.2	83.5	41.0	31.5	20.5	20.7
1974	60.0	98.5	54.1	34.8	26.3	28.9
1975	92.4	159.4	74.7	43.0	36.1	34.8
1976	136.0	221.0	103.7	52.3	47.9	46.6
1977	135.2	225.4	102.4	69.5	52.5	53.3
1978	179.2	291.5	121.9	86.9	69.2	72.0
1979	233.5	402.9	162.5	106.3	95.0	100.0
1980	266.0	437.7	177.2	108.7	115.3	118.2
1981	302.6	492.6	212.8	136.6	138.8	143.7

Source: Administration of Labor Affairs 1972–1982.

demonstrates, the economic rewards for managers and engineers were significantly greater than those for production workers. On average, between 1972 and 1980, managers (including engineers) earned about four times more than production workers. White-collar workers' wages were twice those of production workers. This wage gap is especially striking when compared with other advanced countries, such as the United States and Japan, where the wages of managers were 1.79 times higher than those of production workers (Amsden 1989, 172). On top of regular salaries, white-collar employees in chaebol received 400–500 percent of their monthly wages as annual bonuses (*Dong-A Ilbo* 1/7/1977).

In addition to higher salaries, white-collar workers and midlevel managers received other kinds of economic benefits. Though government welfare benefits were almost nonexistent (national spending on social welfare was less than 1 percent of GNP in Korea), white-collar workers and managers employed in large firms received substantial benefits through employers. These benefits included housing loans, retirement benefits, subsidies for their children's tuition, and other family-related support, as well as health insurance (Koo 2001, 207). Often, large corporations provided recreational facilities for employees and their families. In return for their serving as the main social welfare provider, the state offered corporations tax deductions and controlled the price of agricultural products in order to curb wage drift and inflation (Song and Hong 2008). Increasing wage levels and access to diverse material benefits provided by employers created conditions under which particular occupational groups began to develop into a middle class. As the Korean economy experienced explosive growth, the majority of employees enjoyed virtual lifetime employment. Being an employee at chaebol meant being guaranteed a comfortable middle-class lifestyle, presumably for life.

With industrialization and economic growth, Korean society witnessed an increase in the number of educated, skilled employees, including engineers, technical experts, and managerial workers in big businesses, banks, and the public sector. Representing Korea's growing technological excellence and enhanced global position in the world economy, the rise of the new middle class showcased the economic success that the Korean state had achieved. The middle class that had existed only in discourse started to emerge and gain in number.

The Middle Class Living a "Modern" and "Cultured" Life

The middle class not only represented an idealized, productive, and frugal lifestyle, both at home and at work, but also symbolized improved living standards and national affluence. In fact, from the time the government implemented the Five-Year Plan of Economic Development in 1962, Korea saw remarkable economic growth. Per capita GNP rose from $82 in 1961 to $1,647 in 1979, a twentyfold increase over eighteen years (Korean National Statistics Office 1998, 116). The most remarkable growth was in exports, which exploded from $119 million in 1964 to $15 billion in 1979, an increase of 12,600 percent in two decades (Korean National Statistics Office 1995, 323). As the entire economy grew, the average income rose quickly. The average monthly income for all urban households was 28,180 won in 1970.[15] This rose to 194,749 won in 1979, which was almost a sevenfold increase in only ten years (Korean National Statistics Office 1998, 111). Wages increased by 40.3 percent in just one year, between 1978 and 1979 (Administration of Labor Affairs 1979, 17). The rapid increase in real wages for ordinary citizens brought about a flood of changes in Korean culture, particularly in housing and consumption.

Rapid economic growth led to a construction boom that transformed the urban landscape. Modern apartment complexes were built as "vanguards" of new residences and symbolized modern middle-class lifestyles. As Laura Neitzel notes about Japan's postwar *danchi* housing[16] construction, new apartment complexes became not only a physical built environment but also an ideological one that provided a powerful vision and social imaginary of an attainable middle-class lifestyle (2016, 26). Similarly, in Korea, apartment construction was promoted by the state and elites as innovative living space. At a ceremony marking the completion of the Mapo apartment complex in 1964, President Park praised modern apartments as instruments of national modernization, an alternative to the rural backwardness of the old feudal system (Gelézeau 2007, 130). From the 1960s onward, the government encouraged apartment construction for middle-class families, and the mayor of Seoul announced in 1966 that the city government would build 40,000 apartment buildings for middle-class citizens (*JoongAng Ilbo* 5/25/1966). Yet until the mid-1970s apartment living was still unfamiliar among most Koreans, and the preferred type of residence was a single-family house (N. Chun, Yang, and Hong 2009, 149). Large-scale apartment construction was promoted in new neighborhoods—especially in the Gangnam district (which is discussed in chapter 2)—and the particular lifestyles in new apartment complexes were celebrated by architects, social engineers, and journalists.

New apartment buildings replaced old kitchens and dirty toilets with modern conveniences. They were also located in neighborhoods equipped with supermarkets, parking lots, and children's playgrounds. While conventional Korean-style houses (*hanok*) had outdoor kitchens and toilets, the newly built apartments guaranteed the privacy of each family member, incorporating indoor kitchens and bathrooms along with the conveniences of electricity, cooking gas, and running water. New apartment complexes became a symbol of modernity and the new culture of the middle class. Many writers and intellectuals acclaimed the new apartment life: "Compared with our old, traditional houses, the apartment seems much more cultured and even romantic. Whereas our traditional houses did not guarantee any privacy for big families, apartments bring freedom and modernity. *Residents are usually so-called intelligentsia, not factory workers or the poor.* In contrast to maintaining a traditional lifestyle in a house that has not been improved since the premodern period, apartments with gas, hot water, electricity, phones, and mannered neighbors symbolize culture and civilization" (Jinman Kim 1963, 61, emphasis added). Early residents in these new apartments were mostly young, educated white-collar families, as many reports indicated. More than half of the new apartment residents were college graduates and worked at big business firms, in government, and in schools.[17] If they were not rich, they earned stable incomes (O. Kim 1967). This particular demographic composition of apartment residents demonstrated the superior character of apartments relative to traditional types of housing. Apartments and apartment living soon became naturally linked with images of the middle class and its modern and affluent lifestyle.

Just as factories and plants symbolized an industrial nation, apartment buildings embodied urbanity, modernity, and civilization. Living in an apartment also represented a *revolution* in lifestyle that improved the quality of life by heightening energy efficiency and liberating housewives from unnecessary labor. After moving into a new apartment, a housewife reported how convenient apartment living was: "Sleeping in a bed is much more comfortable than on the floor. Since the inside temperature is always around 22°C, we do not need to wear a lot of clothes in the apartment. It is also possible to use hot water whenever I want. Furthermore, the heating system runs on oil instead of coal briquettes, so I do not need to worry about coal poisoning. I do not need to hire housemaids to help do chores around the house, and going out is really convenient, as the apartment is watched by a security guard" (*Chosun Ilbo* 12/11/1970). As pointed out by many apartment-dwelling housewives, the biggest advantage of apartment living was the convenient lifestyle. They did not need to worry about the security of their homes or the dangers of coal, and because they could manage without hired help, they actually cut household expenses. Furthermore, apartments were much easier to keep clean than traditional Korean houses. Modern heating methods meant that they did not have the storage and dust problems caused by coal briquettes. While traditional houses were considered dark and dingy, modern middle-class apartments symbolized brightness and cleanliness (Lett 1998, 116). The convenience of living in apartments became associated with modernity and civilization and became more popular among the well-to-do.

Living in modern apartments also meant using modern household goods. The washing machine, the refrigerator, and the black-and-white TV, called "the three sacred treasures" (*samsin'gi*),[18] symbolized in the late 1960s the everyday revolution of domestic electrification and mass consumption. The presence of *samsin'gi* certified the identity of the individual household as a "modern family" (Yoshimi 2006, 77). Although these electric appliances were still luxurious items for an ordinary family at that time, they rapidly entered Korean homes, especially those of urban middle-class families. According to a 1978 newspaper survey of middle-class white-collar citizens—employees who had worked in the government, banks, and business firms for more than ten years—every respondent had a television set at home; 96 percent of respondents owned refrigerators; 64 percent owned washing machines; 42.7 percent owned pianos; and 2.7 percent owned cars (*Kyunghyang Shinmun* 11/17/1978). What were luxury items in the 1960s had become more common among urban middle-class families in the 1970s. In the 1960s, television sets had been quite rare among urban households; now they were universal. As table 1.3 shows, in 1970 less than 5 percent of urban households had refrigerators, but that proportion jumped to roughly 50 percent in 1980. Household washing machines were virtually unknown in 1970, and less than 2 percent of households owned them in 1975, but by 1980 about 16 percent of urban households owned washing machines. The increase in TV ownership was most dramatic, rising from 6.4 percent in 1970 to almost 90 percent by 1980. Throughout the 1970s, owning such consumer goods became more and more common, and this phenomenon went national.

The increasing availability of these household durables provided strong evidence not only that consumerism was emerging as a way of life but also that the extreme poverty of the early 1960s had dramatically decreased. The increasing social and cultural prominence of the urban middle class brought

Table 1.3. Ownership rates for major household goods (% by household)

	TV		Telephone		Refrigerator		Washing machine	
Year	Whole Country	Cities	Whole Country	Cities	Whole Country	Cities	Whole Country	Cities
1970	6.4	13.7	4.8	8.6	2.2	4.5	–	–
1975	30.2	44.4	9.6	13.5	6.5	11.7	1.0	1.9
1980	86.7	90.9	24.1	30.3	37.8	51.5	10.4	16.1

Sources: Kyŏngje Kihoegwŏn 1970, 1975, 1980.

with it the rise of consumer culture. While in the official discourse of the 1960s the urban middle class contributed to national modernization through its frugality and discipline, in the 1970s it was again the nation's savior—but this time through its adoption of "cultured" consumer lifestyles.

Yet the dominant discourse on mass consumption and consumer culture, such as apartment living, home electrification, and car ownership, was more aspirational than reflective of reality. Though it was true that more and more household consumer durables were being purchased by the end of the 1970s, the discourse on consumerism remained a national imaginary promoted by the government, intellectuals, and the mass media. Through the "hegemonic" representation of consumer culture and middle-class lifestyles, the state and intellectuals set the terms of Korean development and modernization.

Aspirations to Join the Middle Class

Although the image of the urban middle class signified the bright side of high economic growth in Korea, the majority of factory workers still suffered from low wages and long working hours under miserable conditions. Industrialization led to economic expansion for the whole country, but the benefits were far from equally distributed. It is widely recognized that Korean workers were subject to extreme capitalist exploitation, were forced to work long hours, and were paid low wages (J.-J. Choi 1997; Deyo 1989; Koo 2001). Korean workers worked the longest hours in developing countries: 52.3 hours a week in 1970, up from 50.3 hours a week in 1960. However, their wages did not keep pace with the increasing hours. Though the government trumpeted the rapid increase in real wages during these two decades—around a 10 percent rise in annual real wages in the 1970s alone (J.-J. Choi 1997, 332)—the growth in wages for production workers was extremely small. Hagen Koo notes that a large proportion of Korean manufacturing workers were paid wages below subsistence levels throughout the 1970s and even into the first half of the 1980s (2001, 58). The average income for production workers was 25 percent lower than the national average (Administration of Labor Affairs 1979). Though mainstream development scholars often celebrate Korea for achieving both growth and equity—high economic growth with relatively low social inequality—the dismal working conditions that most manufacturing workers faced at that time tend to undercut such assertions.

Mostly led by female factory workers, Koreans in the 1970s started organizing independent, democratic labor unions with the help of religious activists (Christian churches, for the most part) and progressive intellectuals and demanded more humane working conditions on the shop floor (Soonok Chun 2003; Koo 2001). Nonetheless, throughout the Park regime, the number of strikes remained extremely low, and the patterns of labor resistance were localized with no significant signs of large-scale resistance (J.-J. Choi 1997).[19] Obviously, the state's strict labor repression and the rapid pace of industrialization at least partly explain the workers' silence and the underdevelopment of working-class identity. At the same time, however, the state's promise of upward mobility and improved living standards as an eventual payoff for short-term pain and sacrifice also played a role in preventing massive resistance. The state, as well as many intellectuals, argued that the growth of national wealth would result in a trickle-down effect, ultimately benefiting the entire population evenly (Lim 1973, 60). The slim hope of upward mobility and escape from miserable working conditions sustained factory workers as they endured poverty.[20] Despite rising social inequality, the increased enjoyment of leisure and consumption of new household commodities by the small but growing middle class symbolized what modern life could be for those not yet a part of it. State promotion of the discourse of upward mobility and the visibility of consumption during the two decades of industrialization seemed to promise everyone a middle-class lifestyle in the near future.

Images of the urban middle class played an ambivalent role in accomplishing state aims. On one hand, they served to disseminate an official state ideology of frugality, discipline, and self-reliance. On the other hand, they also created consumerist dreams, showcasing improved living standards and thus bolstering the regime's political legitimacy. Although the state and some intellectuals disapproved of conspicuous consumption, widespread purchase of the latest gadgets and leisure goods by the middle class led the Korean nation into the new modern world. The urban middle class was in the vanguard of introducing and disseminating the rationalized culture of modernity. It was ironic that the state promoted extensive mass consumption as the reward for enduring a life of discipline and austerity. In this respect, images of the middle class might seem contradictory, since they promoted both austerity and consumerism. However, the message was clear: if you work hard and live frugally, you will become middle class and enjoy all the material fruits of your hard-won status.

The Park regime advertised specific features of Korea's future, such as the popular use of consumer goods and expanded opportunity for leisure. The description of Korea's future presented in official state discourse consistently featured middle-class lifestyles, even when they were not explicitly tied to the middle class. In a 1967 speech, President Park declared, "In the 1970s, people will enjoy leisure time with their families, just as housewives will frugally manage their households in modern houses with up-to-date kitchens" (C. H. Park 1973a, 919). In another speech, he argued, "By the end of the Third Economic Development Plan, the typical Korean lifestyle will allow salary men to buy their own cars and go to the suburbs for day trips on the weekends" (C. H. Park 1973b, 1045). In 1978 the ruling Democratic Republican Party (DRP) published a booklet describing the future Korea of 1986 as an affluent nation where most people would be car owners and homeowners enjoying color TVs and phones and traveling abroad: "As economic growth accelerates and industrialization matures, the basic necessities of life will be fulfilled. Beyond simply meeting the basic necessities, everyone will enjoy a higher quality of life. We expect that by 1991, not only will the housing shortage problem be totally resolved, but all citizens will also enjoy decent lives in 'cultural houses' [*munhwa chut'aek*].[21] In the 1980s, our lives will be closer to the level of advanced civilization, with a ready supply of various durable consumer goods, including color TVs, washing machines, refrigerators, electric ovens, and air conditioners" (Minju Konghwadang 1978, 186–87). The ruling party employed some key terms to define its vision of the future Korea, such as "my car age," "technology revolution," and "increased leisure." By portraying significantly improved living standards and incomes, this booklet illustrated the prevailing notion that Korean society was headed toward becoming a predominantly middle-class society.

At the end of the 1970s, many newspaper articles reported on the transformed social landscape, focusing on the weekend leisure boom and car ownership. Celebrating the improvement in living standards, these articles detailed how ordinary citizens had escaped from poverty and built better lives for themselves. "My car" (*maik'a*) and "my home" (*maihom*) were two common expressions that began appearing in newspapers or magazines in the late 1970s. News articles about the increasing number of people taking driving tests and the increasing number of private cars on the streets showed how soon the age of "my car" was approaching (*Dong-A Ilbo* 5/4/1978; *Maeil Kyungje* 12/17/1979). There was a genuine widespread excitement about Korea's newly visible domestic opulence: "Since ten years ago, when the phrase 'the age of my car' [*maik'a sidae*] appeared, the term has been immensely popular. If you go to the DMV in Gangnam, you will be shocked at the number of people taking driving tests. There have been days this year when about 10,000 people tried to take the driving test . . . Salary man Mr. K, who came to pick up his driver's license, told me, 'Think about three years from now. People with "my cars" will not be seen as high class. It is going to be the same as purchasing TV sets when they first came out. In ten years, if you cannot drive, people will take you for a fool'" (*Dong-A Ilbo* 5/4/1978). This "my car" discourse was misleading and did not reflect the current reality: in the 1970s, having "my car" was not common at all. Although domestic production expanded greatly in the second half of the 1970s, from 9,069 cars in 1974 to 112,314 in 1979, throughout the 1970s rates of ownership of private automobiles remained very low (Nelson 2000, 94).[22] Nonetheless, the media lavished attention on "my car fever," and the rapid increase of car owners and drivers received a great deal of positive press. It was important for the state to present "my car" aspirations as a national project, since car ownership was a concrete symbol of an advanced economy. It was said that the popularization of "my car" and the development of the automobile industry were emblematic of the maturity of modernization, as in advanced nations such as the United States (H.-G. Kim 1989, 125). Though not many at the time could enjoy the privilege of purchasing their own cars and apartments, the dominant discourse of "my car" and "my home" reinforced the fantasy of becoming middle class. While income inequality had been rising since the start of industrialization, continued economic growth and visible economic prosperity generated a perception of mass culture and mass consumption. The predominant urban images in the mass media, showing high-rise buildings and apartments with streets full of cars, might have been deceptive, but they symbolized Korean modernity and civilization opening a new era.

Rapid economic growth led Koreans to assess their current situation optimistically, especially with respect to class identity and mobility. Several national surveys conducted at the end of the 1970s show that ordinary citizens increasingly identified themselves as middle class. For example, according to a poll of 2,000 households conducted by the Ministry of Culture and Public Information (Munhwa Kongbobu) at the end of 1977, the overwhelming majority of respondents (86.8 percent) believed that their living standards were those of the middle class (*Dong-A Ilbo* 2/8/1978; *Kyunghyang Shinmun* 2/8/1978). On the other hand, social scientists, who measured the proportion of the middle class using objective indicators such as occupation, income, and homeownership, estimated that the middle class included no more than 30 percent of the Korean population (Hong 2005; K. Kim 1993). The survey results show that middle-class self-identification was hugely overrepresented; in Marx's terms, Korean citizens had developed a false class consciousness. This excess of middle-class identity could be interpreted as a result of anticommunist state ideology that repressed working-class identity, as previous scholars have noted (H.-Y. Cho 1998; K. Shin 2004). Yet the surge of middle-class identification by the end of the 1970s also shows that Koreans had become optimistic as a result of the economic progress made since the 1960s. Although it would have been difficult to believe immediately after the coup in 1961, the Park regime had succeeded in reshaping Korean self-perceptions, creating a national identity based on economic modernization and middle-class identification. In the public perception, a comfortable, "cultured" lifestyle had shifted from being virtually unobtainable to being within almost everyone's reach.

The growing ubiquity of cars, apartments, and summer vacation trips, viewed as quintessentially middle class, helped to establish the rising standard of living as a point of national pride. The survey conducted by the Ministry of Culture and Public Information also found that rapid economic growth led to increasing national pride among the public: the majority (88.8 percent) agreed that the Korean economy would be self-sufficient soon, and over half (52.4 percent) expected that it would be comparable to the most advanced economies (*Dong-A Ilbo* 2/8/1978; *Kyunghyang Shinmun* 2/8/1978). Public confidence in the economy also led to an increasingly positive perception of the government's performance: the majority (80.4 percent) believed that corruption had become less common than four or five years before.[23] Yet the national optimism and confidence about the improving lives and upward mobility of the middle class obscured an increase in social inequality. While some radical student groups and intellectuals criticized state policies that resulted in uneven economic development and advocated redistribution for greater social equality, their claims could not effectively compete with the state's discourse of high economic growth and modernization. Despite increased mobilization and organizing capacity toward the end of the 1970s, anti-regime struggles and resistance mostly remained at the local level and were unable to mobilize people on a larger scale.[24]

With the help of intellectuals and the mass media, the authoritarian state created and disseminated a specific vision of national development that was embedded in middle-class discourses about comfortable and modern life-styles. By doing this, the state successfully generated widespread societal support for its developmental projects. Near-universal membership in the middle class had become the national goal to be met in the near future. The Park regime successfully created the middle class as a new national identity and strongly linked this class identity to peace and prosperity.

In this chapter I have investigated how the idea and imagery of the middle class were promoted in Korea. The creation of the Korean middle class was a political and cultural project: while the urban middle class was still embryonic in the early stages of industrialization, it was represented as the social mainstream in the mass media and official discourse. Through the projection of particular images of the urban middle class, the Korean state tried to promote national modernization and development. Not only did the middle class serve as the model of an ideal citizenship with moderate and balanced worldviews that would help build a strong, anticommunist nation-state, but its thrifty and economizing lifestyle would, it was believed, contribute to national wealth. Politicians, scholars, and commentators to-gether produced the middle class as a carrier of modernity and civility that would strengthen national identity and the political legitimacy of the state.

In tandem with embodying forms of social discipline such as hard work and frugal living, the middle class also symbolized material affluence and the new consumer culture reflected in apartment living, home electrification, and the leisure boom. This modern, "civilized" middle-class lifestyle was celebrated in the mass media as evidence of successful economic development and material progress. While the actual middle class was still a small (though increasing) segment of the population, images of the new middle class in the mass media created widespread social aspirations in the 1970s. In this sense, the middle class was more a product of dominant discourse and social imag-ination than a reflection of socioeconomic reality in Korea.

The rise of middle-class identity and the inexorable spread of consumer culture in the 1970s suggested that Korea was recovering from the tragedy of the Korean War and moving toward peace and prosperity. These develop-ments implied a social mobility wherein anyone could rise to a higher station in life (Fernandes 2006), given enough hard work and strenuous effort. Thus, the increase in claims of middle-class identity played a role in concealing a rise in social inequality and in strengthening social homogenization, at least for a while, which helped the state smooth the process of development and modernization.

Chapter 2

The Rise of "Gangnam Style"

Real Estate and Middle-Class Dreams, 1978–1996

Hyundai Apartment in Apgujeong-dong is an equal society of desires
and a socialist heaven of fashion.

—Ha Yu, *Param Punŭn Nal Imyŏn Apkujŏng-dong e Kaya Handa: Yu Ha Sijip*
(We Have to Go to Apgujeong-dong When It Is a Windy Day)

The five of us lived in hell and we thought of heaven. There wasn't a single
day that we didn't. Because each and every day of our life was insufferable.
Our life was a war. And in that war, every day, we were losers.

—Se-Hee Cho, *Nanjangi ka ssoa ollin chagŭn kong*
(A Little Ball Launched by a Dwarf)

In 2012 the song "Gangnam Style" made the Korean pop star Psy a global sensation. Few listeners outside Korea knew that the song parodies the lifestyle of a district in Seoul called Gangnam. Since the late 1970s Gangnam has, within Korea, served as an icon of rapid economic development and affluent lifestyles. Having benefited greatly from rising real estate prices and planned urban development, Gangnam has become one of the wealthiest and most expensive districts in Korea and embodies prosperity, social status, and high culture. Psy mocks Gangnam for its superficial materialism. The song reflects Koreans' ambivalent views of Gangnam. On one hand, it is an aspirational place, and ordinary Koreans are envious of the district's residents and dream of moving there themselves. On the other hand, many feel that much of the wealth possessed by Gangnam residents has been acquired unfairly or undeservedly through unearned income from housing price inflation.

The anthropologist Denise Lett remarks that the urban middle class in contemporary Korea is usually understood as being synonymous with people living in Gangnam and/or residing in high-rise apartment complexes (Lett

1998, 102).[1] Indeed, Gangnam was the place where, in the 1970s, huge, expensive apartment complexes were born and popularized and where the typical Korean middle-class neighborhood as it is now understood was created. Yet the history of Gangnam reveals the irony of Korean capitalism and the Korean urban middle class. Conventional wisdom holds that the middle class is a merit-based group with educational credentials and technical job skills. Although these traits do partly characterize the middle class, the Gangnam case demonstrates the *speculative and contingent* characteristics inherent in the scramble for middle-class status. Many of the first-generation middle class in Korea were able to accumulate wealth and acquire class mobility through homeownership and real estate investment due to the real estate boom and subsequent skyrocketing housing prices. The apartment lottery system (*ap'at'ŭ punyangjedo*) was an important policy that aimed to promote homeownership by providing middle-income families with apartment units for affordable prices. However, the apartment lotteries in Gangnam were subverted by speculators and opportunists who drove up housing prices. Those lucky enough to win a Gangnam lottery (often by manipulating the system) eventually profited from housing price inflation—leaving behind many others who did not enjoy such an opportunity and producing a collective sense that class mobility was a matter of luck rather than hard work and merit. While development scholars praise Korea for achieving both economic growth and equity (Diane Davis 2004; Kohli 2004; Teichman 2012), when it comes to housing policy, the state did not effectively manage housing distribution, which became a major source of social inequality. Statistics reveal the severe inequality in housing and real estate in Korea. Compared with the national income inequality index, real estate inequality is extremely high (0.747) (N.-G. Son 2008, 205). Looking at the process of Gangnam development helps us to understand how this particular kind of inequality became more widespread in Korea and how becoming middle class went hand in hand with apartment construction and real estate investment.

By examining urban development in Gangnam, this chapter aims to highlight a spatial dimension of middle-class formation: how urban development creates differentiated residential space and how residents in particular spaces foster common economic and cultural orientations. Exploring how the middle-class space and middle-class culture of apartment living were manufactured, I argue that state-directed urban redevelopment plans and state-sponsored homeownership programs provided the material conditions under which a nascent urban middle class could improve its standard of living. By promoting massive apartment construction, initiating a government-subsidized housing program (the apartment lottery system), building infra-structure, and strengthening the school system, the government transformed Gangnam, once a nearly empty area with low property values, into a district of middle-class apartment residents. Gangnam residents, in turn, cultivated middle-class lifestyles in high-rise apartment complexes. Sharing similar life-styles with their neighbors and employing gatekeeping practices to separate themselves from outsiders, apartment residents tried to create their own living space and to develop distinctive identities.

In this chapter, I focus on the era from 1978 to 1996, during which the Gangnam area started to be developed and the first generation of the Gang-nam middle class materialized in Korean society. Despite an emerging scholarly interest in Gangnam and apartment living in recent years (for ex-ample, M.-R. Cho 2004; Sang-In Chun 2009; Gelézeau 2007; J. Kang 2006; N. Kang 2004; H.-G. Kim 2004; H.-C. Park 2013), few studies focus on the interactions between the living space and the formation of the middle class. By documenting the lives and experiences of the middle class as shaped by the housing market, this chapter aims to contribute to a critical understand-ing of the nexus among urban redevelopment, the housing and real estate market, and class formation and identity in Korea.

Gangnam as Representative Middle-Class Space

Gangnam literally indicates the area south of the Han River (*gang* means "river," *nam* means "south"), as opposed to Gangbuk (north of the Han River). While Gangnam can be defined in different ways—from the narrow-est Gangnam-gu to the broad south of the Han River, throughout this book I refer to Gangnam as including three administrative units of Gangnam-gu, Seocho-gu, and Songpa-gu, which are usually adopted by the media and represent Gangnam's typical characteristics, a space of economically affluent, highly educated residents (see map 2.1).[2]

Gangnam has come to symbolize the wealth, social status, and prestige of the Korean upper middle and middle classes; it is the center of finance, education, fashion, and information technology and provides access to good school districts and convenient living environments (see figure 2.1). Gang-

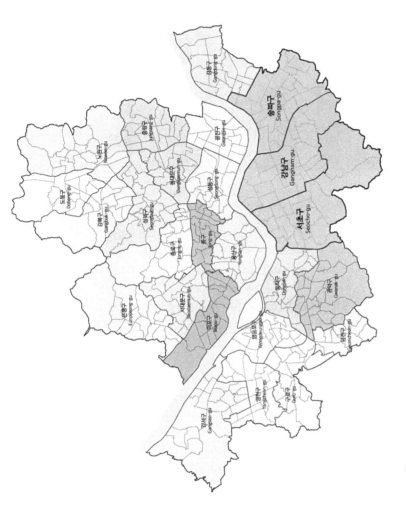

Map 2.1. The Gangnam district in Seoul.
Source: Seoul Research Data Service (http://data.si.re.kr/).

Figure 2.1. The current landscape of Gangnam.
Source: https://jmagazine.joins.com/monthly/view/305431 (accessed 12/11/2016).

nam's status as the most desirable residential district in Seoul has served to maintain its high rents and housing prices and has attracted many affluent middle-class families. An address in Gangnam has become a status symbol. Gangnam-gu has a budget three times larger than the average in other administrative units in Seoul and a very well-maintained infrastructure. Gangnam has the highest apartment price per *p'yŏng*[3]—twice as much as the average in Seoul, and four times as much as some other areas (N. Kang 2004, 65). It is home to 37 percent of the members of the National Assembly and 39 percent of top state officials (*JoongAng Ilbo* 1/16/2002). The mass media produce hegemonic images of Gangnam as a place of upscale apartments and conspicuous consumption of high-end designer products. These images create widespread social aspirations to live in Gangnam, and they endow Gangnam's residents with symbolic power (Bourdieu 1989), a pride in what they view as the superiority of the way they live. In this sense, Gangnam is a symbolic and idealized space that suggests a model for middle-class living and creates desires for upward mobility.

One might ask why Gangnam is considered a middle-class space instead of upper class or elite. It is true that some pockets of Gangnam contain wealthy segments of the population, as signified by luxurious high-rise buildings and conspicuous consumption, and many wealthy people have moved there because of the images of affluence that Gangnam is associated with. Though the luxurious images of Gangnam predominant in mass media might give an impression that Gangnam is an elite space, most inhabitants of Gangnam would not be categorized as upper class based on measures of occupational prestige and social status broadly used among sociologists (Wright 1985) to identify the middle class. Following these measures, the middle class consists of occupational groups such as white-collar employees or professionals who are highly educated and earn stable salaries. Gangnam's biggest occupational groups are highly educated professionals and white-collar employees, who can be identified as primarily middle class. As of 2013, more than half of residents in Gangnam-gu were professionals (34.6 percent), white-collar workers (22.4 percent), or managers (8.6 percent). These figures are much higher than the average in Seoul (where professionals account for 25.3 percent of the population, white-collar employees 20.2 percent, and managers 4.2 percent). At the same time, Gangnam is clearly not working class: 32.3 percent of its residents have received a higher education (college and above), and less than 10 percent of residents are manufacturing workers (Gangnam-gu 2014, 61). When Gangnam was initially developed in the late 1970s, the residents were mainly white-collar families whose breadwinners worked at big corporations, at banks, and in the public sector. In short, Gangnam's demographic composition indicates that the majority of residents have been relatively well-paid, salaried employees and their families—the backbone of the new middle class.

Gangnam epitomizes the ways in which high-rise apartment complexes became an essential component of middle-class life in Korea. Before Gangnam, the urban space in Korea had been more mixed and had not been spatialized by different classes. In the mid-1970s, as new apartment complexes were being built on a large scale in Gangnam, rural, low-income residents were displaced and instead white-collar families with stable jobs and incomes resided there. Apartment residents with similar socioeconomic characteristics lived together, shared similar lifestyles, and formed an identity around their living space. The rise of Gangnam exemplifies the process by which the idea of the middle class materialized in the living space and by which urban space became increasingly stratified.

In contrast to its current reputation as a middle-class space, Gangnam's past was very modest. Prior to the 1970s, the center of the city was in Gangbuk, and there was little demand for housing in the undeveloped Gangnam area. How was this insignificant, sparsely populated district transformed into a Korean status symbol? Tracing how Gangnam was created and how it became what it is now can help us to understand how state and urban policies shape the character of urban space and class configurations.

A Mega State Project: The Birth of Gangnam

In the 1970s, Seoul, the capital of Korea, was experiencing a rapid population increase and suffering from an accompanying housing shortage. Between 1960 and 1970, the population had doubled, from 2.45 million to 5.5 million, and by 1988 it had doubled again, reaching 10 million.[4] Because of state-driven industrialization, more and more people left their rural hometowns and migrated to big cities, particularly Seoul, for better opportunities. This explosive population increase in Seoul created a number of problem areas, including transportation, housing, and the environment. The housing shortage was particularly serious. For example, in 1960 more than half of all households in Seoul lived in a single room (*tank'anbang*), and it was quite common for multiple families to share a house.[5]

In the face of increasing population pressure and the subsequent shortage of housing, the Park Chung Hee regime started looking into developing Gangnam and relocating some of the population there. Until the early 1970s land in the Gangnam district was cheap, used mostly for pear orchards and mulberry fields. The population in 1963 was only 14,867 in what is now Gangnam-gu and 12,069 in what is now Seocho-gu. (As of 2014, Gangnam-gu's population was 583,446 and Seocho-gu's 454,288.)[6] The current heart of Gangnam was then completely rural, and some Gangnam neighborhoods even lacked an appropriate sewage system until the early 1980s. In the 1970s, Gangnam was not connected to the center of the city and was isolated because of its poor infrastructure. Public transportation, public phones, and post offices were completely lacking. Gangnam's isolated location and lack of social infrastructure made it nearly uninhabitable and unappealing to most Seoul citizens.

The government tried to promote Gangnam's development by enacting laws, stimulating the real estate market, and building basic social infrastructure. It simultaneously acted to curb the growth of overpopulated Gangbuk by restricting construction of new department stores, schools, and bars there (J.-M. Son 2005, 229) and provided significant tax exemptions for urban projects in Gangnam (S.-H. Chang 2004, 60). At first, the city government tried to make Gangnam the hub of transportation and administration. All the major transportation facilities, including bus terminals, were moved from Gangbuk to Gangnam. Starting with the Third Han River Bridge in 1969, the government constructed a number of bridges connecting Gangnam and Gangbuk and designed second and third subway lines to penetrate the Gangnam region (J. Kang 2006; J.-M. Son 2005). Major government and business offices were relocated to Gangnam. The Supreme Prosecutors' Office and the Supreme Court were soon followed by the Korean Customs Service, the Korean Electric Power Corporation, and the Foreign Service Offices (Seoul Metropolitan Office 2012, 23). At the time, the decision to promote Gangnam seemed unsound, yet the government invested a large amount of resources in developing Gangnam to incorporate it into the city.

In tandem with relocating major facilities to Gangnam, the government promoted massive apartment construction there, designating about 25 percent of the district's land for this purpose (J.-M. Son 2005, 231). At that time, apartment living was still alien to most Koreans. Until the late 1960s, there were roughly thirty apartment buildings nationwide, accommodating approximately 1,000 households in total (Seoul Metropolitan Office 1983). The large-scale construction of apartments beginning in the mid-1970s changed the cityscape, introduced Koreans to apartment living, and cultivated middle-class identities through the manipulation of residential space. To provide a better residential environment, the government also encouraged the building of amenities in Gangnam to appeal to potential residents, including medical facilities, libraries, parks, and department stores.

Last but not least, the government relocated elite high schools from Gangbuk to Gangnam by offering the schools better land prices. Beginning in 1976, several such schools made this move. Though many people were still reluctant to leave Gangbuk, the relocation of elite schools triggered a large-scale migration of middle-class families to Gangnam.

In sum, the development of Gangnam was a large state project aimed at resolving the housing problems and population pressures of Seoul. It was carried out through quick and aggressive top-down measures. By investing resources and providing infrastructure, the state was trying to transform Gangnam into the center of the city.

The Making of Speculative Gangnam: The Alliance between the State and Chaebol

Gangnam's development and apartment complex construction went hand in hand. By building new residential districts in Gangnam, the government tried to alleviate the housing shortage in Seoul and, at the same time, to disperse the population, which was intensely concentrated in the northern district. This was an important task for the authoritarian state, inasmuch as providing decent housing was directly related to social and political stability. In 1972 the Ministry of Construction set the ambitious goal of building more than one million housing units between 1972 and 1981 (Gelézeau 2007, 91). To achieve that goal, the Korean government implemented massive housing construction projects, particularly large-scale apartment complexes. Given Korea's small land area, policymakers regarded building large apartment buildings as the most viable way to provide more housing (Korean Housing Corporation [hereafter KHC] 1992, 493). Seventy percent of housing constructed in the 1970s consisted of apartment complexes accommodating more than 2,000 households, and apartment buildings accounted for up to 90 percent of newly constructed housing in the 1980s and the 1990s (Gelézeau 2007, 91). Between 1975 and 1979, 17,108 apartment units were constructed in the Gangnam area, and between 1981 and 1985 a total of 40,319 apartment units were constructed in Gangnam (Seoul Museum of History 2011, 42). As of 1985, apartments accounted for only 26.5 percent of all domiciles in Seoul as a whole, but 72.7 percent of domiciles in the Gangnam district were apartments.

In the early 1970s, the public enterprise KHC (Taehan Chut'aek Kongsa)[7] led colossal apartment construction projects in Gangnam. Seoul's first large-scale middle-class apartment complex in Gangnam's Banpo neighborhood was built between 1971 and 1974 (KHC 1992, 380). While previous apartment complexes contained no more than 1,000 to 1,500 households, the Banpo apartment complex accommodated up to 4,000 households and 15,000 people (ibid.). After the Banpo project, there were even larger developments, such as the Jamsil complex. Called Jamsil New Town, this complex on the east side of Gangnam hosted 20,000 households and 100,000 residents (KHC 1992, 130–31). Under the slogan "180 days of strategy of housing construction," 280,000 construction workers were mobilized, and it took only two years, from 1975 to 1977, to complete this project (ibid.; J.-M. Son 2005).

These huge apartment complexes built in Banpo and Jamsil were very different from the small-scale apartment buildings constructed previously. They had particular features to provide comfortable and convenient living for residents. The units ranged from 22 to 44 *p'yŏng* (approximately 783 to 1,566 square feet) in area and targeted relatively affluent families. The KHC built apartments with larger units because policymakers were afraid that building apartments for the poor would lead to the formation of inner-city ghettos (D.-G. Lim and Kim 2015, 156). As self-sufficient communities, these large apartment complexes were equipped with facilities such as schools, shopping centers, grocery stores, gyms, playgrounds, and green space (J.-M. Son 2005). This model set the terms for later apartment construction and became a new, alternative way of middle-class living.

Though public enterprises such as the KHC built some gigantic apartment complexes in Gangnam in the 1970s, their target constituency typically had incomes *above* the average, even among those in relatively smaller units in Jamsil (Gelézeau 2007, 97). The Korean government prioritized investment in heavy industry and lacked the resources to directly provide affordable housing for the majority of the population. It therefore mobilized private developers, including chaebol, to build housing (J.-C. Kim and Choe 1997, 115). According to Kim and Choe, 67 percent of new housing was supplied by the private housing industry in 1975 and 79.9 percent in 1980 (ibid., 116–17). The government required these developers to charge affordable prices for the apartments (N.-G. Son 2008, 77). However, as building bigger apartments was more profitable and brought higher return rates (see table 2.1), private developers focused on building larger and more expensive apartments

Table 2.1. Construction companies' profit per *p'yŏng* on apartment sales (1 *p'yŏng* equals 35.58 square feet)

Size (unit: *p'yŏng*)	77	50	45	38	34	13
Construction cost (unit: 1,000 won)	565	414	419	407	407	251
Selling price (unit: 1,000 won)	690	500	500	491	476	266
Return rate (%)	21.9	20.8	19.3	20.6	17.0	2.3
Company (developer)	Sunkyung	Samik	Samik	Woosung	Woosung	KHC

Source: Hyun 1978, 144.

targeting the middle or upper middle class. Thus, housing policy favored more affluent social groups and sponsored homeownership for those who could afford to buy and live in brand-new buildings.

Chaebol that participated in the apartment construction business in Gangnam were among the biggest beneficiaries. While chaebol are recognized as the motors of Korean economic growth, it is less well known that they have made significant profits from apartment construction and land speculation in the course of industrialization. The Korean government provided many incentives to chaebol to attract them to the apartment construction business. Not only did the government offer affordable land prices to companies for apartment construction, but it also granted tax exemptions (D.-G. Lim and Kim 2015, 158). Yet these private developers benefited the most from an apartment lottery system launched in 1977. Under this system, developers could sell apartment units even before they were completed; the slogan was "Distribution first, construction later" (sŏnbunyang, hugŏnsŏl). Anyone wanting to buy a new apartment had to open an account and deposit money with the Housing Bank, the exclusive manager of the Korean apartment lottery system. Chances of winning the lottery depended on the number of years in advance deposits were made. For example, those who made deposits two years in advance were assigned to the first class, and those depositing one year in advance to the second class (Gelézeau 2007, 93). Someone who drew a lot that gave them a chance to purchase an apartment had to pay in full before they moved into their unit. Construction companies could receive the deposits and lump-sum installments of applicants even before construction was completed, and they could pay subcontractors for construction materials within forty-five days of completion of construction; at a time of double-digit interest rates, construction companies could easily earn huge interest incomes (Hyun 1978, 140). In addition, the profit rates of construction companies were high: selling prices were usually twice as high as production costs, and the rate of return could amount to almost 40 percent (ibid., 142).

Because of these financial advantages, the apartment business was always lucrative for construction companies, and a number of firms grew rapidly through housing construction. For example, Woosung and Hanshin, which started as small construction-supply companies, quickly became well established chaebol by building apartment complexes in the Banpo and Seocho areas in Gangnam (J.-S. Shin 1976). Hyundai, which was best known for its large construction contracts in the Middle East, also built a large-scale apartment complex in Apgujeong that accommodated 3,000 households (Gelézeau 2007, 39). Taking advantage of government support and high demand in apartments, companies that invested in the apartment business in the 1970s and 1980s made enormous profits.[8]

Chaebol gained tremendous benefits by selling apartments in Gangnam and other areas. This construction business also opened a way for them to earn huge revenues through real estate speculation. A combination of Park's large-scale heavy industry promotion, large-scale construction of apartment complexes, and an influx of dollars from construction projects in the Middle East stimulated the real estate market in the mid-1970s. As a result, most chaebol saw a promising prospect in real estate investment.[9] They capitalized on government-subsidized financing and used the loans to purchase land for speculative purposes. By 1978 chaebol owned an enormous amount of real estate, and 70 percent of the land they owned had nothing to do with their core businesses (*Dong-A Ilbo* 10/4/1978). Chaebol often bought much more land than needed, let it sit idle, and greatly benefited from steeply rising real estate values (T.-S. Chung 1978, 137). Chaebol's involvement in land speculation was systematic: several chaebol employed special real estate teams that reported directly to the owner (*Dong-A Ilbo* 4/15/1991). These teams collected information about what areas were being targeted by the government for development and recommended real estate buys on this basis. Such confidential information was obtained through connections with state officials and politicians. The Hyundai apartment scandal in 1978 demonstrated how close the ties between state officials and chaebol were: a lottery of Hyundai apartments in Apgujeong was fixed so that elites, including politicians, state officials, prosecutors, and journalists, won. Originally, Hyundai had gotten approval to build apartment buildings in the Gangnam area under the guise of providing affordable housing to non-homeowner employees (*Kyunghyang Shinmun* 7/4/1978).

As with Hyundai, chaebol often colluded with politicians and government officials who tried to use apartments as extra properties. In exchange for information on development projects, chaebol offered politicians and government officials bribes and opportunities for speculating on land. As the economic boom continued and large-scale construction projects proliferated in the late 1970s, chaebol enjoyed astronomical profits from the resulting increases in land prices. Chaebol focused on investing in the real estate sector more than the industrial sector: in the first half of 1988, the thirty largest chaebol invested US$911 million in real estate but only US$730 million in industry (B. Park 1998, 280). By 1989 the thirty largest chaebol owned land amounting to 140 million *p'yŏng* (larger than three-fourths of the land area of Seoul); real estate owned by the three largest chaebol (Hyundai, Samsung, and LG) was valued at around 5.5 trillion won (H.-C. Park 2013, 37–38).[10] Investing in real estate was an easy and common road to profit for large Korean firms.

One might wonder why the Korean government did not regulate the real estate market but instead let chaebol speculate on land. Contrary to typical images of the Korean developmental state as wielding great power and maintaining a relatively efficient bureaucracy, the government did not try to regulate chaebol's undisciplined speculative activities in real estate because it was the beneficiary of chaebol's land speculation. According to a former urban planner and state official, Jung-Mok Son, part of the profit from real estate speculation was funneled to politicians through their political campaigns (J.-M. Son 2003).

The government in its complicity with chaebol had no interest in regulating the real estate market, and as a result Korea experienced a dramatic increase in land prices. Gangnam was the site that experienced the most dramatic increase. As figure 2.2 shows, the price of land in Gangnam increased a thousandfold between 1963 and 1979 while in Gangbuk prices increased only by twenty-five times in the same period (J.-M. Son 2005, 236). Over just seven years in the 1970s, the land values in Hak-dong, Apgujeong-dong, and Sinsa-dong in Gangnam increased twentyfold, twenty-five-fold, and fiftyfold, respectively. The real estate boom in Gangnam in turn fueled more investment, thereby further increasing real estate prices and rendering Gangnam synonymous with greed and high-rolling speculation.

As vast apartment construction projects targeting middle-income families were completed in Gangnam and land values there increased rapidly, the new urban landscape dramatically changed perceptions about apartment living and Gangnam. When apartments were first introduced in the early 1960s, they were viewed as low-quality housing for low-income families. The Wau Apartment incident in 1970—the poorly constructed building collapsed three months after completion, and thirty-three residents died (*Maeil Kyungje* 4/9/1970)—strengthened negative images of apartments. An apartment was not considered proper housing for the middle or upper middle classes. However, most apartment construction projects in the 1970s included larger and higher-quality apartments and advertised modern, Westernized living for educated, salaried middle-class families. Thus, apartments began to lose their associations with cheapness and low quality and became increasingly associated with the middle class. With massive apartment construction and other urban development projects such as subways, new roads, and high-rise office buildings, Gangnam changed the cityscape within a single decade. In contrast to Gangbuk's old, bustling, narrow, and winding streets and neighborhoods, the cityscape in Gangnam was orderly and clean: streets and roads were wide and straight, and the atmosphere was modern, with newly constructed buildings and facilities. There were more parks and green space along the Han River. Lands once almost abandoned, seemingly worthless and far from the heart of Seoul, suddenly became its most promising district, showcasing new high-rise modern apartments that contrasted with the rest of Seoul.

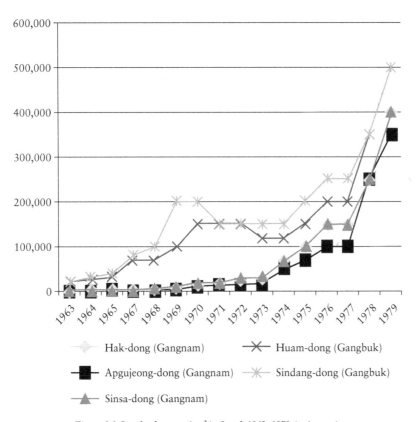

Figure 2.2. Land values per 1 m² in Seoul, 1963–1979 (unit: won).
Source: J.-M. Son 2005, 236.

Large-scale urban development in Gangnam led by private developers was a process in which "space, property, and housing—the constitutive elements of real estate" became a "commodity, an object whose most relevant characteristic is its exchange rather than its use value" (Yates 2012, 777). Promoting unbridled speculative development, it was a process by which lands and living space became subordinated to profit making and the logic of the market. Public housing did not exist until the late 1980s; in the meantime, most non-homeowners suffered from unstable housing tenure as real estate prices skyrocketed. Unlike Korea's other East Asian rivals, such as Hong Kong and Singapore, which have very large public housing systems (46 percent for Hong Kong and 86 percent for Singapore in 1987) (Castells et al. 1988), housing construction in Gangnam and state-sponsored homeownership benefited only the relatively affluent, failing to provide more affordable housing for lower-income families and to stabilize housing tenure for the larger segment of the population.

Becoming Apartment Owners in Gangnam: Real Estate Investment and Class Mobility

Gangnam became an attractive new destination for many relatively well-off families. New, modern apartment complexes, urban developments including new subway lines and other facilities, and rising real estate values made Gangnam very appealing. The institution of the apartment lottery system promoted homeownership for white-collar families and gave them a golden opportunity to buy homes in Gangnam and to increase their property values. Becoming apartment owners was an important aid to their climbing the economic ladder and joining the middle class, because they could gain windfall profits from rapidly rising real estate prices in Gangnam.

As housing prices escalated sharply with the real estate boom—much more quickly than wages—homeownership alone powerfully shaped family class trajectories, which in turn affected social inequality. Due to differential increases in real estate values in different areas, people with similar socioeconomic backgrounds or credentials experienced very different economic outcomes. A family that bought an apartment in Gangnam could increase its wealth many times more than others who decided to buy a home somewhere else. Thus, *whether, when, and where one purchased a home* were perhaps the most critical decisions with respect to one's future life chances and socioeconomic conditions.

The apartment lottery system provided an important channel through which ordinary salaried families became homeowners and improved their living standards. As the government controlled apartment prices in the lottery system, lottery winners were able to purchase apartments well below market price. Yet the apartment lottery was run in an exclusive and selective way: as the system required lottery winners to pay a few installments and other fees *before* moving, only those who had stable incomes and could afford to pay a lump sum could benefit from the new system. These were mainly white-collar workers employed at big corporations and banks, government employees, professionals, and teachers. Low-income families were completely excluded by the system. For those who could not afford to pay a lump sum to enter the lottery, an apartment was a prize beyond their reach.

As Gangnam grew and its real estate values swiftly appreciated, Gangnam's apartment lotteries became extremely popular among white-collar families and attracted a huge number of applicants. Applicants included not only non-homeowners but also homeowners who simply tried to purchase additional homes to make fortunes. The chance of drawing successfully in the Gangnam apartment lotteries was low; some popular apartment lotteries in Gangnam reached odds as high as 100 to 1 (J. Chang 1978, 108). It was common to borrow the names of friends or relatives in order to enter multiple times. The high demand for Gangnam apartments made the apartment lottery there even more competitive than elsewhere, and the values of Gangnam apartments increased over time.

Seen as potential investment opportunities, apartment lotteries were soon tainted by mass speculation. Many applicants saw an apartment lottery site as a means of making a profit without even buying an apartment: lottery winners acquired occupancy rights (*ipchugwŏn*) that made them eligible to move into the apartment unit. In the absence of strict regulations, these winners could sell the winning tickets (*ttakchi*) for a high "premium" instead of moving in. Buyers paid very high premiums, often between 2.2 million and 17 million won per unit, for apartments in Gangnam (T.-S. Chung 1978, 129). The premiums were particularly large in some years and often amounted to tens of millions of won (B.-W. Suh 1983, 347). With average monthly income for urban households at only 144,510 won in 1978 (Korean National Statistics Office 1998), such "gambling" could be very lucrative.

Before anyone actually occupied an apartment unit, the tickets might have changed hands as many as thirty or forty times in some extreme cases. According to the Ministry of Construction's report in 1977, only 14.8 percent of apartment residents in Seoul were original lottery winners; most other residents had purchased apartments through real estate brokers (*poktŏkpang*), paying more than the original prices offered at the apartment lottery (*Chosun Ilbo* 1/11/1978). As many applicants took part in the apartment lottery just to gain unearned income from premiums, this fictitious demand for apartments made it more difficult for non-homeowners to purchase homes for affordable prices.

Since apartment properties brought in a far greater amount of money than regular salaries, it was a *rational* decision for those who were interested in earning extra money to invest in real estate. Speculative activities were widespread among many ordinary housewives with entrepreneurial spirits. Ms. Chang, a housewife (born in 1949) who was married to an engineer working in a big construction firm and who lived in Gangnam until the mid-1990s, recalled how the family benefited from real estate investment:

> Speculation [in land or apartments] was not unusual at all. It was very rare to find people who did *not* speculate in real estate. It was common to buy and sell apartments for this purpose. While my husband earned relatively good money, we could become better off through this [real estate investment]. But [what we did] was nothing compared with others who became much richer. At that time, there was no heavy tax burden. By doing this a few times, I could earn a fair amount of money. Six months after I bought [an apartment] for 8 million, I could sell it at 16 million. It was double! I made the same amount of money as my husband earned abroad in a year. Some speculators had twenty or thirty apartments. Those who bought and sold time and again in Gangnam made a tremendous amount of money. (Author's interview conducted in 2008)

As with Ms. Chang, women's nonwage earnings often far exceeded even the salaries of high-earning husbands (Abelmann 2003, 148–49). Stay-at-home housewives' economic activities often produced a significant difference for households whose husbands made similar salaries. These housewives' informal economic activities played a crucial role in class mobility (Abelmann 2003; H. Cho 2002; Ŭn Cho and Koo 1983; Lett 1998; O. Moon 1990; Nelson 2000). Like Ms. Chang, many ordinary housewives bought and sold apartment units and made profits on the increases in real estate values. They purchased extra properties by taking advantage of the *chŏnse* system. Under the *chŏnse* system, renters had to pay a large lump sum in advance to owners (usually half of the property's value), and this money was returned at the end of the lease, usually after two years, when the renters moved out. This unique system in Korea was an informal financial institution in which the tenants loaned lump sum money to landlords for two years with no interest. Thus, a landlord could more readily purchase a second home by leveraging the *chŏnse* amount provided by the tenant.[11] In this way, many entrepreneurial women bought second homes, owning multiple units, all the while benefiting from (and contributing to) soaring real estate prices. With extra money derived from real estate investment, they sometimes invested money elsewhere— buying stocks or bonds or simply putting money in savings accounts that paid double-digit interest rates in this period of high economic growth. Some housewives who were willing to become indebted adopted more aggressive and adventurous strategies, buying multiple apartment units at the same time, which, if prices continued to rise, would bring them windfall profits. Often referred as "Mrs. Realtor" (*pokpuin*),[12] these women seized the opportunity to quickly climb the economic ladder and to amass wealth within a short time.

Those who were less venturesome made unearned incomes simply by moving frequently. Families could buy and sell their homes a few times to take advantage of marginal profits and move into bigger and more expensive apartments, turning apartments into commodities with a high turnover ratio. There was an interesting saying circulated among apartment owners: "One who sells one's apartment in three hours is a speculator [*kkun*], one who does so in three days is a realtor [*ŏpcha*], one who does so in three months is an actual user [*silsuyoja*], and one who does so in three years is an idiot" (*Dong-A Ilbo* 12/15/1982). Among ordinary apartment owners, frequent moving became the norm. According to a 1982 survey of a thousand apartment residents in seven major cities in Korea, 36.9 percent of households had moved three or four times before purchasing the apartments they currently lived in; among these people, 54.9 percent were planning to move again within four years (*Dong-A Ilbo* 12/15/1982). Even apartment owners who did not consider themselves speculators jumped on the bandwagon and tried to make profits by selling and buying apartment units a few times. A journalistic depiction of this common practice illustrates the differences in family wealth it could bring:

Mr. A and Mr. B work at the same company, and their salaries are similar. Mr. A currently lives in a 46-*p'yŏng* W apartment (valued at 80 million won). By contrast, Mr. B lives in a 19-*p'yŏng* Siyoung apartment (valued at 20 million won). If we consider only the apartment prices, Mr. A's wealth is four times bigger than Mr. B's. Just five to six years ago, A was living in a 17-*p'yŏng* apartment. But the puzzle is easily solved. Mr. A has moved from one apartment to another five or six times. But Mr. B is ignorant of the real estate market and thinks that moving is a hassle. Yet this small difference between Mr. A and Mr. B made a huge difference in their wealth. (B.-W. Suh 1983, 356–57)

Those who simply moved to a new apartment in Gangnam could take advantage of skyrocketing apartment prices and became owners of expensive properties. Apartment prices could increase by as much as 30 percent in just a few months. For example, between January and March 1978, apartment prices rose by 40 percent, single-family home prices by 30 percent, and land prices by 20 percent (*Chosun Ilbo* 3/24/1978). Between 1964 and 1984, consumer prices in Korea increased by 11.5 times, while land prices increased by 108.4 times in the whole nation and 171 times in big cities (S.-H. Chang 2004, 58). The real estate price increased more dramatically in Gangnam. It was common to witness apartment prices in Gangnam increase manifold times between the mid-1980s and mid-1990s, often fourfold or more (Gelézeau 2007, 141). The prices of some popular apartments in Gangnam—for example, those in Banpo—increased by millions of won overnight in the early 1980s; the price of a 34-*p'yŏng* unit in the Woosung Apartments increased to 48 million–53 million won on February 5, 1983, up from 38 million–49 million won just two days before (B.-W. Suh 1983, 341). Based on these statistics, one can easily conclude that those who were able to purchase an apartment, especially in Gangnam, could also accrue large windfall gains from increases in property values.

Families who moved to Gangnam *by chance* could get ahead much faster than those who ended up settling somewhere else. A family's seemingly arbitrary decision strongly affected the household's class horizons and subsequent financial conditions. In her novel *Seoulites* (*Sŏul saramdŭl*), the famous Korean novelist Wan-Seo Park vividly depicts the divergent outcomes produced by where families moved. Two close neighbors and friends, Myunghee and Hyejin, once lived on the outskirts of Seoul. The husbands held the same position in similar companies and earned the same amount of money. The incomes and spending of the two families were almost the same. But after

Hyejin moves into a new apartment in the southeastern part of Seoul—presumably Gangnam—Myunghee notices that Hyejin is spending more and that her clothes have become more expensive. As the value of Hyejin's new apartment increases quickly, the two families' economic conditions diverge:

> Hyejin did not worry about borrowing 2 million won to make up for her living expenses. She was not afraid of having debts and was not annoyed by her husband's meager salary. Rather, it was a completely new and surprising experience just to witness how her property values increased by 2 or 3 million won every month by doing nothing. The new apartment was like a goose that lays golden eggs in a fairy tale. Hyejin started spending more money, keeping up with her neighbors. Since she no longer struggled in her daily life, she felt that her way of speaking and behaving had become more elegant, and living felt more pleasant. (W.-S. Park 1989, 179)

Simply moving to a new apartment in Gangnam put Hyejin in a different class position and gave her a different sense of opportunity. One could expect that these two families' life trajectories would be different after a few years in these different locations, as their properties' values would have diverged drastically over time. Moving to Gangnam did not mean simply having appreciating housing values; it also meant access to insider information that was difficult for outsiders to obtain. Social networks at churches, mothers' meetings at their children's schools, and neighborhood associations were all good places for obtaining information about real estate investment. In particular, when networks included women whose husbands were government officials or worked in real estate, others in the networks could collect valuable information. Using this information, Gangnam residents found better opportunities for real estate investment. There were many people who moved to Gangnam by chance, but once they moved, their social networks and connections provided exclusive information and gave them much greater opportunities to increase their wealth. Therefore, seemingly arbitrary decisions to move to Gangnam created structural inequality between Gangnam and non-Gangnam residents over time.

Those who bought homes in Gangnam, either after making careful decisions or by chance, benefited tremendously from housing price inflation, climbed the social ladder, and acquired a solid middle-class status. Yet this haphazardly managed and speculative housing market produced widespread demoralization among those who did not benefit from the system. Many who had not gotten a chance to purchase an apartment were frustrated and infuriated—both by those who abused the system and by the government, which did not manage the system properly. While most non-homeowners tightened their belts, lived frugally, and saved money for the apartment lottery, those who had the means could apply for multiple units and had a better chance to win the lottery than others. Non-homeowners felt that homeowners who took advantage of the system deprived them of the opportunity to become a homeowner. A novelist who lost in the lottery wrote about his feelings: "After finding out that we did not win the lottery, my wife was very disappointed and cried hard. In fact, I was not exactly upset that we did not win the lottery. Rather, I was enraged and even felt betrayed by our neighbors, those who managed to apply for tons of units, won multiple apartments, and sold the occupancy rights instantly, getting high premiums. Those are the ones who trampled on our aspirations to be homeowners and snatched our opportunity away" (I.-H. Choi 1977). Whereas Gangnam apartment owners witnessed their apartment prices rise quickly and celebrated their wealth, non-homeowners had to watch their dreams of becoming homeowners vanish and the possibility of upward social mobility recede. The real estate boom in Gangnam also created a sense of relative deprivation among those who instead purchased homes outside Gangnam. They could not make sense of Gangnam residents' success, which was determined by "simple luck" and the social inequality shaped by differential real estate prices. A sense of relative deprivation became particularly strong when they witnessed their colleagues or friends who were in similar socioeconomic conditions quickly climb the economic ladder through real estate investment. Seeing Gangnam's property values increase much faster than their own, many non-Gangnam homeowners regretted not having made the "right" decisions.

The real estate boom in Gangnam produced people who hit the jackpot through real estate investment there, overshadowing the dark side of uneven urban development. The housing conditions of many low-income families did not improve at all: in 1985, 40 percent of families in Seoul lived with one or more other families, and the poorest 30 percent of the population averaged two square meters of living space per person and three families per house (Asian Coalition for Housing Rights 1989, 90). The squatter settlements, mostly located on hillsides, were demolished on a large scale in order to build high-rise apartment buildings, and in this process millions of people had to bear the brunt of forced eviction and displacement without proper compensation. The compensation they received equaled only a few months' rent. They were forced out of the homes they owned or rented, and many households were evicted two or more times. The eviction process was often violent, as developers hired thugs to forcibly evict tenants and crush protesters opposing the demolition. More than 90 percent of those evicted did not obtain an apartment in the redeveloped site: even though they had the right to move into the new apartments in principle, they typically could not afford to buy one, and sold the right to speculators or real estate brokers (ibid., 91). Se-Hee Cho's renowned novel *A little ball launched by a dwarf* (*Nanjangi ka ssoa ollin chagŭn kong*) powerfully illustrates the brutality that the urban poor experienced in the course of urban redevelopment and depicts contradictory experiences of both middle-class citizens and the urban poor: it was an age of possibility and prosperity for the affluent middle class, who could take advantage of their resources and experience upward mobility; yet, under the name of urban redevelopment and beautification, those who occupied the bottom rung of society were deprived of their homes and communities and were pushed to the outskirts of the city.

Creating Educational Fervor in Gangnam

Education played an important role in making Gangnam attractive to middle-class families and maintaining high housing prices there. Currently, Gangnam serves as the hub of the private tutoring industry, which is valued at $20 billion annually in Korea. In 2013 Gangnam-gu had the most cram schools[13] (2,014) among Seoul's twenty-five districts, twice as many as any other district.[14] And two other districts in Gangnam (Songpa and Seocho) have the second and third most cram schools (1,176 and 1,008, respectively). Currently, many families live in Gangnam, or want to move there, for their children's education, as its schools are more academically oriented, its students are more competitive, its parents are better-informed, and many good cram schools are located there. Gangnam's educational reputation has kept real estate prices high and is a direct outcome of government policy that relocated elite schools to Gangnam in the late 1970s.

Because the traditional hierarchical order and dominant elites had been completely destroyed by colonialism, land reform, and the Korean War, the major channel for social upward mobility following the war was education. Graduation from prestigious universities guaranteed social status and economic wealth for a lifetime. Getting into elite middle schools and high schools was critical to making this possible, and the competition for admission to these schools was fierce. Students aged twelve or thirteen endured intense entrance exams. Sending their children to prestigious schools was an important family project for most Korean parents. State officials and urban planners expected, correctly, that moving elite schools to Gangnam would make the area appeal to the many parents who were willing to sacrifice much for their children's success; moving the schools did, in effect, move many families to Gangnam (Seoul Metropolitan Office 2012).

Most of the top schools at that time were located in the heart of the city, Gangbuk. When, as part of the Gangnam development program, the government ordered the elite schools in Gangbuk to move to Gangnam, most alumni and students, who had strong pride in their schools, did not want the schools to leave. The plans were carried out despite this opposition. The government offered many incentives to convince elite schools to move to Gangnam. For example, it not only subsidized construction but also helped to provide lower land prices and larger sites for schools to build on. In addition, the government promised schools that it would build paved roads and an appropriate sewage system and offered the schools tax exemptions (Seoul Metropolitan Office 2012, 27).

Before 1974 the school system was entirely stratified into top-, second-, and third-tier schools. In 1974 the government announced the standardization of all high schools and abolished entrance examinations for top schools (J. Kang 2006, 94). Students had previously competed to get into schools on the basis of their exam scores, but after the exam system was abolished, students were assigned to schools based on their home addresses. Even though the exam system was abolished, parents believed that getting into *formerly* elite schools was still better for children, as the schools' reputation was good, the teachers were excellent, and the entire environment would be academically strong, motivating their children academically.

After Kyunggi High School, the most prestigious school, moved to Gangnam in 1976, other elite schools, such as Huimun High School, Sukmyung Girls' Middle and High Schools, and Seoul High School, moved to the new area in 1978–1980 (J. Kang 2006, 94). Some second-tier schools, anticipating that relocation to Gangnam would in itself strengthen their reputations, decided of their own accord to move to the area. Most elite schools followed the government's decisions. Between 1976 and 1990, eleven elite high schools left their original sites and settled in Gangnam (Seoul Metropolitan Office 2012, 29). The ban on private tutoring implemented in 1980 further strengthened the importance of schools, causing more people to want to move to Gangnam to take advantage of its better schools. By the mid-1980s, Gangnam's School District Eight (*p'al hakkun*) had become known as a district of "rising" elite schools (*sinhŭng myŏngmun'gyo*) with a reputation as a shortcut to the elite universities. The five high schools with the most students admitted to the top three universities in Korea (Seoul National, Yonsei, and Korea University) between 1984 and 1986 were all in District Eight (J. Jung 1988, 548–49).

These events made parents all the more determined that their children go to school in Gangnam, causing an even greater influx of new residents. As of 1985, about 30 percent of Seoul's total population had moved within the past five years, but the figure was 89 percent in Gangnam. The trend was even greater for high school students: in the mid-1980s, the number of high school students increased by 1.2 percent in Seoul but by 57.5 percent in Gangnam (H.-G. Kim 2004, 19), strongly suggesting that families were moving to Gangnam for educational purposes. Indeed, most of my informants who live (or lived) in Gangnam told me that the principal reason they moved there in the 1980s was for their children's education. They believed Gangnam's schools would expose their children to a more academically competitive environment that would better prepare them for college entrance exams. Many parents moved to Gangnam when their children were in elementary school so that they would later be assigned to elite high schools. It was not uncommon for parents to borrow an address from friends or relatives in Gangnam in order to send their children to the schools there (*Kyunghyang Shinmun* 8/13/1982).

The relocation of elite schools to Gangnam played a decisive role in accelerating the movement of families to the district. Increased demand for apartments further raised prices, and many schools struggled to accommodate the influx of students. Because of the large numbers of children transferring to Gangnam schools, long waiting periods—from six months to a year—became an issue, as did overcrowded classrooms (*Dong-A Ilbo* 9/21/1984). Nevertheless, Gangnam has become by far the most popular destination for middle-class parents whose biggest concern is their children's education.

People Like Us: Cultivating Middle-Class Identities
in Apartment Complexes

Massive apartment construction in Gangnam created a middle-class place and cultivated middle-class identities by congregating people with similar socioeconomic backgrounds in specific apartment complexes. Apartments became vehicles through which residents adopted similar lifestyles and, at the same time, distinguished themselves from non-apartment residents.

Apartment residents in Gangnam were a fairly homogeneous group consisting of young, educated white-collar families who preferred convenient, Westernized lifestyles. According to surveys conducted around the 1970s and 1980s, Gangnam apartments were inhabited mostly by highly educated white-collar families (S.-S. Chang and Kim 1994; Seoul Metropolitan Office 1996). For example, among apartment residents in the Yeongdong neighborhood in 1973, 76.8 percent of household heads had some college education or above (Seoul Metropolitan Office 1996, 612). White-collar workers were the largest occupational group, followed by civil servants and small-business owners. Further, their income level was relatively high: more than half earned between 50,000 and 100,000 won a month, more than most working-class families. Before Gangnam was developed, it had the highest percentage of poor residents in Seoul, but after the binge of apartment construction, this fell to less than 1 percent (Seoul Metropolitan Office 1996, 605). Thus, Gangnam development displaced the poor in this region and resettled relatively young, affluent white-collar families in new apartment complexes.

New apartment complexes provided middle-class families with a space in which to fashion a convenient and Westernized lifestyle. Apartment living, with its elevators, hot water, and emphasis on cleanliness, symbolized "civilization" and modernity, an advance on old and dusty traditional neighborhoods. Furthermore, it also meant being "cultured" (*kyoyang itta*) or acting "properly"—apartment residents who were generally educated kept their neighbors at arm's length. Unlike traditional community life, where everybody knew everybody else's business, apartment living guaranteed privacy from one's neighbors. Apartment living served as a class marker that distinguished "civilized" apartment residents from "unenlightened" and less-privileged others.

At the same time, new middle-class identities became reinforced and reproduced through a distinct "cultural milieu" of apartment complexes that promoted similar lifestyles among their residents. The standardized layouts of apartment units in a complex and the similar socioeconomic status shared by residents led them to pursue similar lifestyles. Apartment residents learned what and how to consume through their neighbors. In order not to fall behind their neighbors in status, they would purchase similar sizes of cars and brands of household commodities and decorate their interiors in similar styles. If one's neighbor purchased a Hyundai Sonata, for example, one would purchase a similar car, or a larger one, to save face. "Keeping up with the Joneses" meant not only homogenized consumption patterns but also a strengthened sense of belonging among apartment residents.

Though apartment residents as a group had similar lifestyles and dispositions, differences in apartment size played an important role in shaping class identity. In general, apartments within a complex were similar in size. Therefore, which apartment complex one lived in indicated the size of the apartment one could afford; it was a marker of one's class standing, financial conditions, and spending power. The anthropologist Bonggil Lim remarks on how segmentation and hierarchical order were created among apartment residents in Gangnam depending on their apartment sizes:

> There is a hierarchical order between large and small apartments; residents call those who live in bigger apartments high stratum [*koch'ŭng*], those who live in smaller apartments low stratum [*chŏch'ŭng*]. Residents of apartments larger than 40 *p'yŏng* are high executives in the government, banks, and chaebol, and professors; residents of apartments smaller than 30 *p'yŏng* are relatively young and are small-business owners, teachers, and white-collar workers. There is a large difference between cars the two groups of residents own. While high-end cars are the norm in "high-stratum" buildings, compact or low-end cars are predominant in "low-stratum" buildings. There are many two-car owners in apartment buildings with units larger than 47 *p'yŏng*, and some people own foreign cars or hire a chauffeur. Experienced security guards work for high-stratum buildings, whereas newly hired guards work for low-stratum buildings. Because of this, there are some tensions between the groups of residents. (Bonggil Lim 1992, 116)

Apartment size not only shaped class identification of adults but also played a critical role even among children, affecting how they made friends and shaping their social circles at school. It could be difficult for children living in smaller apartments to mingle with those living in bigger apartments.

"What is your apartment size?" was a common question among schoolchildren, and some parents advised their children to play with children living in similar-sized apartments. A famous literary critic identified this obsession with apartment sizes as a particular mentality that apartment residents shared (Hyun Kim 1978), wherein those who lived in bigger apartments felt superior to those in smaller ones. Moving to a bigger apartment was a means by which many families hoped to save face. Apartment size was a new calibrator of social class and success as well as a symbol of one's cultural level.

Despite the existence of hierarchy and stratification among residents living in different-sized units, most Gangnam apartment residents were well off, considered to be members of the middle class, living relatively comfortable and cultured lifestyles. Promoting a sense of belonging among apartment residents, apartment complexes also delineated clear boundaries between insiders and outsiders, that is, apartment residents and nonresidents with lower socioeconomic status. Apartment residents, who believed that they pursued modern and culturally advanced lifestyles, tried to exclude "natives" (*wŏnjumin*), those who had lived in the neighborhood before apartments were built. Most *wŏnjumin* were involved in the informal economy, had meager incomes, and could not afford to live in the newly built apartment buildings. These native residents were stigmatized as poor, uneducated, and uncultured. Middle-class apartment residents believed that the presence of *wŏnjumin* in their neighborhoods lowered the "cultural" level of the area and thus apartment prices as well. The "quality" of an apartment or neighborhood was shaped by how many native residents lived nearby. In order to maintain their property values, middle-class apartment residents had to prevent these "low-class" native residents from entering their own "paradise" and to stop their children from playing with "native" children. Soo-san Han's novel titled *Door [Mun]* vividly describes through the eyes of *wŏnjumin* children how the new apartment residents viewed and treated the "unruly" *wŏnjumin* and tried to exclude them from their apartment complexes:

> Children living in apartments left our school. I didn't see them at church any longer. They had their own school in the apartment complex. Their own church, near the shopping center, was much bigger and taller than ours. After they disappeared from our school, I heard women living in apartments call us children of "*wŏnjumin*." "Hey, you are *wŏnjumin*'s children, aren't you? Our children are not your friends any more. You are not allowed to come

here. You *wŏnjumin* should hang around your own neighborhood." We came to learn things little by little. Even if we washed our faces and wore clean clothes without mud, our faces were much darker than those living in apartments. And from the word *"wŏnjumin,"* we were naturally reminded of cannibals [*siginjong*]. At least in our minds. The ladies living in apartments must have thought that we were cannibals. (S. Han 1982, 93–94)

As one can see in this passage, native residents were often looked down upon by apartment residents as barbarous, dirty, and uncivilized. Because of their dangerous and inferior characteristics, native residents were an imminent threat to middle-class apartment residents, disrupting a peaceful and civilized apartment life. Thus, native residents and their children were the ones to be separated from the apartment residents. Through gatekeeping practices against *wŏnjumin,* apartment residents tried to protect their own space from unwanted "intruders." The gates, walls, fences, and security guards clearly separated "insiders" from "outsiders." At the same time, these visible spatial differences and physical boundaries created sharp psychological distances and boundaries between apartment residents and nonapartment residents. As Li Zhang puts it, "Highly visible spatial demarcation externalizes and foregrounds previously invisible or less pronounced socioeconomic differences" (2010, 120).

Exclusion of outsiders, in turn, strengthened insiders' identity and solidarity. Apartment residents were "comrades" who shared precious information about the real estate market and who had a common interest in securing their apartment values. Neighborhood associations and women's associations within apartment complexes held meetings and took collective actions to protect their interests. It was common for neighborhood associations in Gangnam to circulate handouts among residents that asked them not to sell apartments below certain prices or to organize opposition against a church's moving into an apartment complex, based on concerns about noise (*Dong-A Ilbo* 12/15/1981). They acted quickly against events that might lead to a decline of their apartment prices. Wan-Seo Park's *Seoulites* illustrates how shared common economic interests created a strong sense of community and fellowship among apartment residents: "The young housewives with whom Hyejin made friends in her new apartment complex were mostly her age and very friendly. They were all reliable and frugal partners who shared the secrets of windfall income with Hyejin. When apartment prices were stagnating, they united and spoke up in a neighborhood meeting so that they could ensure that the prices of their own units stayed at a certain level" (W.-S. Park 1989, 180). Living together, interacting with each other, and taking actions together led to the formation of emotional bonds among them and developed a sense of collective identity. As E. P. Thompson remarks, "Class cannot be defined abstractly, or in isolation, but only in terms of relationship with other classes" (1966b, 357). Collective actions of apartment residents *against* any groups or attempts to lower their property values could be seen as a sort of class struggle of middle-class people, similar, in this sense, to working-class people going on strike on the shop floor. The class identity of Gangnam apartment residents was articulated through defending their common interests in maintaining home values and distinguishing themselves from nonresidents.

Living in an apartment in Gangnam meant being middle class, affluent, and even cultured, a class marker to which non-Gangnam residents aspired. The creation of Gangnam and middle-class living space demonstrated the process by which salaried white-collar families fashioned affluent, Western-ized lifestyles based on apartment living. These lifestyles suggested a new standard and model for middle-class lives, yet the process by which they were formed was often accompanied by exclusionary practices of apartment residents, creating clear physical and psychological boundaries and distances between apartment residents and nonresidents and between Gangnam and non-Gangnam residents—the production of space as class struggle (Lefeb-vre 1991). By spatializing middle-class residents in a particular urban space, Gangnam's development created a stratified spatial order.

Currently, living in Gangnam and owning a home there are out of reach for most ordinary citizens because housing prices have skyrocketed between the 1970s and 2015. Through the case of Gangnam, I have illuminated how massive apartment construction materialized the particular concept of the Korean middle class beginning in the mid-1970s. Providing apartment units on a massive scale through the lottery system, the Korean government al-lowed ordinary salaried, white-collar families to become homeowners and to accumulate wealth. My research on Gangnam demonstrates that the con-cept of social classes, including the urban middle class, should be understood in terms of spatialized configurations. New cultural milieus produced by apartment complexes cultivated new lifestyles and dispositions among the residents and defined becoming middle class in Korea. Spatial form and geography, in addition to objective conditions such as income, occupation, and education, play a crucial role in shaping class identities.

Yet the speculative and exclusive bases for middle-class formation in Gangnam produced a distorted outcome. The state's failure to enforce the rules in the housing and real estate markets permitted large-scale speculative activities among ordinary citizens. As a result, apartment prices kept rising sharply, continually exacerbating housing inequality. In the midst of the real estate boom, many families who happened to purchase homes in Gangnam and invest in real estate could make astronomical unearned increments, while leaving behind the others who did not. The rise of the speculative Gangnam middle class became the source of a sense of deprivation and frustration for many low-income non-homeowners who were excluded from these benefits. The particular ways in which Gangnam residents achieved middle-class status through real estate investment and housing price inflation ironically weakened the notion of the middle class as a product of open opportunity and merit.

Epilogue: After Four Decades of Development, Gangnam Is an Exclusive and Distinctive Place

Currently referred to as a "special district," Gangnam has become an exclusive space where only the select few can live because of its unimaginably high housing prices. The ever-increasing housing prices have made the barriers to moving into Gangnam higher. Yet new, upscale housing developments in Gangnam attract the wealthy from other towns and districts. Gangnam's high real estate values, excellent school district, and convenient living environment make it an aspirational place; Gangnam symbolizes an affluent, desirable, and cosmopolitan lifestyle, creating a sense of superiority among its residents and, at the same time, a sense of envy among those who do not share it. Thus, Gangnam is not simply a physical space; it also has cultural and symbolic dimensions, distinguishing Gangnam residents from the rest of the population.

The distinctive and dominant images of Gangnam, which are represented and circulated by the media and also perceived by outsiders, are ones of material affluence and conspicuous consumption. Often, living in Gangnam is synonymous with being rich and being on the upper rung of the social hierarchy. As many homeowners in Gangnam have been able to benefit from skyrocketing housing prices and to make unearned incomes, their standards of living are more likely to be better than those living somewhere else, all else being equal. The average apartment prices in Gangnam-gu are the highest in Korea: as of 2008, the price per *p'yŏng* was 23.91 million won, 3.8 times higher than in Eunpyeong-gu (N.-G. Son 2008, 45). The average price of a 33-*p'yŏng* apartment in Gangnam-gu was 790 million won, while the average price for apartments of the same size in the twelve other districts in Seoul were less than 300 million won (ibid.). Starting in roughly 2007, chaebol such as Samsung and LG have redeveloped apartment complexes, and their brand names drove real estate values even higher. Newly redeveloped, upscale apartment complexes in the Banpo and Jamsil neighborhoods have strengthened Gangnam's affluent image, and the price of an apartment in those complexes can easily be US$1 million.[15] Tower Palace, a luxurious high-rise apartment building with the highest real estate values in Korea, marks Gangnam as a place of the wealthy. Developed by Samsung in the Dogok area between 2002 and 2004, Tower Palace displays the wealth, power, and social status of the Korean wealthy and elite. Its convenient living environment, including a gym, a pool, screen golf, a sauna, restaurants, and a shopping center, makes it possible for the residents to get everything they need at their buildings without even going outside (E. Cho 2007). Exclusive membership of the facilities and an extensive security system preclude the entry of "strangers." The residents form "fortified enclaves," as Teresa Caldeira (2000) puts it—exclusive, enclosed, and privatized space where their privacy and comforts are protected by private guards, surveillance cameras, and monitoring systems. Luxurious towers in Gangnam and the astronomical prices paid for the units strengthen Gangnam's particular image as a place of prerogatives of the rich and create *psychological* boundaries dividing Gangnam and non-Gangnam residents further.

Gangnam's material wealth also makes it a bastion of conspicuous consumption and high-end tastes. This consumption first appeared among the youths in Apgujeong-dong in the early 1990s. Surrounded by material affluence, many youths from this neighborhood had particular consumption patterns and lifestyles: they enjoyed foreign cultures in McDonald's, cafés, and Japanese-style bars; they became fashion trendsetters by investing in high-end designer brands; they drove their own cars, mostly foreign brands; and they were more open-minded about sex and more expressive about their desires (Lee and Oh 1992). Many of these youths spent some time abroad for schooling or travel and were fully exposed to foreign cultures through satellite TV and foreign magazines. This indulgence in pleasure seeking and conspicuous consumption led Gangnam to be seen as a site of materialistic and pretentious culture. Consumption behaviors that appeared in Gangnam often became the target of public criticism. However, despite these negative views of Gangnam, the district has been a fashion leader and has set style trends in Korea—in particular, the Apgujeong and Cheongdam neighborhoods, which feature many high-end designer boutiques, upscale department stores, and plastic surgery clinics.

Negative depictions of Gangnam as a place of wealth, extravagance, and exclusion, Gangnam residents believe, are nothing but biased viewpoints that take behaviors of a minority as representing the whole. They believe that such "prejudiced" ideas simply betray the aspiration to live in Gangnam and envy of Gangnam residents. All my informants in Gangnam argue that the images of Gangnam that are projected by the media often distort the "real" Gangnam. Though some neighborhoods contain the superrich or Korea's elites, they say, many people in Gangnam are ordinary middle-class citizens and salaried employees who happen to own a home there. They protest that those who own only one apartment in Gangnam do not even benefit from housing price inflation, as they live there without selling. Though Gangnam residents argue that they are not as rich as others would think, they have a sense of superiority associated with living in Gangnam. It comes not from owning high-value properties but from Gangnam's *cultural level* (*munhwa sujun*). First, Gangnam residents often make distinctions between well-organized Gangnam and bustling non-Gangnam. They usually perceive areas outside Gangnam as disordered—with narrow roads, bustling streets, and a less-clean environment—and Gangnam as well ordered, with wide, straight roads. Thus, Gangnam is considered a more developed and civilized place. Second, Gangnam residents believe that those who live there tend to be more cultured and well-mannered because of its demographic composition—highly educated and professional. They often describe areas outside Gangnam as less civilized and less sophisticated. One of my informants identified being highly educated and professional, prudent (*sinjung*) and not capricious, and hard-working as characteristics of Gangnam residents. Contrary to media reports, they argue, most Gangnam residents do not engage in conspicuous consumption and are even frugal. Because of the cultivated manners that Gangnam residents purportedly share, they believe that Gangnam is also the best place to raise children. They would tell me about their children in their thirties who grew up in Gangnam and who currently have strong identities as Gangnam residents. They fear moving out of Gangnam when they get married, not only because they are attached to the place where they were raised and grew up but also because moving outside Gangnam feels like falling behind and even failing. There is an underlying assumption that living in Gangnam is a status symbol. In many cases, this second generation of the Gangnam middle class resettles in Gangnam with the financial help of their parents, and Gangnam residents acknowledge that it is almost impossible for young people to buy or rent an apartment there on their own. This is exactly where one can see class reproduction taking place.

Many of my informants shared stories of friends and neighbors who once lived in Gangnam but moved to new towns such as Bundang and Yongin between the years 1995 and 2005—the losers who did not make the "right" decision. After these people sent their children to college, they usually moved to suburban areas, looking for a spacious and less-bustling environment. It is a story of lamentation and regret: Gangnam's real estate values kept appreciating, while real estate prices dropped in other areas. Now, even if they would like to come back to Gangnam, they can no longer afford to move there. Many people regret having sold their Gangnam apartments and moved somewhere else. Unlike Gangnam friends and residents with whom they once shared similar economic conditions, their property values have diminished dramatically, and they feel as if they have experienced significant downward mobility—a feeling of loss.

Gangnam's development fulfilled many people's aspirations to live in attractive apartment buildings and to have a middle-class lifestyle. Yet its development over the past four decades, in the form of a construction boom, was the basis for a speculative craze. Real estate prices in Gangnam after 2001–2002 increased even more quickly than in previous decades, and purchasing a home there became almost impossible for outsiders. Gangnam as a cultured, privileged, and exclusive urban space therefore cannot be separated from Korea's uneven urban development process.

Chapter 3

THE BETRAYED DREAM OF THE KOREAN MIDDLE CLASS, 1997–2015

Status Anxiety and the Collapse of Middle-Class Myths

> Did you just say you wanted to have a baby?/ . . . /You make me scared/ . . . /
> I am from a poor family, I am not smart, and I don't have any savings/ . . . /
> I am a high school graduate, and you graduated from a mediocre
> college/Do you think it makes sense to have a baby?/You and I, we already
> have a hard time making ends meet.
>
> —JUNGSIGI BAND, "HOW DARE YOU SAY YOU WANT A BABY"
> (AGI *RŬL* NAK'O SIP*TTANI*)

In 2015 I interviewed Mr. Yoon (age seventy-one), a former banker. After thirty years at the same bank, he retired from his position as vice president in 2002, at the age of fifty-seven. He had always worked for the same employer, which is not uncommon among his peers. Based on his successful career at this bank, he worked for other small companies for a few more years before completely retiring.[1] He received 260 million won for his retirement (from the bank), and, more importantly, he invested in real estate while he was working. He also owns two apartments in Gangnam. The income from these apartments allows him to enjoy a carefree post-retirement life, and he rents an apartment near Mount Bukhan because he loves to hike. He keeps himself busy hiking, traveling, and spending time with friends and family members. Seeing his former colleagues, who failed to manage their finances (*chaet'ek'ŭ*)[2] as well as he did and now experience money problems as a result, he feels extremely fortunate to be secure.

By way of contrast, a few years earlier this story appeared in a daily newspaper:

Mr. Kim, now fifty-three years old, retired from Kookmin Bank in December 1998, at the age of thirty-nine. It was when countless people were forced to retire early after the financial crisis in 1997. Without regard for rank or age, 2,790 employees, 20 percent of the employees at the bank, lost their jobs like Mr. Kim did. Now he makes a living frying chickens at a traditional market in Seoul. Before this, he opened a small gallery, a fertilizer plant, and a stationery store, but all failed. When he ended his second business in 2001, he had to sell his 30-*p'yŏng* apartment. Now he and his wife and their two children live in a smaller two-bedroom rented house. Business at his chicken restaurant is getting worse and worse. When he opened the restaurant in 2008, there were nine other chicken restaurants at the market. Now there are twenty-nine chicken places. He worries about his two children's college tuitions. When I asked him about how to save money for his later years, he was irritated, saying, "Look, it is already tough to pay the rent for my business. How can I think about planning my later years?" He says, "No matter how hard I have tried for the last fifteen years, I have only found that things are getting worse," and that "nine out of ten who retired from the bank at that time live like me." (*JoongAng Ilbo* 11/20/2012)

These two tales about members of the Korean middle class are typical of those one currently encounters in the Korean mass media or in daily life. One reflects the well-to-do lifestyle enjoyed by a relatively small, cosmopolitan class, whereas the other captures the more fragile and vulnerable existence experienced by a much larger, downwardly mobile segment of society. Though these two images contrast sharply, each is a common representation of middle-class existence. Can both of the depicted groups be categorized as middle class, despite their divergent living conditions and states of mind? If so, how can one make sense of this complicated and somewhat contradictory nature of the middle class? And why do we see this fragmentation within the middle class?

This chapter looks at what we might call the unmaking of the Korean middle class. In the face of globalization and recent economic changes, what has happened to the Korean middle class, a celebrated, mainstream social group that rapidly expanded along with the nation's economic development? A discourse on "the crisis of the middle class" (*chungsanch'ŭng wigi*) has dominated Korean society since the economic meltdown of the late 1990s. Both ruling and opposition parties have called for a "remaking" of the middle class, and many research institutions and news outlets have addressed the plight of the "squeezed middle class." Research findings confirm that the middle class has shrunk dramatically: as defined by income, the middle class included 67 percent of all Korean households in 2010, down from 75 percent in 1990 (Hyundai Research Institute 2011).[3] With respect to perceptions, only half of the population (52.8 percent) identified themselves as members of the middle class in 2010, and almost as many (45.3 percent) believed that they belonged to the lower classes (Korean National Statistics Office 2011). Middle-class identification is now much lower compared with thirty years ago. In 1989, for example, more than 60 percent of Koreans believed that they lived a middle-class lifestyle (*Dong-A Ilbo* 1/23/1989). The decline in middle-class self-identification is in contrast to an improvement in objective economic measures and spending power over the past thirty years. Through a variety of survey results, one can readily see that both the actual size of the middle class (based on income) and middle-class consciousness have been decreasing for the past twenty years.

As these news reports and research findings demonstrate, more and more middle-class citizens are anxious about their economic situation and worry about downward mobility. Yet it is also true that a small segment of the middle class has a luxurious existence, embodied by large apartments in Gangnam, consumption of products from high-end designers, educational credentials from foreign institutions, and extensive transnational experience. This chapter explores what forces have shaped these complicated dynamics within the middle class over the past two decades and how these changes have shaped the ways in which becoming middle class is understood in Korea. Some might argue that the phenomena of the "squeezed middle class" and "polarization within the middle class" are universal in countries with advanced economies, such as the United States, western European countries, and Japan, where economic restructuring and cuts in welfare programs have affected the middle class negatively and created acute social inequalities (Alison 2013; Cooper 2014; Ehrenreich 1989; Newman [1988] 1999; Zunz, Schoppa, and Hiwatari 2002). While I agree that economic recession and neoliberal policies have negatively affected the middle class through massive layoffs and wage reductions, I also emphasize domestic policy dynamics' shaping of the living conditions of ordinary citizens and patterns of social inequality over time.

I analyze two different yet interconnected processes that have conditioned the overall decline of the middle class and differentiation within the Korean middle class. First, economic restructuring and neoliberal economic policies have led to changes in employment. Job insecurity and forced early retirements at private firms put ordinary salaried families in a vulnerable situation. Second, increased expenditures on housing and after-school education have placed a major financial burden on middle-class families. These two major causes of increased spending prevent families from saving money for the future, which can engender a heightened sense of anxiety. While the first change can be commonly observed in other countries that also suffer from a lack of stable jobs, the second phenomenon is more an outcome of specific policies and should be understood in a particular historical and social context. This chapter argues that these two external and internal factors together accelerated differentiation and fragmentation within the middle class. The upper segment of the middle class possesses stable assets and properties, and its material conditions remain relatively intact during economic recessions. Many in this group have benefited from soaring real estate prices and have accumulated greater wealth, which helps their children reproduce their parents' class positions. The rest of the middle class consists of salaried employees or small-business owners, who are more likely to be downwardly mobile during economic downturns. Precarious job conditions and financial burdens make the latter group worry about their own and their children's futures. The precariousness they experience on a daily basis leads to a pervasive feeling of anxiety and distress.

The Short Heyday of the Korean Middle Class

After three decades of industrialization and economic growth in Korea, the 1980s inaugurated an era of affluence and consumerism. Because of a favorable international economic environment, the economic boom lasted the full decade. As a result, the authoritarian Chun Doo Hwan regime (1980–1988) was able to showcase successful economic performance. GDP per capita (in current US dollars) increased from $1,674 in 1980 to $5,438 in 1989, more than tripling within a decade (World Development Indicators, 1980–1989).

Over a longer term, household disposable incomes had increased explosively, from 68,400 won in 1963 to 15,010,800 won in 1992, a ninefold increase after adjusting for inflation (Korean National Statistics Office 1993, 60). By the late 1980s, acquiring a middle-class lifestyle had become more common. Equated with car ownership, vacations abroad, and life in modern high-rise apartment buildings, the middle class embodied economic progress and was a source of national pride.

Middle-class homes were equipped with every kind of modern appliance and device. A survey conducted in 1987 showed that more than 90 percent of middle-class households had refrigerators, color TVs, telephones, gas ovens, and cameras. More than half had pianos, and 42 percent had cars (W. Han, Kwon, and Hong 1987, 13). The consuming middle class portrayed in the mass media in the 1970s was not an aspiration any longer; it was now a reality. Rising incomes and increasing consumption of household goods led many families to feel that their standard of living had significantly improved. Although there were some criticisms of the growth-oriented economic model, mostly related to rising social inequality and the daily struggles of the urban poor, nobody could deny the achievements of economic development evidenced by material affluence and the rise of consumerism.

In the context of such material progress, many white-collar workers joined pro-democracy protests in 1987 and helped anti-dictatorship movements overthrow the authoritarian regime and achieve electoral democracy. The successful hosting of the Seoul Olympic Games in the following year seemed to prove that Korea had overcome economic hardship and had joined the ranks of advanced nations. As Korea progressed economically and politically, there was a new sense of confidence and national pride.

Children of middle-class families who were born in the 1970s were the first generation that had not experienced any economic adversity. Having grown up in material affluence, these young people were major customers at global fast-food chains and consumers of foreign-brand products. In the 1990s it was popular among middle-class youths to eat at Pizza Hut, McDonald's, or T.G.I.F. and to buy expensive Guess jeans, Polo shirts, and Nautica jackets. It became common for college students to travel abroad during the summer to the United States or Canada for language training. Consumption in this period was not simply a way of meeting needs but also a way of pursuing personal desires and expressing identity. Conspicuous consumption became more common among upper- and upper-middle-class citizens—purchasing bigger cars, upscale household appliances, and foreign-brand clothing and cosmetics was a way of revealing their social status. Playing golf (especially for middle-aged men), having resort memberships, and going on vacations abroad became popular among middle-class families. While typical, these forms of "conspicuous" or "excessive" consumption (*kwa-sobi*) were often condemned by the mass media as social evils and signs of moral decay. Many news articles criticized the lavish behaviors of the "Orange Tribe" (*orenji chok*)[4] for disrupting social harmony and producing a feeling of class resentment (*wihwagam*).

Prosperity and optimism reached their peak in the early and mid-1990s, when the Korean economy matured to a level comparable to those of other advanced nations. Korean citizens did not need to worry about the basic necessities of life and could afford to enjoy diverse leisure and cultural activities. Poverty still existed, yet it was part of the distant past to many upwardly mobile young people. Gross national income per capita topped US$10,000 in 1994, and Korea joined the rich countries' club, the OECD, in 1996. Korea had finally become a mass middle-class society. Consequently, Koreans were optimistic and confident about the future. In one survey in 1994, 80 percent of respondents said that they belonged to the middle class, and 70 percent anticipated that they would have a financially stable lifestyle for a lifetime (*Maeil Kyungje* 1/24/1995). This period was indeed an era of abundance and uplift. Yet the feeling did not last long.

The Debt Crisis and the Collapse of a Social Contract

For many of those who were taking a middle-class life for granted, the events of one day in 1997 meant that they would enter a completely different world from what they were accustomed to or had anticipated. On December 3, the Korean government accepted the terms of a huge International Monetary Fund (IMF) bailout to rescue its staggering economy. It was a critical moment for Korean society, as the economy was completely restructured and the rules of the game were changed. As a condition for receiving IMF bailout funds, the Korean government was required to carry out extensive and thorough internal reforms in the finance and corporate sectors. Many powerful chaebol with enormous debts were restructured through mergers and acquisitions; underperforming banks and financial institutions had to be closed down; firms in the public sector were required to privatize; and government institutions were downsized. In 1998 the Korean economy recorded a −5.7 percent growth rate.[5] GDP per capita, which had reached US$13,254 in 1996, fell dramatically to US$8,133 in 1998.[6]

However, it was on ordinary citizens' shoulders that the biggest burden of the dismal economic situation fell. The IMF reform package made labor flexibility a central issue, and it required massive layoffs (J.-J. Choi 2002, 169). Many workers lost their jobs overnight or were pressured into "voluntary" early retirement (*myŏngye t'oejik*), and even those who survived the layoffs had to face huge wage reductions and worried about being laid off suddenly. The number of unemployed more than doubled, from 658,000 in December 1997 to 1.7 million in December 1998. The unemployment rate reached 8 percent in 1998, up from 2.6 percent in 1997 (OECD data, 1997–1998). The number of people under the poverty line was 7.63 million in 1996 but increased to 10.3 million in the first quarter of 1999 (*Hankyoreh* 11/15/1999). Rising unemployment was accompanied by sharply falling real wages; 74 percent of families experienced a reduction in income because of the economic crisis (Hong 2005, 3).

Labor reform not only meant layoffs in the short term; it entirely changed practices in the labor market. In the face of economic catastrophe, employers were not required to guarantee secure, permanent employment for workers. Both the Korean government and corporations often blamed labor inflexibility for causing inefficiency and burdening the economy (J.-J. Choi 2002). In the name of labor flexibility, most business firms reduced the number of permanent jobs and instead hired workers with lower pay, little job security, and no benefits. This new practice completely broke with the "iron rice bowl" system that had commonly guaranteed full-time employees permanent job security and extensive benefits. In the new regime, the norm of "lifetime jobs" disappeared. Instead, nonstandard or nonregular employment (*pijŏnggyujik*) proliferated as an increasing proportion of the working population was employed temporarily or on short-term contracts.[7]

The growing number of nonregular workers and their precarious economic circumstances have become a major social issue.[8] Nonregular employment, including limited-term, part-time, and atypical workers, has made up more than half of total employment since the early years of the twenty-first century, and the percentage of nonregular workers in the service industry is even higher, estimated at 60 to 90 percent (Yu-Sun Kim 2004). Korea's share of nonregular workers is large compared with other OECD economies. They account for 51.9 percent of the Korean labor force, considerably higher than in the Netherlands (45 percent, the next highest among OECD countries), the United Kingdom (28.4 percent), and the United States (16.1 percent) (Yoonkyung Lee 2015, 190).

In addition to temporary employment and insecure labor contracts, nonregular workers have more disadvantageous working conditions than their regular counterparts. Nonregular workers are paid on average 51.3 percent of a regular worker's hourly wage for the same labor (Yoonkyung Lee 2015, 192). Average weekly working hours are longer for nonregular workers: regular workers' hours were considerably reduced, from an average of 47.1 hours in 2000 to 41.8 hours in 2003, whereas the hours of nonregular workers were only moderately reduced, from 47.5 hours in 2000 to 44.1 hours in 2003 (Yu-Sun Kim 2004, 30–31). Moreover, "overwork" (working longer than fifty-six hours per week) is more common among nonregular workers, who tend to work longer to make up for their low pay: 21.8 percent of nonregular workers overwork, compared to only 13.3 percent of regular workers (ibid.). On top of lower wages and longer work hours, nonregular workers are rarely eligible for fringe benefits such as retirement benefits, bonus pay, overtime pay, and paid holidays, all of which are available for most regular workers.

The new economic landscape after the economic crisis, with its large-scale layoffs and reductions in permanent employment, had a tremendous impact on the lives of ordinary middle-class families, who had to adjust their lives to survive in a new environment. Many middle-aged employees in the corporate and financial sectors lost their jobs and had to search for new jobs relatively late in life. Their children also faced intense competition for a limited number of jobs. Their economic predicament was captured in two dominant phenomena: displaced and downwardly mobile middle-class families and young people condemned to nonregular employment, often represented in popular discourse as the "880,000 won generation" (*p'alsip p'almanwŏn sedae*).[9]

Many of those who had been categorized as members of normal middle-class families before the crisis suddenly encountered joblessness and economic adversity. People who thought they had secure jobs with decent salaries found that their comforts had come to a sudden end with the economic crisis. The crisis hit employees in the financial sector particularly hard.

Working at a bank had been considered the basis for promising stable, middle-class lives for the employees and their families. By the end of 1998, many workers in their late forties and early fifties lost their jobs in the financial sector. In 1998, five banks and ninety-seven financial institutions went bankrupt, and the surviving ones had to implement severe restructuring by laying off 20 percent of their employees—68,500 with jobs in the financial sector became unemployed (*JoongAng Ilbo* 11/20/2012). Many media stories showed how the lives of bank employees, paradigmatic middle-class white-collar workers, dramatically changed with joblessness. Titled "The Age of New Poverty" (*sinbin'gon sidae*), one news article describes how a young couple that had a promising future experienced an unexpected economic calamity:

> At 5:30 a.m., in the darkness before sunrise, Chungsik Park (age thirty) sneaks out of his in-laws' home, where he and his wife are staying for free. His destination is Yeongdeungpo Market. He haggles over the prices of vegetables, then delivers them to one of the Korean restaurants nearby. Around 11:00 p.m., he cleans up the restaurant and closes it. From 6:00 p.m. until late evening, he sells baked sweet potatoes as a street vendor near the Moonrae Park. Yet all he earns is around 500,000 won every month. His wife, Seung-A Han (age twenty-five), who is seven months pregnant, works thirteen hours a day and barely makes 700,000 won per month. Until last June, when both of them were laid off, this couple was on a roll, making 50 million won a year. In the year and a half since then, they have joined the ranks of the poor. Even if they work so much that they get only three hours' sleep at night, they cannot escape the poverty that strangles them. He has lost a lot of weight: he is now down to 65 kg, from 80 kg. (*Hankyoreh* 11/15/1999)

In the late 1990s, it was not uncommon to see similar newspaper stories about the downward mobility of displaced white-collar workers and mid-level managers. Formerly privileged middle-class employees who anticipated a comfortable lifestyle for a lifetime, they now realized that everything that had sustained their lives—secure jobs, good salaries, and satisfactory careers—was long gone. Though lump-sum retirement payments and savings helped get them through the rough times, it was hard for them to find jobs at their age, especially after being unemployed for several months. As time passed, their savings eroded, and they started to be frightened. Unemployment compensation was not nearly enough to support the expectations for middle-class teenage children, such as private after-school tutoring and nice clothes. Fathers who were discarded by their employers and could not afford to meet their families' needs any longer began to view themselves as incapable and incompetent. Mothers entered the labor force to pay the bills and cover the family expenses. Many had been stay-at-home housewives for most of their adult lives and therefore lacked experience and stable employment histories; these mothers could find only temporary part-time jobs as cashiers or domestic workers, with wages that could not be stretched far enough.

Despite continuing efforts to reverse their situations, many discovered that there was little they could do to prevent their descent. They realized how challenging it would be in their current situation to maintain the lifestyle that they had previously taken for granted. Now they were experiencing unending insecurity, depression, and fear about their uncertain futures. As Katherine Newman points out in her study of the downward mobility of the American middle class, "Occupational dislocation may occur suddenly, but its consequences can take six or seven years to become fully evident, depending upon the resources the families can tap" ([1988] 1999, 97). At first, the damage is largely confined to the loss of a job, as the unemployed worker tries to maintain a sense of normalcy in the family realm. As jobless weeks turn into months, money becomes tighter and tighter until any pretense of normality disintegrates, and the whole family suffers, bringing about acute family discord—often leading to family breakdown or divorce. Some end up with a mounting burden of debts. They are often under intense strain and suffer from depression. In the worst cases, distressed people choose the most extreme way of escaping from the strain: committing suicide. Since the economic crisis and massive layoffs of the late 1990s, the suicide rate has rapidly increased.[10] Though it is difficult to single out one cause of suicide, severe depression from financial hardship is surely an important factor. The laid-off not only lose the economic comforts and security that they had enjoyed but also start doubting their capabilities and self-value. As everything collapses before their eyes, they feel helplessness and despair.

Many downwardly mobile middle-class families end up in poverty and suffer from emotional distress, but they all struggle to cope with new situations. They try to find ways of rebuilding their lives. Having learned that it is not easy to find a job as stable and well-paying as the ones they have lost, and that employers are often not eager to hire workers in their forties or fifties, many displaced managers choose to open small businesses, usually small restaurants, franchise bakeries, or convenience stores. The "fried chicken hypothesis," a sardonic joke recently circulated on the Internet, references this trend: whatever you choose for your career, however "fancy" and middle class it may be—computer programmer, engineer, architect—you will end up owning a fried chicken restaurant. The joke mirrors a bitter economic reality in Korea, where many professionals, corporate executives, and even venture capitalists are eventually forced to become self-employed workers because of early forced retirements or layoffs from large conglomerates or because their own companies have gone bankrupt.

Alejandro Portes and Kelly Hoffman (2003) point out that self-employment has become a place of refuge for public servants, salaried professionals, and other skilled workers displaced in the labor market in Latin America. Similarly, in Korea, many displaced white-collar workers or corporate managers enter into self-employment. The self-employment rate among those over fifty years of age has increased since the late 1990s. As of 2013, more than half of self-employed workers (3.29 million people, 57.1 percent) were in their fifties and sixties (Economically Active Population Survey 2013). Many of the elderly population are "pushed" into self-employment after retirement, as it can be quite difficult to find regular salaried jobs at their age. Given that they still need to work to make a living and support their children, they enter into forms of self-employment that do not seem to require highly skilled labor, in-depth knowledge, or business know-how (KB Research Institute 2012; G. Kim and Cho 2009). They usually invest all or nearly all of their money in self-employment ventures, including their retirement severance pay, and use their homes as collateral. In addition, most owners start their businesses by borrowing a considerable amount of money from relatives or friends or take out bank loans. They hope this alternative path will bring them a new, promising future. Yet this can soon turn out to be a naïve and in fact risky decision because of intense competition in a saturated market, and a lack of experience and preparation can easily lead to failure. As many statistics reveal, their expectations of regaining their previous "normal" lives are often not realized through self-employment. Overall, they make low incomes in low value-added businesses, such as small retail shops and restaurants, and their employment is unstable, vulnerable to high bankruptcy rates.

These inexperienced small-business owners face challenging situations. As more and more small businesses enter the market, competition among them becomes fierce. Indeed, the number of self-employed workers in Korea is very high in comparison with other countries. Currently, 6.8 million, almost 30 percent of the working population, are self-employed (OECD 2016).[11] Not only is the self-employment rate in Korea the fourth highest among OECD countries (after Turkey, Greece, and Mexico) and much higher than the OECD average of 15.8 percent, but it is also significantly higher than in countries whose per capita incomes are similar to Korea's, such as Taiwan (19.5 percent), New Zealand (20.8 percent), and Spain (20.2 percent) (Yun 2011). In order to survive in the saturated market, most of the self-employed work extremely long hours. On average, the self-employed worked 55.72 hours per week in 2007 (Kum et al. 2009, 68). As of 2004, 68 percent of the self-employed worked six or seven days per week (ibid., 65). Yet the long work hours do not bring stable incomes, and most of the self-employed suffer from economic vulnerability. Most self-employed households earn low incomes, rendering it difficult to make ends meet. In 2013 around 27 percent of self-employed workers earned a net monthly income of less than 1 million won (around US$900), and almost 80 percent earned less than 3 million won (US$2,700) (Small and Medium Business Administration and Small Enterprise Development Agency 2013). It was also common for self-employed workers to earn nothing or to run deficits, leading to higher household debt rates among the self-employed population. The household debt of the self-employed accounts for 43.6 percent of the country's total household debt. The average amount of household debt of self-employed workers (100.16 million won, about US$93,000) is almost twice that of salaried workers (51.69 million won, about US$48,000) (T.-I. Kim 2014).

Tough financial situations make self-employed workers vulnerable to business failure. A 2016 survey showed that 40 percent of small businesses fail within a year, and the rate is even higher in the accommodation and food sector (45 percent) (*Yonhap News* 1/24/2016). Seventy percent of small businesses go out of business within five years. These stunning statistics indicate how vulnerable the self-employed are to debt. Contrary to their hope that they will be able to make enough money to support their families, they may end up at greater financial risk, with increasing debt and in danger of living in poverty in their old age. In the face of a saturated market and intense competition, they are concerned on a daily basis about how to make things work out and how much longer they can maintain their businesses. The precarious status of the self-employed in Korea—"uncertain, unpredictable, and risky from the point of view of workers" (Kalleberg 2009, 2)—means that it is challenging for displaced workers to make their alternative paths work out and to avoid downward mobility.

Some empirical studies suggest that only a small segment of the middle class is able to sustain their status over time, and that once they are displaced from full-time jobs, they are more likely to fall into poverty. Using a life course approach, Kwang-Yeong Shin (2015) examined social mobility in Korea between 2001 and 2011.[12] Around 65 percent of permanent, full-time, middle-class employees in their thirties and forties remained in the middle class after ten years; one-third, however, slid down the class ladder. This trend was more striking among older people. Only 27 percent of Koreans in their fifties remained in the middle class after ten years. The other 73 percent became unemployed or underemployed in their sixties. Without pensions or savings, those who also lack full-time employment are extremely vulnerable to poverty in their later years.

While middle-aged citizens experience a "fall from grace"[13] through, as Newman ([1988] 1999) describes it, "economic dislocation," young adults struggle with a lack of opportunities and unattainable dreams. Except for the small segment of young people who go to prestigious colleges and get permanent, well-paying jobs, young workers in their twenties are irregularly employed and are paid much less than regular employees. Current popular culture is full of representations of the problems of young students and workers from less-privileged backgrounds. For example, the popular Korean TV series *High Kick* (*Haik'ik*) features a young character named Jinhee, a twenty-four-year-old college graduate in Seoul who is looking for a job.[14] Because of recent increases in college tuition, she has to take multiple leaves of absence during her undergraduate years. She lives in a modestly furnished, cramped room in a *kosiwŏn*[15] building with ten other people. She cannot even find a temporary job to pay her rent. Her bachelor's degree does not make her stand out in Korea's highly competitive job market, where she must compete with graduates of top Korean and US universities who have international experience and are fluent in English. In her college years, she worked hard to earn a high GPA, attain high scores on English tests, and get other certificates to make her attractive to potential employers. Despite these lengthy and painful efforts, her qualifications are not good enough. She is several months behind on her rent and is in danger of being kicked out by her landlord. A generation ago, most college graduates like Jinhee could find a decent job, have some savings, buy a home, and join the middle class without difficulty. The steep rises in income and living standards brought about by the economic boom are unlikely to be seen again. In the new economy, the prospects for becoming middle class for those not from privileged backgrounds are dim.

Many young people without financial support from their parents have to work several part-time jobs to pay tuition and bills. Those who struggle daily to make ends meet are further disadvantaged in the job market when competing with their peers who can afford to invest in strengthening their résumés (accumulating their spec [*sŭp'ek*][16]) by studying for English tests, working as interns, and getting related certificates. Thus, a small number of young people are able to acquire decent, full-time jobs, while the rest become nonregular workers or are underemployed, leading a precarious, insecure life.[17] "Precariousness" also prevents many young adults from leading a life independent from their parents. They cannot enjoy a real adulthood, marked by marriage, parenthood, and a "real job," and their baby boomer parents are bearing the financial burden of supporting their grown-up children (Newman 2012). Even dating and socializing with friends seem like luxuries, and they expect to give up having romantic relationships, getting married, and having children.

Members of the younger generation are frustrated that their hard work and efforts do not yield more returns and that qualifications that once would have made them competitive—a good education, fluency in foreign languages, and adeptness at new technology—seem to count for nothing. The anthropologist Hae-joang Cho notes that this "spec" generation, which grew up under intense competition that began in childhood, now fears falling behind and, as a result, avoids uncertainty and risk (Hae-joang Cho 2015, 448). Wishing to live safe and normal lives without financial concerns, a substantial number of college graduates want to become civil servants and teachers—jobs that are not necessarily exciting but that guarantee stable incomes and job security. While most young people search for ways to live relatively safe lives, more-frustrated ones cope with the situation in a different way. Fed up with living an intense, stressful life with no leisure time, and seeing no prospects for a better life in Korea, they search for a better life in a foreign country. Kang-Myung Chang's novel *Because I hate Korea* (*Han'guk i sirŏsŏ*), one of the best-selling books in 2015, traces the adventures of Kyena, a woman in her late twenties who decides to quit her job and immigrate to Australia. Not born into a rich family, having graduated from a mediocre college, and not particularly good-looking, Kyena feels that she is not competitive enough to survive in Korea. Rejecting the pursuit of mainstream success in Korea and leaving her family and friends behind, Kyena takes menial jobs (as a waitress and cleaner) in Australia, believing that this will provide a better quality of life. Though things do not go smoothly there, after a few years of hard work, Kyena finally acquires Australian citizenship and gets the job as an accountant that she has aspired to have. She finds happiness and life satisfaction in a foreign country—something her own country could not offer.

In the era of the debt crisis, belief in class mobility and the "self-made man"—once seen as part of the social contract during the period of high economic growth (Koo 2012)—seems to have faded away. It is now accepted that "lifetime jobs" (*p'yŏngsaeng chikchang*) are no longer available and that many people have to prepare for retirement even in their late thirties or forties. Newly minted graduates face intense competition for a limited number of jobs. With the deregulation of the labor market, job insecurity and precariousness have become a new norm—one can be easily disposable at work during the economic downturn—that defines the majority of the Korean population. This new economic landscape has made joining the middle class and maintaining middle-class status much more difficult. The current discourse on the "collapse of the middle class" or the "middle class in crisis" is clearly related to job precariousness and stagnating incomes, but it is also about the heightened sense of anxiety and insecurity widely shared by so-called middle-class citizens. Even for those who have relatively stable employment and decent incomes, a sense of economic security is not easy to achieve because of rising housing and education costs that have intensified both financial and emotional burdens.

Unstable Housing Tenure and Financial Insecurities

Along with job security and income, housing has been an important factor shaping class status and inequality as well as a source of a sense of relative deprivation and social injustice. The dramatic change in property values has created a deep divide between those who own their homes and those who do not. Even among homeowners, the location and market value of their homes can produce an acute sense of relative deprivation. For relatively young families in particular, housing issues can become quite grave. Housing prices soaring beyond their reach have forced them to pay an unsustainable share of their income for rent, which can badly damage their quality of life.[18]

The problem of unaffordable housing is now common in cities around the world because of speculative urbanism and subsequent skyrocketing of housing prices. Urban scholars have argued that neoliberal globalization and urbanization have facilitated and evolved gentrification. Gentrification is no longer simply residential upgrading and slum clearance. It is "a crucial urban strategy for city governments in consort with private capital in cities around the world" (Smith 2002, 440). As the partnership between transnational capital and local governments promotes mega-developments in urban centers, and as real estate markets become "vehicles of capital accumulation" (ibid., 446), real estate prices have often seen manifold multiplication in mega-cities in developing countries, such as Mumbai, Kuala Lumpur, and Rio de Janeiro, as well as in Western metropolises (Fainstein 1994; Nijman 2000; Smith 2002). In these cities, it is the flow of transnational capital and foreign investment in partnership with local states that has promoted neoliberal urbanization and led to skyrocketing real estate prices since the 1990s.

In Korea, however, the phenomenon of real estate speculation and steep housing price increases was not primarily an outcome of neoliberal globalization but rather a consequence of processes beginning in the late 1960s: an ongoing economic boom, rapid urbanization, and, most importantly, a lack of real estate regulation (B. Park 1998; H. Shin and Kim 2016; J.-M. Son 2003; N.-G. Son 2008). As discussed in the previous chapter, the state and chaebol were complicit in the explosion of the real estate market: chaebol found tremendous benefits both from participating in the construction business and from speculating on land; state elites also benefited from speculation by chaebols, since part of the profit was funneled to them through their political campaigns (J.-M. Son 2003). As a consequence, speculative urbanism in Korea generated outrageously high housing costs, severe spatial inequality, and a distorted economic structure. The Gini index in real estate is extremely high, reaching between 0.6 and 0.8 (S.-H. Chang 2004, 69). In 2007 total real estate values in Korea were 5.7 times higher than the national GDP and 19.3 times higher than the annual national budget (N.-G. Son 2008, 44).

Unaffordable housing is a problem not only among low-income families but also among middle-class families. The overheated real estate market has escalated housing and land prices sharply since the 1970s, and wages have failed to keep up with the costs of owning or renting a home. Figures 3.1 and 3.2 show that between 1986 and 2015, housing prices have more than doubled and apartment prices have more than quadrupled.[19]

These trends mean that property ownership and homeownership have determined family welfare by shaping divergent paths to accruing wealth and, in turn, future life chances. Those who happened to buy a home (or homes) in the right neighborhood at the right time secured valuable assets for themselves and their children, whereas those who failed to do so missed great opportunities for increasing their wealth quickly and are highly conscious of their relative deprivation. Given the critical importance of housing in influencing one's economic conditions and state of mind, addressing housing issues is crucial to understanding the current conditions of the Korean middle class.

Differential increases in apartment prices create dramatic differences in asset values for people who otherwise have similar attributes. The following

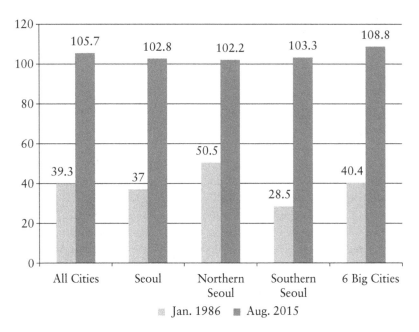

Figure 3.1. Changes in housing purchase prices, 1986–2015 (2013 = 100).
Source: Korean Housing Price Survey, Koomin Bank, 1986–2015
(http://nland.kbstar.com/quics?page=B025949).

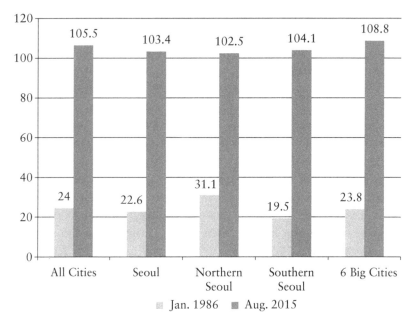

Figure 3.2. Changes in apartment purchase prices, 1986–2015 (2013 = 100).
Source: Korean Housing Price Survey, Koomin Bank, 1986–2015
(http://nland.kbstar.com/quics?page=B025949).

case demonstrates this pattern for two people who had the same rank at the same company:

> Both Deputy Team Head P (age forty-one) and Deputy Team Head J (age forty-two) started working at T Industries in the same year. Both have similar salaries, around 52 million won a year. Both bought 33-*p'yŏng* [1,174.2 square foot] apartments in 2001. P bought an apartment for 270 million won in Jeongja-dong, Bundang,[20] while J purchased an apartment for 240 million won in Gil-dong, Gangdong-gu.[21] After five years, their destinies were quite different: P's apartment value went up to 1.1 billion won, but the worth of J's apartment reached "only" 620 million won. There was still not much difference in their incomes, but the difference in assets became enormous. Though he earned nearly the same wages as J and purchased a similar-sized apartment for a similar price, P now belongs to a different social class, with assets 500 million won greater than J's assets. (N.-G. Son 2008, 202–3)

Though both P and J benefited from buying an apartment, as both their apartments grew in value, the degree to which their apartments could be converted to cash when sold is very different. This financial divergence due to real estate prices becomes much sharper when comparing those who bought homes in Gangnam with those who bought homes elsewhere.

Ms. Ahn's case illustrates how her choice of buying a home in Gangnam thirty years ago made a huge difference in her property values relative to her friends who did not. A sixty-four-year-old retired elementary school teacher, Ms. Ahn owns an old 45-*p'yŏng* (1,601 square foot) apartment in Gangnam. Though her husband passed away a few years ago, her lifestyle is quite stable and comfortable: about 3 million won of pension and an allowance from her daughters every month make her life financially secure. Most importantly, her old apartment, her only asset, is now valued at almost 1.8 billion won (about US$1.6 million). The prime location and the possibility of reconstruction (*chaegŏnch'uk*)[22] in two years make her apartment more valuable, and she believes that the price will go up to 2 billion won right before the reconstruction. While she often feels relative deprivation compared with neighbors who own multiple apartment units or other real estate properties in Gangnam, she is much better off than her friends or former colleagues. She is the only one among her friends who has settled in Gangnam. Those who own similar-sized apartments somewhere else have property values less than half that of Ms. Ahn's apartment. When Ms. Ahn moved to Gangnam looking for a better school district for her children thirty years ago, Gangnam was more affordable. Her first small, 17-*p'yŏng* (604.9 square foot) apartment cost 40 million won in the mid-1980s. Having benefited from the real estate boom in Gangnam, she was able to sell her old apartment for a much higher price than she had paid. She then moved to a bigger apartment twice before settling in her current home. She feels fortunate to have made the "right" choice, staying in Gangnam. Some of her friends had owned homes in Gangnam, but when, in the early years of the twenty-first century, they thought their property values were at the peak and there would no longer be increases in property values in Gangnam, they sold their apartments and moved to new towns outside Seoul, such as Bundang and Yongin, where they could live in newer apartments in a quieter environment. Soon they realized they had made a huge mistake. For example, one of Ms. Ahn's friends bought a bigger apartment for 1 billion won (about US$907,441) in Yongin after selling her home in Gangnam to look for more space and a quieter neighborhood. Though she seemed somewhat satisfied with living there, her apartment value recently dropped to 600 million won (about US$544,464). Her old apartment, which she sold for 1 billion won, is now valued at 1.3 billion won. Whenever the friend comes to Gangnam and thinks about her "wrong" choice, she cannot but feel bitter about it. If she had kept her apartment in Gangnam, her current property value would be twice as high. Although she herself made a handsome profit selling the Gangnam apartment that she had bought for a much lower price many years before, she still feels deprived relative to current apartment owners in Gangnam and regrets not having made a "smarter" choice.

While the real estate boom provided some homeowners with great opportunities to increase their property values and accumulate family wealth, it meant that others who did not have enough resources to buy a home now suffer from an increasing burden of housing costs and unstable housing tenure. As a result of skyrocketing housing prices, it takes 18.6 years of saving for the average Korean salary man to afford a 33-*p'yŏng* apartment in Korea as a whole, 29.1 years to afford one in Seoul, and 44 years to afford one in Gangnam (N.-G. Son 2008, 92). It is now virtually unimaginable that an ordinary salary man could become a homeowner relying solely on his own salary. Many people who planned to buy a home after years of saving, thereby avoiding large bank loans or the need to borrow from friends or relatives, have seen their dreams of becoming a homeowner fade away. Looking back, they feel they should have taken out large loans in order to buy a home; their conservative strategy of avoiding risk by avoiding debts turned against them. Minsup Choi and his colleagues provide an example: "In the past, people tried to buy a house when they had accumulated a lump sum of money after years of savings. It is the opposite these days. You can only own a home if you are willing to carry a lot of debt. If you can secure a home with loans, it will be yours at a certain point after paying them off. But if you want to wait until you have enough money [to buy a home outright], it is not going to happen. By the time you have a sufficient amount, the price will have gone up; if you reach that price with even more saving, the price will go up yet again. You will never buy a house that way, given the structure [of the market] in Korea" (M. Choi et al. 2010, 28). There exists a significant difference between those who have gone into debt to buy a home and those who have not purchased a home at all. The latter are busy trying to find ways to cover the *chŏnse*[23] increase every two years, while the former are at least free from that concern and, in most cases, are able to benefit from the increase in real estate values.

Non-homeowners struggle to find affordable places to live, and the cost of renting a home (*chŏnse*) has increased even faster than the cost of purchasing one. Between 1986 and 2008, housing prices have increased by 125 percent, whereas *chŏnse* prices have increased by 263 percent (N. G. Son 2008, 94). The average *chŏnse* price for an apartment in Seoul was 312.6 million won (US$290,270) in 2013, equivalent to 5.66 times the average urban household income of 55.27 million won (*Maekyung Business News* 2/24/2014). These extremely high housing costs are challenging for young people; it is almost impossible for them to rent an apartment in a big city without family support. Parents' financial resources therefore significantly affect children's life trajectories and class horizons.

The cases of Hyerim and Jihyun demonstrate how parents' financial resources affect housing tenure and, in turn, life chances and state of mind. Both Hyerim and Jihyun can be seen as members of the middle class in terms of education and occupation. Both went to prestigious colleges and have solid white-collar jobs. Yet they feel very differently about their life situations. Hyerim, thirty-six years old, has been an employee of the Korean government for ten years and married another government official. She lived in the United States for two years, earning a graduate degree with government sponsorship. In Korea, she and her husband rented a 32-*p'yŏng*, three-bedroom apartment north of the Han River in Seoul, which cost 200 million won. When they got married in 2007, they did not have much in savings, like other ordinary couples, since they had just started their careers as civil servants. Their parents gave them about 100 million won to help them get an apartment *chŏnse*, and they took out a bank loan for the rest of the amount, 50 million won. After two years, when they renewed their lease, the landlord asked for an increase of 50 million won. They had to take out another loan. While Hyerim and her husband were away in the United States for two years, the *chŏnse* prices increased rapidly—now the rent for the same apartment has increased to 380 million won (US$344,827), and the couple worries about how to get an apartment when they return to Korea. While she thinks that her situation is not that bad, given that both she and her husband hold secure jobs, she feels relative deprivation when comparing herself with her colleagues or friends who do not need to worry about housing because they can rely on their parents' support:

Many of my friends' parents or their in-laws bought or rented an apartment for their children when they got married.[24] In those cases, the couple has more room to use their salaries somewhere else—like savings or *chaet'ek'ŭ*. Their starting point is different from ours. I feel behind compared with them. For us, after paying all this money, such as interest to the bank, the tuition for my child's preschool, and food and utilities, there is nothing left for savings. Though other people think that we have nice jobs and do well financially, I am not satisfied with our financial situation. I don't think our hard work pays off at all. How do we manage our money [*chaet'ek'ŭ*]? Well, I wish we could have that money to invest somewhere.

Most of my informants in their mid-thirties agreed that it makes a huge difference if parents have the financial ability to help their children purchase a home. They commonly told me that, as a result of extremely high housing prices, starting a family from scratch is extremely challenging. Even if Hyerim and her husband can be categorized as core members of the middle class based on their jobs and household income, their housing situation—being susceptible to sudden rent increases and struggling to find an affordable home—makes Hyerim anxious about her future.

Unlike Hyerim, Jihyun does not need to make expenditures on housing. A PhD, Jihyun (age thirty-six) works at one of the largest companies in Korea. While her salary is similar to Hyerim's, she has a more easy-going and comfortable lifestyle. Jihyun owns an apartment in Bundang that her parents bought for her and does not have any debts. Jihyun's father was a judge, but it was her mother who amassed the family wealth through real estate investment. Her mother converted the small house in Gangnam that they lived in into a low-rise building (*tasedae chut'aek*) in order to rent out more units when they left Gangnam, and, in the meantime, managed to buy apartments for all of her children. The apartment Jihyun inherited from her parents gives her both financial resources and peace of mind; she owns a property valued at 550 million won and does not need to worry about paying off debts from *chŏnse* or a mortgage. This financial security also gives her some freedom, including freedom to choose a spouse free from financial considerations: "To be honest, if I hadn't had this apartment from my parents, I might not have gotten married to my husband. The fact that I own my apartment made me feel reassured. If I hadn't owned my apartment, I would have considered my potential spouse's financial situation more seriously, that is, whether his parents could afford to buy an apartment for us. But this apartment allowed me to choose my husband free from that worry." Despite the attributes that Hyerim and Jihyun share, such as education level, intelligence, and career-related expertise, the points at which they now stand are different. While Hyerim and her husband need to be frugal in order to afford an apartment (though their parents helped some) and to pay off their loans, Jihyun and her husband can get ahead and spend their money on more pleasurable things. In twenty years, when Hyerim and her husband are still paying off the loans for their home, Jihyun and her husband may already have enough savings for retirement. In this sense, one's long-term well-being may depend, in part, on whether one's parents have managed their finances successfully. Expressing frustration, Hyerim asked me, "What kind of middle class cannot afford their own homes and worry so much about increasing *chŏnse* prices?" High housing costs and their rapid increases have made many young, ordinary white-collar workers' living conditions unstable.

So far, housing policies in Korea have failed to effectively regulate real estate speculation and to provide affordable housing for non-homeowners. Despite continuous housing construction, the overall housing status of ordinary citizens has grown more and more unstable over the years. The homeownership rate declined from 72 percent in 1970 to 55.6 percent in 2005 (N.-G. Son 2008, 188). Nak-Gu Son notes that of 5.87 million newly built houses, only 54 percent were bought by non-homeowners, with all the other purchasers having previously bought at least one home (ibid., 191). This trend becomes more obvious in expensive Gangnam neighborhoods. According to an examination conducted by the Korean National Tax Services, in nine apartment complexes in Gangnam, where the average apartment purchasing price increased by 690 million won between 2000 and 2005, 60 percent of those who purchased apartments already owned three or more homes (ibid., 189). This stunning fact reveals that many newly built or reconstructed homes were used for speculative purposes to increase wealth rather than being purchased by non-homeowners as homes.

The housing market in Korea has created economic winners who invested in real estate and made huge profits. At the same time, it has created losers on a large scale who cannot afford to buy a home and who suffer from unstable housing situations. At the height of increases in both housing and rent prices, the housing problem creates anxiety and daily adversity even among many white-collar corporate employees who are considered to have decent jobs and who make good salaries. Housing insecurity adds another layer of economic and emotional burden for middle-class citizens.

Status Anxiety and the Educational Project of Middle-Class Families

Along with the housing situation, paying for education is another financial burden that many middle-class parents must carry. Over the years, spending on private after-school education has increased. Getting into a prestigious college has been the key to individual success and upward mobility in Korea since the Korean War. In the past, access to education was relatively egalitarian; it was not uncommon that the children of poor families got into elite universities and joined the middle class. But opportunities for social mobility through education have decreased in recent years. As the private education market expanded and ordinary families mobilized more resources to send their children to prestigious colleges, the competition grew fiercer, and children who received more private tutoring and after-school exam-prep classes—those whose parents had the ability to pay for extra preparation—gained the advantage in college entrance exams. Consequently, high spending on children's education has become a huge financial burden for ordinary middle-class parents.

Although access to prestigious colleges in Korea has always been competitive, it has become more so over time, as the private education market has expanded. In 1974 the elite secondary school system was abolished, and students were randomly assigned to schools on a residential basis. In 1980 private tutoring was also banned. These measures strengthened the public schooling system.[25] In 1989 the Roh government lifted the ban on private tutoring and allowed students to go to cram schools (J. Kang 2006, 119). Since then, the private education industry has boomed, and some "star" teachers at cram schools now earn a great deal of money. Attending expensive after-school exam-prep schools became a virtual requirement for getting the highest scores on college entrance exams. The relatively egalitarian education system collapsed as middle-class and upper-middle-class families began to rely on private tutors and cram schools to give their children an educational advantage (Koo 2007, 11). The economic crisis in the late

1990s exacerbated this competition in the field of education. Economic restructuring due to the crisis caused many white-collar employees to lose their jobs, sparing only a few groups, such as civil servants and schoolteachers, and, importantly, those with elite college degrees. This taught many parents a painful lesson that caused them to worry about their children's future success and job stability and to increase investment in education, which, in turn, further intensified competition for getting into a top college.

The private education market in Korea is a $20 billion a year industry in a country with a total government budget of $375 billion a year.[26] In addition to regular schooling, almost 70 percent of all students, including preschoolers, go to cram schools or obtain private tutoring (Korean National Statistics Office 2015). The average monthly expenditure on private education per household is 242,000 won ($220).[27] Another survey on private education in Korea shows that spending on private education amounts to 19.2 percent of the average monthly household income and 25.6 percent of average monthly expenditures (Hyundai Research Institute 2007). Surprisingly, 26 percent of parents work second and third jobs solely to afford private education (ibid.).

Certainly, spending on tutoring and cram schools correlates strongly with household income: the higher the household income, the greater the proportion of it spent on private education. For example, as of 2014, in households whose income was more than 7 million won a month, 83.5 percent of children were receiving a private education, with the spending per student at 428,000 won a month (Korean National Statistics Office 2015). This contrasts starkly with children in households whose monthly income is below 1 million won a month: only 32.1 percent receive private education, and the spending per student is only 66,000 won. Thus, education becomes an uneven playing field where children from richer families are more likely to be academically successful because they get more private education. News articles have reported that students from wealthy neighborhoods, particularly in the Gangnam area, are more likely to get high scores in college entrance exams and to be accepted into elite universities (*Chosun Ilbo* 1/28/2015; *Hankyoreh* 8/14/2014).

While middle-class parents invest heavily in educating their children, this does not mean that only money matters. Educating children is a significant family project among middle-class families. There is a popular sardonic saying about the educational fervor in Korea: "What's required for children's success is grandparents' money, mothers' information, and fathers' non-interference."[28] The saying reflects the real importance of family support for children's educational progress. To succeed in the education race, all family members need to be mobilized. Since educational costs are enormous, the father's income alone is not enough. It is also important that the grandparents have the financial means to support their grandchildren. The role of mothers as the primary managers of children's education is also crucial. They have to network with other mothers; collect information on the best cram schools, private tutors, or national college exam policies; organize their children's after-school schedules; give them rides to cram schools; and monitor their progress closely on a daily basis. This becomes a full-time job for many middle-class mothers.

A notable emphasis is placed on teaching children English. As Korea has become more integrated into the global economy, fluency in English has emerged as a valuable part of career development. While taking English lessons at cram schools in middle and high school and studying abroad in English-speaking countries were common among college students in the 1990s, the recent pattern is for children to start learning English very early, at age two or three in some cases. English has become a class marker, a sign and site of "cosmopolitan yearning" (S.-J. Park and Abelmann 2004). Not only do parents spend tremendous amounts on English education (it is now a $6 billion a year market)—for instance, by enrolling their children in "English kindergartens"[29] or hiring native English speakers as tutors—but they also spend summers with their children in English-speaking countries and enroll their young children in summer camps or programs there.

One interesting phenomenon that attests to the obsession with English education is the rise of "wild geese families" (*kirŏgi kajok*). As a strategy for raising "cosmopolitan" children, mothers accompany their children on study-abroad programs in English-speaking countries such as the United States, Canada, Australia, or New Zealand, while fathers remain in Korea and send money to their families overseas (Uhn Cho 2005; Finch and Kim 2012; Y.-J. Lee and Koo 2006; Park and Abelmann 2004). This unique form of family life is further evidence of the prevalent notion that anything should be sacrificed for the sake of children's education. Parents' desire to provide an English education starting from an early age and thus make their children globally desirable subjects has led to what amounts to an educational migration from Korea. This new strategy has become popular among middle- and upper-middle-class families who possess the requisite economic and cultural capital (S.-J. Park 2009). Parents who are themselves highly educated and have had international experience—be it living abroad for family reasons, studying abroad for the short term, or working overseas at a multinational firm—are the most likely to employ this "globalized" strategy for their children.

Through investing in education, middle-class families attempt to prepare their children for a globalized, competitive environment, as they believe educational credentials are the most valuable assets in an age of economic uncertainty and unstable labor markets. Wealthy families, in contrast, own "the ability to ensure class reproduction through inheritance of wealth or business ownership" (Koo 2016, 450), so that their children can be well off regardless of their work qualifications or credentials. Unlike their wealthy counterparts, children of middle-class families—including the children of high-income professionals and corporate managers—still have to go through a competitive process in order to maintain middle-class status, even if their parents' wealth often helps them. Moreover, given the lack of a strong social safety net or welfare system in Korea, individual competitiveness and self-development are critical for survival. When everybody participates in the education game, even those who are critical of the Korean educational system and the education frenzy among parents do not dare to completely abstain from the game, out of fear of their own children falling behind.

As a result, the intense competition in the education race not only puts immense pressure on young children but also drains parents financially and causes them emotional distress. Excessive spending on after-school education creates a distorted household economy in many middle-class families. While wage increases have been slow, the costs of after-school education have increased rapidly. In one 2007 survey, 76.8 percent of respondents agreed that their spending on after-school education was a financial burden, with only 8.4 percent answering that the cost did not affect their household economy at all (Hyundai Research Institute 2007, 11). The financial burden resulting from after-school education leads to lower savings rates and has negative impacts on parents' preparation for the future (Hyundai Research Institute 2007). Except for wealthy families (those whose annual household income is above 100 million won), most households reported reducing their saving in order to spend on children's after-school education. In addition to high hous-ing expenses, then, the increasing cost of children's after-school education causes middle-class families to struggle to map out a long-term plan.

As spending on housing and after-school education has increased and real wages have remained almost the same between 2000 and 2015 (Y.-S. Kim 2015, 149), seemingly high-income earners feel that covering all expenses is challenging. Major newspapers feature stories of middle-class citizens who struggle to save money for later in their lives:

> Mr. Lee (age forty-six), who works in finance as a senior manager, is the breadwinner of a family of four, including a stay-at-home wife, a son in the ninth grade, and a daughter in the seventh grade. He earns 4.5 million won a month, but he says, "My family doesn't belong to the middle class." After making payments on a housing loan, private insurance, and utilities and giving some money to both his parents and in-laws, his family has only 2.5 million won. From this they must pay 1 million won for the children's private tutors. In the end, they have a monthly disposable income of only 1.5 million won. Mr. Lee says, "According to official government statistics, I am middle class. But our living standards cannot be that of the middle class." (*Chosun Ilbo* 8/17/2013)

With 1.5 million won of monthly disposable income, after paying for basic necessities, Mr. Lee's family—a typical Korean middle-class family—does not have enough money to spend on leisure activities such as family travel or vacation or, more importantly, to put aside as savings. The effort to try to give a better future to their children through education enhances the finan-cial strain. In this way, many ordinary families feel trapped by rising ex-penses and see no better future given their stagnating incomes.

In sum, objective conditions since the economic crisis have dramatically changed in such a way that it is more difficult to do things that are under-stood as middle class. The accumulation of family wealth and the improve-ment of living standards that occurred during the era of high economic growth are no longer part of middle-class expectations; instead, most ordi-nary middle-class families struggle to find affordable housing and to pay their children's educational expenses. And even maintaining this status quo is not guaranteed: they are acutely aware that if they lose their jobs they will immediately lose everything, as they have observed in the situations of their colleagues and friends. Middle-class status feels quite precarious—as if they are on the brink of falling into poverty if something goes wrong.

Disillusioned with Becoming Middle Class

Objective economic conditions are important criteria when delineating so-cial classes. Yet social class is not simply a matter of material facts. It is also a *lived experience* of shared beliefs and dispositions (Katznelson 1986). Without talking about fear of falling out of the middle class, feelings of insecurity, and anxiety, it is difficult to discuss the current conditions of the Korean middle class. Since the economic crisis, the Korean word *puran* (meaning uneasiness, anxiety, or nervousness) has been used in the mass media to describe the state of mind among middle-class citizens. Many people who seem to earn stable incomes and appear to be doing well financially often share this feeling of anxiety. Having looked at their predecessors who expe-rienced early forced retirement and who fell out of the middle class, they realize that their current status is a fragile thing.

This shared sense of anxiety can be found in a low level of self-identification with the middle class. Far fewer people identify themselves as middle class than are identified as middle class on the basis of official statis-tics. Figures 3.3 and 3.4 reveal two things. First, the size of the middle class using both objective and subjective criteria has decreased over time. Second, there is a huge gap, almost 20 percent, between the official count of the middle class and subjective middle-class consciousness. This gap between the two measures is partly due to the exaggerated official count of the middle class. Because official statistics measure the size of the middle class *only* by income and do not include other factors, such as total assets and liabilities, official counts tend to overestimate the percentage of the middle class in the general population. Additionally, the definition of the middle class as people with 50–150 percent of the median income does not take account of the high cost of living. Whether or not the middle class is being identified with the appropriate objective measures, these figures show that fewer and fewer people perceive their standard of living as middle class. Many believe that they need more economic resources to have a sense of security, given unstable employment conditions, high living costs, and lack of social security benefits. Without enough economic resources and backup such as savings, pensions,

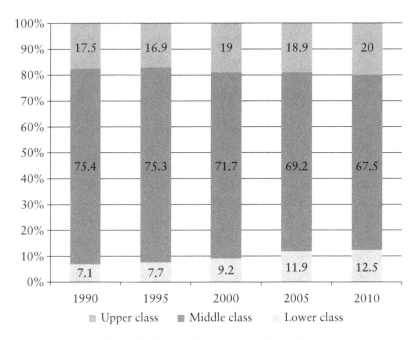

Figure 3.3. Changing class structure in Korea (%).
Source: Korean National Statistics Office,
Household Survey Data, 1990–2010 (www.kostat.go.kr).
Note: The upper class is defined as those who make more than 150 percent of the median income. The middle class is defined as those who make 50–150 percent of the median income. The lower class is defined as those who make less than 50 percent of the median income.

and real estate they feel they could suddenly plunge into an abyss when emergencies crop up.

What has exacerbated anxiety and fear of falling among white-collar salaried families is the growth in the income and wealth gaps and accelerating differentiation *within* the middle class. Social class is a *relative* concept—how people locate themselves in comparison to others within the structure of inequality (Wright 2008, 331). Thus, when social inequality worsens, most people rank their relative position lower in the structure of inequality. Various measures confirm that income distribution and social inequality in Korea have worsened over the years, particularly after the economic crisis. For example, income inequality, which had been stable before the economic crisis, worsened in its wake, from 0.251 in 1995 to 0.307 in 2012 (T. Lee 2015).[30] According to the OECD, in 1984 the 10 percent best-compensated

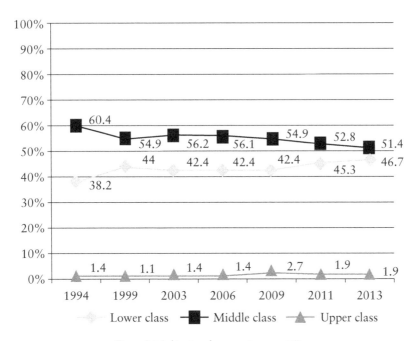

Figure 3.4. Subjective class consciousness (%).
Source: Korean National Statistics Office, Social Survey, 1994–2013.

Korean workers were paid 4.6 times what the bottom 10 percent were paid. In 1994 the difference had dropped to 3.6 times but by 2008 had risen again, to 4.8 times (OECD 2011), higher than the OECD average and third worst for income inequality among OECD countries. By 2013 the average income of the top 10 percent of Koreans was 10.1 times higher than that of the bottom 10 percent, also above the OECD average (9 times).

More important than these numerical indices of income inequality is the feeling that most ordinary white-collar employees have of falling behind, as an upper segment of the middle class has become visibly wealthier than the rest. The composition of the middle class has become more diverse, differentiated, and stratified since the 1990s, significantly as an effect of the economic crisis (Fernandes 2006; Koo 2016; Robison and Goodman 1996). Those with financial resources were able to take advantage of the crisis, which provided an excellent investment opportunity to purchase stock and real estate, whose prices had dropped (Koo 2016, 445).

They benefited tremendously when the real estate and stock markets rebounded, while other middle-class citizens were left anxious about their uncertain futures.

Currently, two groups comprise the upper segment of the middle class, which is much better off than the rest of the middle class. A first group consists of professionals, such as lawyers, doctors, and bankers, who have advanced professional credentials and scarce occupational skills and who earn much higher incomes than regular salaried employees. Taking advantage of their rare knowledge and expertise, these professionals accumulate wealth easily based on the high salaries they can command. Passing the extremely competitive bar or civil service exams and pursuing these elite professions has often been considered the best channel to upward mobility (*ch'ulse*).[31] Since only a small number of people can pass these exams and have these jobs, they enjoy social status and prestige as well as material benefits. These professionals form exclusive social networks that give insiders privileged access to resources and information while effectively excluding outsiders and blocking access to their benefits (Parkin 1971; Tilly 1998; Wright 2008).

The second group comprises those who successfully invested in real estate and can draw income from ownership of extra properties—whether an officetel (*op'isŭt'el*),[32] a commercial space in a big building, or a regular apartment. Thanks to the real estate boom, many ordinary families made great economic gains by these means. Given that most citizens—excepting government employees, schoolteachers, and college professors—do not have strong pension benefits in Korea, monthly rents or lump-sum payments deposited by tenants provide a crucial source of steady income that serves as a buffer in emergencies. Those who own extra properties are generally better off than non-property owners, but those who were able to aggressively invest in real estate in booming areas were the biggest winners, and, as a result, they are rarely affected by economic downturns. In comparison to the first upper-middle-class group, the occupational composition of this group is relatively diverse. It includes professionals, but also bureaucrats, small-business owners, and ordinary white-collar employees. Those who had resources and social connections through their occupations were able to invest in real estate and buy extra apartments more easily than others, but it was not uncommon to see ordinary housewives of white-collar workers or civil servants shrewdly invest in real estate and climb the economic ladder. More broadly, those who happened to move into booming neighborhoods for particular reasons—for example, children's education, proximity to workplaces, or family networks—had privileged access to networks and information about the real estate market through their neighbors and friends.

These two groups comprising the upper segment of the middle class are not necessarily separate and non-overlapping. By taking advantage of their connections and access to information, many professionals and corporate managers with high incomes were able to easily expand their wealth through real estate investments. Members of the upper fraction do not need to feel insecure, since their financial resources and extra assets insulate them from precarious economic situations. Comparing the affluent lifestyles and economic security that the upper middle class enjoys with their own situation, most salaried families in the middle class feel that their material conditions are not favorable enough to allow them to lead a comfortable lifestyle— including having a nice apartment and some savings, and taking a vacation abroad—and share the relative deprivation.

When it comes to children's life chances, the difference between the upper segment of the middle class and the rest becomes larger, and most middle-class citizens are anxious about the uncertain futures of their children. Clearly, when parents have more financial resources, they give their children financial support during major life events such as getting married or purchasing a house. Most of my informants in Gangnam acknowledged that they provided financial support to enable their children to settle nearby after they got married. As we have seen in the case of Jihyun in the previous section, children who have more-affluent parents start their lives from a better position than others, all else being equal.

Yet class is reproduced not only through economic and financial positions. Rather, parents' financial assets can often be transformed into children's cultural and social capital, as Pierre Bourdieu (1984) demonstrated with respect to French society. Parents can invest their greater economic and cultural resources in making their children's education better and their children more competitive in school and beyond. By participating in various extracurricular activities, going to better cram schools, and having private tutors, children with more parental resources have a better chance of excelling in school. In addition, traveling abroad and participating in academic programs there help these children acquire fluency in foreign languages and turn them into more global and cosmopolitan subjects. With full family support that frees them from many worries, these children can focus on studying for college entrance exams and building more competitive résumés for getting a job after college.

The following two cases featured by the Korean daily newspaper *Hankyoreh* exemplify how parents' class positions significantly shape children's life chances:

> Seung-woo Kim (age thirty-one) lives in a 63-*p'yŏng* [2,273.3 square foot] apartment in Jamsil [the east side of Gangnam], owned by his father and currently valued at 2 billion won (US$1.8 million). His father is a senior manager of a construction company and earns 300–400 million won (US$260,000) a year. Seung-woo graduated from the University of Michigan, majoring in economics. In 2010, after two months back in Korea, he found a job with a foreign financial company, where he earns 30 million won (US$33,800) annually. He is now preparing to take a CPA exam. Though his degree in the United States and his fluency in English gave him a competitive edge in getting his job, he does not believe that money automatically brought him these advantages. Convinced that only self-motivation and hard work will result in success, he studies for an hour every day before going to work and for an additional eight hours on the weekends. (*Hankyoreh* 2/21/2012)

> Seoyoung Kim (age twenty-five) is a manager of customer representatives at a call center in Seoul. She is paid about 1.7 million won (US$1,500) a month, of which she gives 1 million won to her parents, who have a hard time making ends meet. Her father's grocery store has gone bankrupt twice, once when she was in fifth grade, and then again in her senior year of high school. When she was young, her father obtained a loan to start a grocery store in the city of Guri, Gyeonggi Province, but when the economic crisis hit Korea in 1997, his store was a casualty. The family had to move three times to avoid debt collectors. After working hard to save money, her parents opened another store in the city of Pocheon, also in Gyeonggi. This time, a Super Supermarket (SSM),[33] owned by a chaebol, opened nearby, and her parents lost most of their customers. Seoyoung had to drop out of college in 2006 after only a semester. Working several part-time jobs at the same time, she was eventually able to pay off her parents' debts. It was 2008 when she found her current permanent job. (*Hankyoreh* 2/19/2012)

The above cases show how parents' class positions are transmitted to their children and how the children are positioned to remain in the same class unless something unexpected happens. On the surface, it seems that the difference between Seung-woo and Seoyoung in merits, such as educational degrees and skill sets, determined their access to different jobs, which explains Seung-woo's belief that self-motivation and self-development are the important components of success. However, it is not difficult to see that their parents' class positions were conditions underlying the development of these merits. In the Seung-woo's case, his parents' wealth helped him to get a college degree and develop English fluency in the United States, which in turn helped him land a nice job. By contrast, Seoyoung's parents' difficult economic situation did not allow her to finish her college degree, and she had to assume her parents' debts. Although she was fortunate in that she was able to pay off the debts and found a permanent position, she might have been much better off now if her parents had been able to support her financially. In the future, Seoyoung's life may improve, given the drive she demonstrated as she worked hard and paid off the debts. Yet to reach Seung-woo's position, Seoyoung would have to make much more effort than Seung-woo would. It is also likely that both of them will marry someone with a similar background. Seung-woo's parents will no doubt help him to purchase a house when he gets married, whereas Seoyoung will have to save money on her own. In the absence of a major misfortune, Seung-woo will almost certainly have a comfortable life. For Seoyoung, even staying in the same position will not be easy, because her job is not prestigious and is vulnerable to economic recession, and she does not have a financial cushion to fall back on in an emergency.

Figure 3.5 shows Koreans' expectations of social mobility in the future. In 2015 only 21.8 percent of respondents believed that class mobility would be possible within their own generation, and only 31 percent expected that their children's generation would do better than their own generation. The majority of the population—including middle-class citizens—shares strongly negative beliefs about the possibility for class mobility, and over time this pessimism has become even stronger. Witnessing how social class is passed down from one generation to the next and how the wealth gap becomes larger over the years, fewer and fewer citizens hold optimistic views about upward mobility.

In the past, Korean society was believed to afford ample opportunity for class mobility. The Korean War and land reform demolished the existing

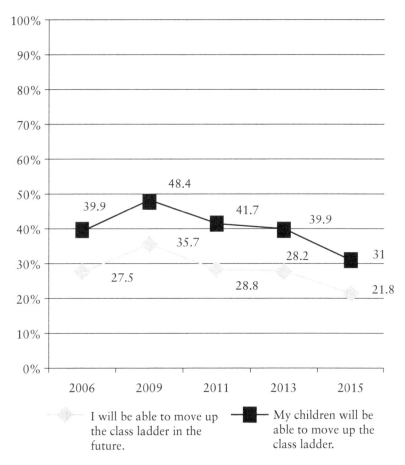

Figure 3.5. Perceptions about intra- and intergenerational social mobility.
Source: Korean National Statistics Office, 2006–2015.

class structure and created a relatively level playing field. In the course of industrialization, people were able to pursue economic gain with almost no
structural barriers, and many rode the economic wave of that period and
accumulated considerable wealth. It was common to encounter stories of
people who had once barely earned a living later becoming millionaires, such
as Chong Ju-yung (the founder of Hyundai) and Kim Woo-Choong (the
founder of Daewoo). Such stories were widely circulated and consumed, and
it became an indestructible myth that anyone could achieve success using
only one's bare hands, strong will, and incessant effort. Although the acqui-

sition of wealth was often fraught with corruption and favoritism, and although the degrees of economic success were different among different groups of people, most ordinary citizens benefited in some way from an era of material improvement. Many people from poor families climbed the social class ladder and joined the middle class. The middle class was also a symbol of optimism and possibility: those who worked hard would earn decent salaries that would allow them to purchase an apartment and to invest in their children's education so that their children would also enjoy middle-class status. The promises of middle-class status led Koreans to harbor hopes for a better future.

After a generation, however, this myth of class mobility was crushed. The opportunities that existed in one generation suddenly disappeared in the next. Even college graduates have limited job opportunities, and the jobs do not secure promising futures. Even those who have decent permanent jobs feel anxious about their circumstances after retirement. They invest a lot of money in their children's education, but the children's chances of joining the middle class are not as good as they were a generation ago. With stunted wage growth, lack of job opportunities, and enormous housing and education costs, living a middle-class life has become more challenging. For those not born into wealthy families, the chances of getting ahead will be very small. Many therefore feel that they live on an uneven playing field and that their ceaseless efforts will never pay off. As the channels of class mobility become much narrower than they once were, relative deprivation prevails, and feelings of frustration become stronger.

Yet a widespread, deep-seated sense of pessimism and frustration cannot be explained only in terms of changes in economic conditions, such as lack of opportunities, and increasing social inequality. It also has to do with the ways in which people *make sense of* how this social inequality and disparity in Korea have been created and maintained. Most people believe that the beneficiaries of economic growth who accumulated wealth and climbed the social class ladder much more quickly than others did so as a result of stretching the rules or manipulating the system. For example, speculators who aggressively invested in real estate and acquired enormous unearned incomes were seen as one of the winners who amassed wealth through less difficult means than hard work and individual effort. And in the next generation, the children of this group could get further ahead than the children of other groups by capitalizing on their parents' class positions. Seeing others with similar starting points get much further ahead through real estate speculation, and seeing the children of these people do better, many cannot help feeling bitterness and relative deprivation. During my interviews, I have often heard those who have failed to make fortunes blame themselves for "not having ridden the waves of the times" when others did. They lament not having made "smarter decisions." "I should have bought a home in Gangnam instead of where we are now," I was often told. "The home that I sold is now worth twice as much," others said. "I shouldn't have sold it that early." While they feel sorry about their missed opportunities, this sense often develops into infuriation with a deeply flawed and unfair system, a scorn for the economic system and the government that did not reward hard work and fair play.

After five decades of industrialization, Korea has joined rich countries with higher per capita GDP, a stunning achievement that no one imagined two generations ago—and yet, despite their objectively improved living conditions, people are disenchanted by an imbalanced economic distribution and limited chances for joining (or staying within) the ranks of the middle class. A once-universal faith in class mobility and a better future has been called into doubt; the social aspirations that once motivated people to work hard to attain their goals have diminished or disappeared. In the absence of security and access to a life of fulfillment, the Korean dream feels shattered, no more than an empty promise.

An overall decline of the middle class and the increasing divide within the Korean middle class—between a small upper segment, which stably sustains a comfortable lifestyle, and the rest of the middle class, which struggles with job insecurity and high living costs and is anxious about downward mobility—have emerged since the Asian financial crisis of the late 1990s. Many studies focus on the role of economic restructuring and labor market changes in explaining the changing dynamics of the middle class. With increasing competition in the global economy and pressure for economic restructuring, corporations have chosen to implement massive layoffs and adopt flexible labor regimes. These economic changes not only decreased the number of decent jobs but also led to diminished job security and forced early retirements. Such shifts created a heightened level of anxiety and economic vulnerability among ordinary white-collar families.

Increasing differentiation and fragmentation within the middle class are in part driven by these global factors, yet this explanation ignores domestic factors such as housing and education policies that have aggravated social inequality and increased the emotional and financial burdens borne by the majority of the middle class over the years. As Thomas Piketty points out, "The history of the distribution of wealth has always been deeply political, and it cannot be reduced to purely economic mechanisms" (2014, 20). Speculative urbanism sharply elevated housing prices and allowed some citizens to significantly improve their fortunes. The property-based middle-class citizens who owned extra properties could get much further ahead than the rest of the salary-based middle class. The unearned incomes won through real estate investment not only provide them with economic comforts and security but also put their children on a better socioeconomic footing. As this chapter has demonstrated, both internal and external factors have contributed to increasing social inequality and the development of heterogeneity within the middle class.

Economic changes and the deepening of social inequality have transformed the middle-class narrative. Formerly dominant narratives of upward mobility and middle-class confidence are increasingly seen as myths. The economic structure that lifted millions of Koreans to middle-class status no longer functions in the same way. Because of the stagnant economy and the almost nonexistent social safety net, middle-class families struggle to formulate strategies to lessen economic uncertainty, finding that their choices are limited. Although rapid economic development through the early 1990s enhanced the livelihoods of many citizens, it also created structural barriers for those who had not exploited their opportunities to the fullest. While those who successfully climbed the social ladder are able to reproduce their class standing through diverse strategies, others who did not benefit from the system feel outraged about what now seems like a closed social structure. Class boundaries have become clearer within the past generation and a half, yet the Korean state has not effectively addressed social inequality and built stronger welfare regimes, to the detriment of the majority of the population, including the vast majority of the middle class.

The remaking of the middle class is an urgent task for state officials and politicians in contemporary Korean society. The presidential debates in 2012 showed that building stronger social safety nets and reviving the middle class had become important agenda items for both conservative and liberal candidates in an election haunted by increasing social inequality and a widening income gap. Creating social aspirations for upward mobility and better lives had once been the driving force of optimism and confidence. When people cannot dream of a hopeful future, when instead they are faced with frustration, limited chances, and a widening social gap, society will face a massive backlash. This is the crossroads where Korean society stands.

CONCLUSION

The Politics of a Downwardly Mobile Middle Class in an Unequal, Globalizing World

A new Korean phrase, "Hell Chosun" (*hel Chosŏn*), went viral in 2015. A multilingual combination of the English word "hell" and a historical term for Korea,[1] the phrase was coined on an ultra-right-wing social media website as a derogatory term describing "backward" and "uncivilized" Korean society and culture. But it soon became widespread and is now commonly used among young people. It expresses a deep sense of dispiritedness, despair, and fury, characterizing Korea as a dystopia rampant with intense competition, inequality, and social injustice. In this "hell," no matter how hard you work and how much effort you put in, you will still never get ahead unless you are born with a silver spoon in your mouth. This shared understanding is directly related to the economic struggles and burdens that younger generations are facing: high unemployment, insecure jobs, and extremely high living costs, including those for housing and education. Precariousness has become a common daily experience for young people all over the world, yet the ways in which young Koreans respond to their contemporary situation are especially pessimistic and fatalistic: they rage against elites and the ruling classes and believe that Korean society is hopeless.

When one considers that Korea's strong, vibrant economy is the envy of most countries, the growing sense among ordinary citizens that Korea's future is hopeless may seem baffling. This pessimistic view results from a sense of dispossession. Abundant opportunities that were once available during the era of high economic growth are now gone, after only a generation. Middle-class status, which was not difficult to attain for an earlier generation given a combination of individual effort, some education, and a decent job, is now a difficult goal for younger generations to achieve. Getting into college, finding a job, and surviving at work all involve intense competition. And even those who are successful in this competition find that buying a home on their own and educating their children are challenging tasks. For young people who were not born into a privileged background, the prospects of having an ordinary life—getting married and having children—are discouraging. To improve their lives, they make extraordinary efforts. For example, Koreans worked the third-highest number of hours among OECD countries in 2014, after Mexico and Costa Rica, 361 more hours per year than the OECD average of 1,763.[2] Yet their hard work and investment in self-development do not necessarily improve their quality of life. Fortune is not an outcome of hard work and competence any longer; one's fate seems to be sealed from the moment one is born. Thus, predominant feelings of pessimism and cynicism among young adults are closely related to the collapse of the "middle-class myth" and to a growing belief that class mobility is not attainable, social inequality is getting worse, and hard work and sweat no longer result in economic rewards. "Hell Chosun" is an expression of hopelessness and wretchedness among young Koreans who cannot find any opportunities in a dog-eat-dog world.

Nevertheless, "Hell Chosun" does not simply reflect the collective frustration about curtailed opportunities and economic hardships of contemporary youth. It also expresses anger toward the ways in which opportunities are given and economic winners are chosen—the unfair and unjust social order that has structurally favored chaebol, power elites, real estate speculators, and others and allowed them to game the system. With almost no structural barriers or regulation, these privileged groups have aggressively pursued material gain. Many who have accumulated enormous wealth are believed to have acquired it by illegitimate and corrupt means, such as giving kickbacks and bribes to politicians. Instead of addressing the flaws embodied in imperfect social institutions and setting fair rules for the game, state elites and politicians alike have preached that young adults need to work harder and cultivate "individual competitiveness." Remarkable economic growth occurred without social safety nets and welfare benefits, leaving many people vulnerable to economic insecurity and uncertainty. The Hell Chosun discourse has emerged as a skeptical and outraged response to an imbalanced and unfair social system and to the Korean state, which has maintained or strengthened inequality and ignored the well-being of the majority of ordinary citizens. The emergence of the Hell Chosun discourse reveals that the collective faith about individual material improvement and social progress has gone to pieces.

The story of the rise and fall of the Korean middle class that I have told in this book is closely connected to the Hell Chosun discourse: What happens when people realize that what motivated them to work harder is a mirage? The celebrated Korean middle class that once symbolized upward mobility and affluence, something that everybody aspired to join, has now become the focus of widespread anxiety and concern. Most studies explain the decline of the middle class as an outcome of globalization and neoliberal economic policies that have negatively affected the labor market and overall working conditions, such as job security and wage levels. Tracing the historical process by which the Korean middle class emerged, expanded, and declined over the past five decades, this book instead demonstrates that the current fragility of the middle class was deeply embedded in the *speculative* and *exclusionary* ways in which it was formed during the era of high economic growth. I have argued that the formation of the speculative and exclusive middle class based on homeownership and real estate investment has produced increasing divisions within the middle class and, in turn, has now made it harder for younger adults to climb the social class ladder. The actual ways in which economic winners were chosen and class mobility was acquired conflicted with state promises of economic rewards for hard work and meritocratic credentials. The speculative route into the middle class produced the widespread perception that class mobility and material gain were the outcome of simple luck and undeserved profits.

Understanding the Politics of Middle-Class Formation in Korea

In order to capture the dynamics of the rise and decline of the middle class over time, this book has addressed three different dimensions of the middle class—social narratives, structural existence, and cultural practices. First, the middle class is represented in public discourses and imagined as a particular social group associated with certain values and images. The middle class in this social narrative produces social aspirations and desires, as well as suffering collective frustrations. Second, the middle class is understood as a structural entity based on income, occupation, and educational level. The middle class from this perspective is a "class in itself" in Marx's term—an aggregate of people who share particular characteristics yet do not own any collective class consciousness. Last, the middle class is the lived experience by which members of a particular group share cultural dispositions, form a boundary through daily interactions against others, and fashion a class identity that is distinctive from other groups. Moving beyond reductionist conceptions of the middle class, this book has tried to disentangle a complex process of middle-class formation and present a more comprehensive picture of the Korean middle class.

In analyzing a historical process of the making and unmaking of the Korean middle class, I have adopted a dialectical approach to bridge political-economic and cultural perspectives. The traditional political-economic approach focuses on economic policies and their outcomes in the structural realm, whereas the cultural approach analyzes consumption practices and performativity in the cultural and symbolic realms. Looking at how ordinary citizens employed specific strategies to enhance their standard of living and how these actions in turn triggered certain outcomes, I have attempted to understand the rise of the middle class in both structural and cultural terms. Middle-class identities and lives are shaped by a dialectical process, structurally formed from above, and articulated and performed from below. The state created structural conditions for the expansion (and decline) of the middle class through policies in housing, education, and employment, and through official discourse. At the same time, operating in the ideological and objective spaces created by the state, middle-class actors pursued diverse strategies to advance their interests. This dialectical approach, looking at interactions between the state and the middle class, structure and agency, and political economy and culture, helps to illuminate the dynamic process of middle-class formation.

It is important to emphasize the vital and intentional role of the state in the making (and the unmaking) of the middle class. Earlier studies have viewed the state as an important influence on class formation (Diane Davis 2004; Fernandes 2006): many governments seek to grow the economy by fostering the middle class. Through various policies such as job programs, housing subsidies, and wage growth, the state shapes the material conditions under which certain groups of people can greatly benefit. As noted previously, the state's promotion of heavy industry created massive armies of engineers, technicians, corporate managers, and office workers, all employed by big businesses that provided high wages and extensive benefits. While these privileged occupational groups were important pillars of the Korean middle class, another critical support was state-sponsored homeownership. By subsidizing the large-scale construction of apartment complexes and promoting homeownership, the state helped white-collar families to become homeowners by making it possible for them to purchase new apartment units below market value.

While previous studies have paid attention to the material and economic side of the making of the Korean middle class, the ideological aspects of the state's promotion of the middle class have been relatively ignored, particularly how the state projects specific images of the middle class and forges particular forms of middle-class identity. Fernandes notes that the rise of the new middle class is a "cultural and *normative* political project" (emphasis in original) in which the middle class serves as "a group that represents the promise of a new national model of development" (2006, xxvii). Likewise, the Korean state tried to construct the middle class as a desirable national subject that embraced the values of discipline, frugality, and political moderatism, a vehicle of ideal and moral citizenship. Given the particular geopolitical situation of the confrontation with North Korea, the South Korean state urgently needed to recover from the intense ideological and political conflicts associated with the war to successfully build a new nation and to outcompete North Korea. In this context, the creation of the middle class as an affluent and ideologically sound citizenry was an important part of the political and ideological state project to consolidate political legitimacy and to survive in the competitive milieu of cold war politics. By disseminating moral values such as hard work, nationalism, patriotism, and self-help, all symbolized by middle-class subjects, the state and political elites alike tried to build a middle-class nation that would redefine national identity and materialize postwar prosperity.

In describing a particular path to middle-class status and middle-class culture in Korea, I have paid attention to the spatial dimension of class formation, especially high-rise apartment complexes in urban areas. We need to understand that these particular spaces were engineered by the state's urban development policies. The production of huge apartment complexes was an outcome of the state's support of private developers, notably chaebol. High-rise apartment complexes in Korea have played an important role in creating wealth for homeowners and fashioning their modern, Westernized middle-class lifestyle. Apartment units were valuable economic assets that brought investment opportunities and financial returns with housing price inflation. At the height of a real estate boom in the 1970s and 1980s, flipping apartments and moving frequently from one apartment unit to another were popular entrepreneurial investment strategies that many relatively affluent families adopted. By making shrewd calculations about when to move and what to buy for the best returns, many families made hefty profits through real estate investment and could quickly climb the economic ladder. Yet differential increases in apartment values in different areas caused material conditions to diverge even among middle-class homeowners and created a larger wealth gap within middle-class families over time. As a source of family fortunes and financial gains, high-rise apartments provided great profit-making opportunities for middle-class homeowners.

In addition to providing economic opportunities for homeowners (and limiting future life chances for non-homeowners), high-rise apartment living became the key ingredient of middle-class culture in Korea. Where one lives demonstrates one's social standing and status, and in Korea, apartment living symbolized cultured and affluent middle-class identity and lifestyle. Apartments that featured green spaces, gyms, lounges, and security systems with CCTV and private security guards displayed their superiority as living space over other types of housing. The demographic composition of apartment residents—young, educated, nuclear white-collar families with salaried husbands and stay-at-home wives—strengthened the image of high-rise apartments as the archetypal middle-class living space. Apartment complexes formed distinctive communities with socially homogeneous members living in standardized units, purchasing similar household items, and having similar lifestyles, which reinforced a sense of belonging among residents. At the same time, the physical boundaries of apartment complexes with fences and gated entrances demarcated an exclusive space by separating apartment residents from outsiders. Cultivating a cultural milieu symbolized by comfort, civilization, privacy, and exclusion, apartment complexes spatialized the middle class in urban space. Yet the emergence and development of middle-class space were often accomplished by bulldozing poor urban communities and evicting many low-income families, to the detriment of social equity, justice, and the rights of the poor.

The case of the Korean middle class analyzed in this book encourages us to revisit earlier scholarship on the middle class, development, and social inequality. First, looking at the historical trajectory of the Korean middle class, this book complements the perspective that emphasizes globalization and neoliberalism in explaining the current decline of the middle class. In this perspective, the common pattern of increasing income gaps and the decline of the middle class is mainly explained by economic restructuring and neoliberal reform. Lack of permanent, decent job opportunities and stagnant wage growth are attributed to neoliberal economic policy changes that reduce labor costs. While such restructuring has exacerbated social inequality and increased economic burdens for middle-class citizens, neoliberalism and globalization cannot explain the variations in social inequality and economic conditions of the middle classes from country to country. My findings demonstrate that the market alone does not dictate the current conditions of the middle class in any given country: domestic policies and a politics of development peculiar to Korea have played a significant role in the making and unmaking of the Korean middle class over the long run. The state and chaebol were accomplices in speculative urban development in the 1970s and 1980s and have kept real estate prices rising for decades. Some families were able to take advantage of this real estate boom, but increasing housing costs have made it extremely difficult for many, especially in younger generations, to purchase homes only with their own salaries and savings and to attain or maintain middle-class status. By examining particular state policies and actions during the course of Korea's economic development and by looking at both external and internal conditions, this book has tried to draw a more complete and accurate picture of the conditions of the Korean middle class in the past and the present.

Second, this book provides a critical understanding of Korean development by challenging the conventional wisdom that emphasizes the bright side of economic development and middle-class formation in Korea (and East Asia). According to the standard narrative, the capable and efficient Korean government successfully promoted rapid economic growth in collaboration with big businesses and, as a result, created a large middle class while maintaining low social inequality. In this perspective, the process of development and middle-class formation is seen as efficient, balanced, and equitable, even though the developmental process was accompanied by some violent aspects such as labor repression and eviction of the urban poor. Contrary to such images of well-organized capitalist development, however, my findings draw a more unbalanced, inequitable picture, in which a lax state simply allowed corporations and individuals to speculate in real estate and pursue material gains with little or no oversight. These circumstances enabled particular groups of people to become homeowners and to take advantage of skyrocketing property values, which in turn resulted in increasing social inequality between homeowners and non-homeowners and between homeowners in booming neighborhoods and those in other districts. As a result of the state failing to properly manage the housing and real estate market, inequality in housing and properties has reached alarming proportions in Korea. Capturing the tensions and contradictions between an official discourse that emphasized merit and hard work on the one hand, and state practices that allowed (and even encouraged) speculation on the other, I have tried to critically analyze the inequities of the state development project and the reality behind the myth that anyone who worked hard enough would be able to join the middle class someday.

Third, this book contributes to the understanding of collective sensibilities shared by citizens who are usually categorized as the middle class by objective measures, yet do not feel that they belong to the middle class. There exists a gap between objective and subjective definitions of the middle class—how the middle class is defined by scholars and the media, and how people view themselves and imagine the middle class. Analyzing how they make sense of both their current situation and the issue of social inequality, I demonstrate what it *feels* like to become and be a member of the middle class in contemporary Korea. Emotions and feelings are also important components in constructing a class identity that cannot be captured solely in terms of material conditions. Portraying widespread feelings of frustra-

tion, anxiety, and outrage, this book sheds light on middle-class sentiments.

The Middle Class, Development, and the State in Developing Countries

The case of the rise and fall of the Korean middle class over the past five
decades provides a good comparative perspective on countries that have experienced a similar socioeconomic transformation. In the past decade, there
have been many studies on the middle class in emerging economies (e.g.,
Baviskar and Ray 2011; Freeman 2014; Heiman, Liechty and Freeman 2012;
Jaffrelot and van der Veer 2008; Lopez and Weinstein 2012; Ren 2013). A
number of studies probe middle-class lifestyles, identities, and consumption,
describing subjects who walk through megamalls and buy brand-new consumer electronics and shiny new cars in Beijing, Mumbai, São Paulo, or any
other megalopolis. These studies tend to focus on globalization and its impact on the middle class as global consumers and neoliberal, entrepreneurial
subjects. Yet the middle class is not merely a consumer group, as this book
has shown; rather, the middle class both constructs and is constructed by
civic discourse, cultural life, economic engagement, and political claim-
making. As a consequence, the middle class is a major socioeconomic force
that plays a crucial role in shaping particular trajectories of development and
domestic politics. The rise of the middle class as "model citizens" helps rein-
force political legitimacy, social stability, and optimism; the decline of the
middle class, however, heightens the sense of frustration, anxiety, and social
inequality, which may bring about social disruption and distrust of politics.

Like Korea, China and India—two giant economies witnessing a middle-
class surge in the midst of socioeconomic transformations—suggest that a
new middle class that embodies individual prosperity and opportunities
plays an important role in legitimizing state-directed economic reforms and
strengthening the state's vision of development. The Chinese case of middle-
class formation in metropolitan cities has many parallels with its Korean
counterpart. Though the Chinese socialist system operated differently from
Korea's, the ways in which state policies favored certain groups of people and
allowed them to rapidly climb the social ladder were similar to what can be
found in Korea. During the Mao period under socialist rule, China was one

of the most egalitarian countries in the world because of the bureaucratic redistribution system. A family's standard of living was mainly determined by the resources of the workplace (*danwei*)[3] rather than by individual rank (Bian 1994; Parish 1984). Under Mao, although material inequalities existed between high-level cadres and ordinary workers, overall living standards were remarkably homogeneous within enterprises. Whether households were headed by a professional or a blue-collar production worker, their family members lived in comparable homes, took the same buses to work, confronted similar food shortages, and faced an equally limited choice of leisure activities and clothing (Deborah Davis 2000, 3). Under socialist rule, most urban adults worked in state-owned enterprises and enjoyed the "iron rice bowl" of lifetime employment, egalitarian wages, and generous welfare benefits (Deborah Davis 1992).

After Mao's death in 1976, Deng Xiaoping suggested a vision of "*xiao-kang* (moderately prosperous) society" as a goal of Chinese modernization, a society where everybody enjoys a comfortable lifestyle. Deng believed that the intense political and ideological struggles of the Mao era had hindered Chinese development and that socialism should instead develop productive power and improve people's living standards. To this end, Deng launched market reform and tried to promote economic growth. To enhance global competitiveness, Chinese leaders emphasized educational credentials and professional skills and dismissed the socialist principles of egalitarianism and class leveling, which were believed to foster a lack of competitive mentality and self-motivation, a reliance on the state, and worker laziness (C. K. Lee 2007; Won 2005). Public sector employees and salaried professionals benefited from the market reform. Not only did urban public employees experience rapid increases in their salaries in the 1990s but they also benefited from housing reform by becoming homeowners. In particular, the massive sale of public housing to employees at highly discounted prices, the availability of "economy housing" (*jingji shiyongfang*, a subsidized form of commercial housing), and "housing provident funds" enabled well-placed public employees to achieve homeownership relatively easily (Tomba 2004). As Luigi Tomba puts it, "Early access to the privatization of housing has become a major discriminant between social actors, and it often determines social status more than income does" (ibid., 6). As these homeowners were able to capitalize on properties that they acquired through subsidized homeownership, professionals and urban public-sector employees experienced rapid upward mobility.

The highly visible gated middle-class communities and consumption practices of the middle class created a new pattern of residential segregation and stratification in urban China. The comfortable, cosmopolitan lifestyles of the new middle class in China exemplify the success of economic reform as well as "neoliberal" values of personal freedom, privatization, and individual responsibility in the postsocialist context. Class differentiation is thus seen as a natural and progressive move away from Maoist egalitarianism (Ong and Zhang 2008). However, at the same time, the rise of the middle class overshadows the decline of the working class in state-owned enterprises in northeastern "rust belt" cities facing unemployment, pay and benefit cuts or suspensions, and the loss of pensions (C.K. Lee 2007), as well as the conditions of migrant workers in cities, who struggle with low wages and long work hours. Once one of the most egalitarian countries in the world under Mao, China now has soaring social inequality, its Gini coefficient having reached 0.46 by 2012, up from 0.21 in the 1960s ("Gini out of the Bottle" 2013). Since the economic reform in 1978, Chinese society has witnessed an increasing number of protests by disadvantaged workers, peasants, and homeowners, a phenomenon often identified as a "social volcano" (He 2003). The increasing socioeconomic differentiation between the affluent few and the rest of the population poses a potential threat to Chinese society. So far, despite increasing social unrest, the Chinese Community Party has successfully managed conflicts, maintaining a high level of social stability. As long as the Chinese government keeps ordinary citizens convinced that there are ample opportunities for upward mobility and that their lives will be better in the future, it can ensure political stability. Yet if this belief declines among ordinary citizens and disillusionment about social mobility begins to prevail, China's political and social stability will be at huge risk.

Along with China, India, another developing country witnessing a rapidly growing new middle class, faces similar problems in contending with new forms of inequality. In the wake of economic liberalization in the 1990s, the new Indian middle class has often been portrayed as highly educated, speaking fluent English, and holding jobs in information technology or the service sector. As a symbol of cosmopolitanism and transnationalism and as proof of India's economic success, the new Indian middle class delivers positive images of economic liberalization and globalization (Fernandes 2006). The Indian state's liberalization policy and its support of the knowledge economy, combined with an educational system that has produced a highly qualified, English-speaking workforce, have created a well-educated professional middle class. High salaries and extensive perks in the new economy make IT workers in particular a consumerist class.

Yet this hegemonic image of the new Indian middle class obscures its complex internal composition. Upwardly mobile IT workers and their families, a new and successful group whose growth the Indian state tries to promote through economic liberalization, constitute only a small part of the middle class (Fernandes 2006; Radhakrishnan 2007). Beyond this much-celebrated, privileged upper segment, the rest of the traditional middle class—including those in public sector jobs—has experienced job insecurity and reduced benefits due to the economic restructuring that has taken place since the 1990s. While the rise of the new middle class seems to support belief in just and equitable upward mobility based on meritocracy, it masks existing inequality and fragmentation within the middle class. The increasing inequality and the anxieties of the lower middle class in India have invited the rise of the Bharatiya Janata Party (BJP) and Hindu nationalism. Tapping the frustrations and economic insecurity of the lower middle class, which has not fully benefited from globalization, the party leaders have provoked anti-Muslim and anti-migrant sentiments and asserted cultural purity and Hindu unity (Fernandes and Heller 2006, 507–8). In the face of accelerated marketization and rising lower-class demands, middle-class politics turns to exclusion and illiberalism (Fernandes and Heller 2006).

Both the Chinese and Indian cases demonstrate that the new middle classes grew with economic reform and liberalization. Yet the middle class is not simply a phenomenon produced by market expansion and economic growth; instead, as a bearer of particular state ideologies in times of economic transformation, the middle class has been shaped by particular state policies. In addition, historical experiences and existing patterns of social inequality shape the specific character of middle classes. Though both states promoted images of the new middle class as a vision of development, only a small segment of the population was able to benefit from state policies. Despite China's and India's visible economic successes and their well-publicized new middle classes, staggering social inequality and wealth gaps have become a challenging characteristic of these and other emerging economies.

In the era of globalization, developing countries face the double challenges of promoting economic growth for development and managing social inequality and conflicts at the same time. As Karl Polanyi noted, the development of capitalism has been shaped by the increasing tension between capital accumulation and social justice, and between economic growth and equity (Polanyi [1944] 1957). Uneven economic development and mounting social inequality, along with the demise of belief in upward mobility, will incur social costs and threaten social stability.

The Future of Middle-Class Politics

The sociologist Göran Therborn (2012) notes that the hopes and resentments of the middle class will shape the politics of the twenty-first century, as the power of the working class and socialism in the twentieth century have disappeared. This book raises further questions about the possibilities of middle-class politics in the globalized world—in particular, how ordinary middle-class citizens in an era of heightened economic insecurity will respond to increasing polarization and social inequality and shape democracy in the world. Previous scholarship has accumulated a great deal of knowledge about the relationship between the middle class and democracy, and many liberals expect the middle class to become the vanguard of democratic reform in developing countries. Yet empirical evidence demonstrates that there is nothing inherently democratic about the middle class and that the role of the middle class in politics is rather "situational" (Hsiao 2006; Therborn 2012). In the current era of downward mobility and glaring social inequality, it still remains unclear whether the increasingly fragmented middle class will forge an important political force in its own right and, if so, what directions it will take in a globalized world—whether it will demand greater social equality and economic reform or turn to reactionary forms of politics, attributing its economic suffering to minority groups.

Around the world, we can observe various patterns of middle-class politics, such as homeowners' activism based on property rights in China, revolution in Egypt, anticorruption campaigns in Hong Kong, antidemocratic and pro-military activism of the conservative Yellow Shirts movements in Thailand, and illiberal Hindu nationalism in India. The global picture of middle-class politics is complicated and even contradictory: for example, the frustrated, dissatisfied middle class, particularly educated youth, took to the streets to demand greater political freedom and economic opportunities and toppled rulers in Egypt, Tunisia, and Yemen during the Arab Spring in 2011 (Bellin 2012; Lust 2011); yet, similar energies, shared by people with the same roots, produced fertile soil for radical fundamentalism at the same time (Castells 2004). Depending on how political organizations and (counter) movement groups utilize and mobilize the frustration and outrage of those who have been educated but feel deprived of their social rights and economic opportunities, the patterns of action and political outcomes can be divergent.

The political situation that the world currently encounters, however, evidences some warning signs and indicates what may come next if national governments fail to embrace the masses and to redress social fractures. The rise of the radical right and ultranationalism around the globe—Brexit, the advent of the Trump administration in the United States, and the rising popularity of extreme right-wing parties in western Europe and their successful functioning as legally constituted governing coalitions—has become a new "mainstream" in institutionalized politics (Berezin 2009; Blee and Creasap 2010; Hochschild 2016; Mudde 2007; Rydgren 2007). The phenomenon of right-wing populism can be seen as a backlash against globalization and neoliberalism by "economic losers"—those who are frustrated with a lack of economic opportunities and precarious employment are attracted to extremist ideas that blame their struggles on immigrants and minorities. The downwardly mobile—ordinary workers, small entrepreneurs, underemployed youths, and midlevel farmers—feel excluded and betrayed by current mainstream politics. In their view, as they suffer and their standard of living deteriorates, mainstream politicians do not seem to care about them, instead embracing the cause of "undeserving" others—immigrants and minorities. These unsettling feelings provide fertile ground for right-wing populists to deploy provocative, exclusionary rhetoric about immigrants taking away "their" jobs and how "undeserving" minorities receive all the welfare benefits. This is a *reactionary* response of the excluded and outraged to the breakdown of the social contract that once promised an improving standard of living and social inclusion through social mobility. Unless the feelings of betrayal and disillusionment widely shared by the downward mobile are properly addressed and as long as there is no long-term public policy that improves the income gap, democracy will be threatened by extremists—as we are currently witnessing.

In the Korean context, my findings suggest that the increasing tensions and conflicts between the property-based, privileged upper portion of the middle class and the rest of the middle class (as well as lower segments of the population) will be an important factor shaping Korean politics. At this moment, we do not know whether the more precariously situated members of the middle class will use individualized strategies to navigate a more competitive economy or if they will instead organize to take collective action against the brutal neoliberal social and economic order. Depending on the economic and social policies adopted by the government, the agendas of political parties, and the issues raised by civil society organizations, we will witness different patterns of middle-class politics. In the midst of global uncertainty, though, one thing is clear: unless the Korean state addresses the socioeconomic insecurities and anxieties of ordinary middle-class citizens, redresses the widening socioeconomic gap, and provides safety nets, Korean society will bear a heavier cost than many imagine. As recently shown in the Hell Chosun discourse, Korean society is currently witnessing signs of social backlash from below.

Notes

Introduction

1. There are a variety of ways to measure the size of the middle class. Official statistics gathered by the Korean National Statistics Office simply use income as the criterion for membership by defining the middle class as those with 50–150 percent of the median income. Though using this definition of the middle class might be controversial and problematic, I am citing it here simply to show rough historical trends.

2. http://www.oecd.org/social/inequality.htm#income. While the Gini coefficient in Korea is still lower than the OECD average, the other two indices are higher than the OECD average. The Gini coefficient is a standard measure of income inequality that ranges from 0 (when everybody has identical incomes) to 1 (when all income goes to only one person). Relative income poverty is the ratio of the number of people whose income falls below the poverty line to the total population; the poverty line is here taken as half the median household income.

3. http://data.worldbank.org/indicator/NY.GDP.PCAP.CD?locations=KR.

4. Chaebol is a Korean word that refers to family-owned big-business conglomerates. *Chae* means property, and *bol* means clans or factions. The word corresponds to the Japanese word *zaibatsu*. With strong support under the authoritarian regimes in Korea, particularly during the Park Chung Hee regime (1961–1979), chaebol experienced

explosive growth and expanded their businesses into different sectors. Chaebol are largely controlled by their founding families. Samsung and Hyundai are examples of Korean chaebol.

5. While most studies look at the positive side of state-business relations in promoting rapid economic development in Korea, David Kang's study (2002) brings up an interesting, understudied subject: rampant corruption and money politics between political elites and chaebol. In contrast to the dominant assumptions found in the developmental state literature that bureaucrats and political elites in Korea were autonomous and neutral, Kang argues that extensive exchanges of favors for bribes between state and business drove policy choices in Korea.

6. Some might question whether the Seoul metropolitan area fairly represents the entire country. It is true that there is a difference in incomes and occupational composition, as well as real estate prices, between Seoul and other big cities and between big and small cities and rural areas in Korea. However, half of the Korean population lives in the Seoul metropolitan area, and the middle class in the Seoul metropolitan area serves as the epitome of the Korean middle class.

7. *Minjung* literally refers to common people or the masses, such as rank-and-file workers, peasants, and the urban poor; but this word has a normative connotation as well, indicating people who are usually marginalized and occupy the bottom rung of the social hierarchy and who carry a potential for instigating social change (or revolution). Influenced by Marxism and liberal theology, antigovernment activists and college students organized *minjung* movements in the 1980s to overthrow authoritarianism. Identifying *minjung* as a true historical subject in opposition to colonialism and authoritarianism, critical intellectuals and college students created a political alliance with workers on the shop floor, helped organize grassroots labor unions, and strengthened pro-democracy movements. For further details, see N. Lee 2007.

8. *Minjung* is a term similar to *sŏmin*: both refer to nonprivileged social groups and those who are economically marginalized, barely making ends meet. Though these terms might refer to similar groups of people substantively, their political implications are different. *Minjung* is the term that has been appropriated by progressive intellectuals and student activists. In this usage, *minjung* were believed to have the ability to transform an unequal and unjust Korean society. By contrast, *sŏmin* is more an everyday, depoliticized term.

9. One can see a similar phenomenon in China. Most Chinese scholars reject Marxist class analysis, replacing it with a Weberian analysis of social status and strata (Ngai and Chan 2008). Chinese scholars have jettisoned the Marxist term "class" (*jieji*) as too reminiscent of the severe social conflicts and backlash of the Cultural Revolution. Instead, they have adopted the Weberian concept of "stratum" (*jieceng*), emphasizing social disparities, mobility, and social harmony rather than a confrontational relationship between the exploiting and exploited. In line with this perspective, other social scientists are addressing middle-class issues.

10. All mass media were severely censored by the government during the authoritarian regimes (1961–1987), but I found that descriptions of economic conditions and state policies were reported fairly accurately and with relatively little distortion.

11. Snowball sampling is a method by which a researcher recruits his/her future research subjects through the current research subjects' introducing their acquaintances.

1. An Imagined Middle Class

1. I have borrowed this word from Raymond Williams (1983), who used it to describe particular words that become central to contention over ideas and values in a certain era.

2. Ironically, the legacy of Japanese colonialism and the Korean War was advantageous to the Park regime. The threat of a war in the Korean Peninsula allowed the state to mobilize all human and material resources in the name of national security. Furthermore, because land reform and the war had destroyed the landed upper class—a group that might have opposed capitalist industrialization—there were no centers of power that could challenge or resist the state's industrial policy (J.-J. Choi 1996).

3. What was interesting was that liberal, progressive intellectuals, even if they did not necessarily favor military rule in Korea, viewed the current situation much as the military did. For example, Suk-Hun Ham, a respected public intellectual, recognized that factionalism and toadyism were the biggest problems that had caused Korea to fall behind and argued that revolution was necessary to address the prevailing problems. Though liberal intellectuals and the military had contrasting political orientations, they adopted the same language.

4. I have borrowed this term from Gorski (2003). He refers to the process of refining and diffusing a panoply of disciplinary techniques and strategies.

5. Eun Heo (2007) argues that two different groups of intellectuals were engaged in producing the discourse of national modernization supported by the state: traditional-conservative and liberal, pro-American intellectuals. The former group, strong supporters of the Park regime, emphasized national identity and patriotism. The latter group, most of whom had studied abroad, emphasized "moral" and "modern" citizenship in nation building. Despite the different ideological-political orientations of these two groups, both were strongly anticommunist.

6. Popular capitalism involves a wider redistribution of privately owned wealth. While this concept is widely used in the West, this Korean version of the phrase was coined by Kim Dae Jung as an alternative idea to the growth-oriented, chaebol-based model promoted by the Park Chung Hee regime. In this theory, all the economic actors should participate equally in decision-making processes, and the benefits should be equally distributed. For further details, see D. J. Kim [1971] 1986.

7. In addition to newspapers, magazines such as *Ch'ŏngmaek* and *Chŏnggyŏng Yŏn'gu* published several academic articles on middle-class issues and national modernization in 1966.

8. I have borrowed this term from Louis Althusser's work (1971) on the ideological state apparatus that is instrumental to propagating the dominant ideology of a given society.

9. In terms of occupational groups, only 6.8 percent of the population could be categorized as middle class (having managerial and white-collar jobs) in 1963. Moreover,

in the early period of industrialization, the wage levels for the majority of the population were still low.

10. Usually translated as rotating credit associations, *kye* originated as a method of mutual aid or public insurance in the agricultural mode of production more than a thousand years ago in Korea. They operate by members making monthly contributions to a common fund and then each taking a turn using the fund. Since formal financial institutions were mostly unavailable to ordinary citizens, people tried to obtain lump sums of money through such informal financial channels. People participated in *kye* in order to receive funds for a special event, such as a child's wedding, buying a home, taking a trip, or starting a business. These *kye* tended to dissolve after one or two years when everyone had had his or her turn at receiving a lump sum (Lett 1998, 71).

11. A Korean thriller, *The Housemaid* (*Hanyŏ*), is a good example of this narrative. Directed by the late Ki-Young Kim, it was released in 1960. It is a story about a housemaid in a middle-class home who has an affair with the husband, destroying his family.

12. The explanation behind Park Chung Hee's decision to transform the regime and to install the Yushin system is a matter of controversy. However, Park himself seemed to be aware of a political and security crisis; the two elections in 1971 showed that formal democratic institutions might have provided a formidable political opposition to the dominant party and a possibility of regime change. Moreover, international factors made Park feel anxious: the United States withdrew 20,000 soldiers from South Korea in 1970 and declined to provide military assistance (I.-K. Chun 2006, 249). Park's response to these events was the inauguration of the Yushin Constitution.

13. The "scientification of all citizens" was a slogan promoted by the Park Chung Hee regime. It not only emphasized science and engineering education at schools but also promoted scientific thinking and rationalized lifestyles in daily life. Eliminating wasteful expenses, planning finances, and rational consumption could be included in this scientification.

14. The Park regime started the New Village Movement (*saemaŭl undong*) in the 1970s. Ostensibly, it sought to promote rural development and improve the living standards of farmers, yet some scholars argue that it was nothing but a political strategy to co-opt the rural sector and to garner political support for the Park regime. For further details, see Y.-M. Kim 2009.

15. The won (*wŏn*) is the South Korean currency.

16. *Danchi* literally means a group of land in Japanese, and refers to a large cluster of apartment buildings. The Japan Housing Corporation (JHC), which was founded in 1955, built large-scale *danchi* housing in suburban areas to provide white-collar families with decent homes between the 1950s and the 1970s. For further details, see Neitzel 2016.

17. According to a survey conducted by the Korean Housing Corporation (O. Kim 1967), 73 percent of apartment head of households were college-educated. In terms of occupation, 35 percent were ordinary white-collar workers, 11 percent were government employees, and 11 percent were teachers or staff at schools.

18. This term was originally introduced in Japan in the 1950s. Inspired by high economic growth and the rapid increase in ownership of home electric appliances in Japan

during the postwar period, Korean intellectuals used this phrase frequently. For further details, see Jongsu Lee 1967.

19. Hagen Koo argues that educational ideology has been a powerful tool in justifying the mistreatment of workers: those who lacked education were seen as inferior and thus undeserving of decent treatment. Even workers who struggled with social discrimination were always self-conscious about their lower educational attainments. Most factory workers expressed a strong desire to "exit" their current situation by talking about their factory employment as a temporary phase in their lives (Koo 2001, 134). The understanding of factory work as "dirty" or low status prevented these workers from developing a working-class identity; instead, they invested in individual improvement, attending night school to acquire cultural skills in order to dissociate themselves from the stereotypical images of factory workers.

20. Borrowing a concept from Hirschman (1970), Koo argues that, while "exit" options were prevalent among workers in the 1960s and 1970s, workers started to voice their rights only later in the 1970s. Supported by church organizations and student movement groups, workers were able to form a class identity and challenge the injustice and discrimination they had experienced.

21. The cultural house (*munhwa chut'aek*) was introduced in Korea during the colonial era. These Western-style houses were popular among educated middle-class families from the 1920s onward. For further details, see Baek 2005 and So 2006.

22. Compared with other countries with generally similar levels of income and industrial development, Korea was unusually short of cars. While there was only one car for every one hundred people in Korea in 1985, Taiwan had one per every fifty people, Malaysia one per twenty, Mexico one per seventeen, and Brazil one per thirteen (Nelson 2000, 95).

23. Given that the authoritarian state strongly restricted freedom of expression and censored all news articles published at the time, it is difficult completely to trust newspaper content. Unfortunately, these are the only in-depth data available for that time period.

24. Some might argue that this was due to the high level of repression. Although this may be true, the situation in the 1980s provides a good point of comparison. Given the similar levels of political repression during the 1970s and 1980s, anti-regime groups could mobilize ordinary people more successfully in the 1980s (leading to political democratization in 1987) than in the 1970s. This implies that repression by itself cannot explain the results of anti-regime protests.

2. The Rise of "Gangnam Style"

1. Apartments in Korea are the same as condominiums in the United States. In Korea the term "condominium" is generally used to refer to resorts. Thus, I use the term "apartments."

2. A gu is an administrative unit of a city, usually comparable to a district. Seoul now has twenty-five gu but in 1960 had only nine.

3. *P'yŏng* is a unit of area commonly used in Korea. One *p'yŏng* is about 3.30 square meters or 35.58 square foot.

4. http://stat-app.seoul.go.kr/sws/sws999P.jsp?ID=DT_B10TAB&IDTYPE=3&A_LANG=1&FPUB=3&SELITEM=1.

5. https://www.si.re.kr/node/52564, accessed September 15, 2015.

6. http://gis.seoul.go.kr/SeoulGis/NewStatisticsMap2.jsp (accessed September 5, 2016).

7. The KHC, a government-backed organization founded in 1962, has played a major role in constructing huge apartment complexes and affordable housing in the nation. Housing policies and projects launched by the KHC appear to have emulated Japanese policies. The Japan Housing Corporation (JHC) promoted *danchi* housing construction in suburban areas for middle-class citizens after the war. For further details, see Neitzel 2016. Korea's huge apartment complexes (*tanji*) seem to have originated from the Japanese model.

8. The apartment construction business is still lucrative and popular among chaebol. Since the 1980s, super chaebol such as Samsung, LG, and Hyundai have dominated this business, although some chaebol that were prominent in the apartment construction line in the 1970s and 1980s collapsed during the 1997 economic crisis.

9. The mid-1970s were not the first time that Korean society saw a real estate boom. The first boom took place in the late 1960s as a consequence of state-directed economic development plans. Rapid urbanization and inflation, along with the construction of the Seoul-Busan express highway in 1968, stimulated the real estate market (N.-G. Son 2008, 26). Land prices in twelve major cities had risen by 50 percent annually between 1965 and 1969; by 1974 land prices were seven times higher than in 1969 (ibid.).

10. The average exchange rate for the US dollar and the Korean won (KRW) was 674 won for one US dollar in 1989. KRW5.5 trillion was valued at US$8.1 billion as of 1989.

11. In principle, the owner has to pay in full to purchase a home. But if she can borrow some money for a short term to pay in full, when her tenant pays a *chŏnse* amount to her, she can easily pay back the debt.

12. *Pokpuin*, a new term that was popularized at the end of the 1970s, literally means Mrs. Realtor, and it refers to housewives who speculated in real estate and made a great deal of money out of it. The typical images of *pokpuin* were of women with several checkbooks in their purses, driving their luxurious cars to apartment lotteries (E. Chung 1978). The behaviors of these women were harshly criticized by mass media as ruining the morale of society and pursuing illegitimate means of making money.

13. Cram schools, known as *hagwŏn* in Korean, are private institutions that provide tutoring for students and help them to get better grades or pass the entrance exams for college. Most students attend one or more *hagwŏn* after school to take extra math, English, or science classes. *Hagwŏn* are a mainstay of the Korean educational system.

14. http://gis.seoul.go.kr/SeoulGis/NewStatisticsMap2.jsp, accessed September 10, 2015.

15. The apartment complexes in Banpo and Jamsil built by the KHC in the mid-1970s were torn down and rebuilt by big-business developers such as Samsung and LG in around 2008–2009.

3. The Betrayed Dream of the Korean Middle Class, 1997–2015

1. It is common for former managers and bankers to work for smaller companies after they "officially" retire from their permanent jobs. Some smaller companies recruit these experienced retired employees, as they do not need to pay them as much as big corporations and financial institutions do. Employees as well like working for a few more years in a less competitive environment before they completely retire.

2. *Chaet'ek'ŭ* is a Korean term that combines *chae* (assets or wealth) and technology. It refers to the technique of managing money or finances to produce more wealth and is used mainly in the context of investment in real estate, stocks, or financial products.

3. Again, this is the most common definition of the middle class in official statistics using income levels (50–150 percent of the median income). Other surveys adopt different definitions, such as 75–200 percent of the median income (in the belief that the bottom line for the middle class in official statistics is too low). In any case, they commonly show the pattern that middle-income groups are shrinking over time.

4. "Orange Tribe" refers to a new generation of young people, often called Generation X, who were from wealthy families and engaged in conspicuous consumption. Driving expensive cars and hanging out in wealthy Gangnam neighborhoods, the Orange Tribes were known for enjoying a sexually active lifestyle.

5. http://data.worldbank.org/indicator/NY.GDP.MKTP.KD.ZG?locations=KR&view =chart.

6. http://data.worldbank.org/indicator/NY.GDP.PCAP.CD?locations=KR&view =chart.

7. Nonregular employment usually includes temporary workers, subcontracted workers, dispatched workers, and daily hires.

8. Defining nonregular workers has been a contested political issue. Various government agencies used their own, varying definitions of nonregular workers until 2002 (K. Shin 2013, 338). The Special Committee on Nonregular Workers (SCNW) established a consensual definition of nonregular workers in 2002, which classified nonregular workers in one of three categories: limited-term workers, part-time workers, and atypical workers. Limited-term workers are those whose termination of employment is predetermined or fixed, at usually less than two years. Some of these positions are renewable but not guaranteed, and many employers take advantage of this fact. Part-time workers are those who work less than thirty-six hours a week. Atypical workers include dispatched workers (workers who have employment contracts with work agencies rather than the companies that they work for), subcontracted workers, special independent workers, domestic workers, and daily workers (K. Shin 2013, 339).

9. The "880,000 won generation" (*p'alsip p'almanwŏn sedae*) refers to workers whose monthly income is about 880,000 won (less than US$1,000). They are usually in their twenties and are not regularly employed, with low wages and almost no benefits. Many are part-time workers in the service sector. This expression was coined by the economist Sukhoon Woo and the journalist Kwonil Park (Woo and Park 2007).

10. Korea has the highest suicide rate among OECD countries; every year more than 10,000 Koreans commit suicide. The suicide rate has been increasing constantly since 1997. In 2010, 31.2 per 100,000 people committed suicide, a 130 percent increase

from 13.6 in 2000 (*Yonhap News* 9/8/2011). Major newspapers constantly report on those who kill themselves because of chronic economic hardship and related family issues caused by unemployment, bankruptcy, and debt.

11. I adopt the definition of self-employment used by the OECD, which includes those who work for themselves, employers (who hire fewer than five employees), and unpaid family workers. Unlike employees who are paid a salary or wages, the self-employed earn profit, in cash or in kind. Currently, there are 4,009,000 people who are self-employed, 1,561,000 employers, and 1,119,000 unpaid family workers (Economically Active Population Survey 2016).

12. In this study, Shin defines "middle class" in terms of occupation and employment. Middle-class status depends on employment in relatively well-paid white-collar, managerial, or professional jobs.

13. Newman defines "fall from grace" as the state of having lost one's place in the social landscape, of feeling that one has no coherent identity, and finally of feeling, if not helpless, then at least frustrated about how to rectify the situation ([1988] 1999, 11).

14. *High Kick: A Counterattack from Short Legs* (*Haik'ik: tchalbŭn tari ŭi yŏksŭp*) is a sitcom that was broadcast on MBC in fall 2011. Many characters are from families who suffer from the economic crisis. The sitcom begins with the bankruptcy of the company owned by the main character; to avoid debt collectors, his family moves to his wife's brother's house.

15. *Kosiwŏn* is a particular form of housing in Korea. *Kosi* refers to national exams, such as civil service or bar exams, and *wŏn* means "building." A *kosiwŏn* is a building with tiny rooms where one can barely fit a bed and a desk. Bathrooms are usually shared by residents living on the same floor. This form of housing originally sprang up to serve those preparing for various national exams, such as civil service or bar exams. Located in neighborhoods conveniently close to schools or to exam-prep institutions, *kosiwŏn* provides a small, convenient space for students to focus on their studies. Since the 1990s, this kind of housing has become an alternative and the most prominent housing type for the low-income single-person households because of the cheap rents. For further details, see Minwoo Jung, 2017.

16. Spec (*sŭp'ek*) originates from the English word "specification." As specifications include a variety of features of consumer products, in Korea, "spec" refers to various desirable components or qualifications that people possess in order to attain long-term, secure jobs. Spec includes many résumé-building activities, such as working as interns during the summertime, obtaining certificates, and achieving high English test scores.

17. This phenomenon is not unique to Korea and is seen everywhere in the globalized world. Many new terms that capture dramatic changes in job arrangements appear in the mass media. For example, the acronym NEET refers to a young person who is "not in education, employment, or training." Similarly, *freeter* is a Japanese expression, a portmanteau of the English word "free" and the German word "Arbeiter" (worker or laborer) that describes the underemployed, who do not hold full-time, permanent positions. These people do not start their careers after finishing high school or college and earn money from part-time, low-skill, and low-paying jobs. These terms capture the lack of access to job opportunities and job security that most young people in the neo-

liberal world have to deal with. Guy Standing (2011) conceptualizes these young, underemployed people as the precariat (a portmanteau of "precarious" and "proletariat"), who suffer from low incomes, insecure lifestyles, and psychological strain.

18. This is also not a new phenomenon in Korea. Non-homeowners had to move frequently to find cheaper rents every two years, as landlords often would increase the rent when the lease period was about to end. Yet many white-collar and corporate employees could buy a home after years of savings. Given skyrocketing housing prices and stagnated incomes nowadays, buying a home has become tougher and tougher for young people.

19. These statistics show only the average prices and their increases, so they do not effectively capture the dramatic increases in housing prices in particularly booming areas.

20. Bundang is located in the city of Seongnam, Gyeonggi Province. Bundang is a newly developed suburban town founded in 1992 in order to disperse Seoul residents to other areas. Many former Gangnam residents have moved there.

21. Gangdong is one of the administrative units, or gu, in Seoul. This district is located in the eastern portion of Gangnam.

22. Since the mid-1990s, reconstruction has become common. Reconstruction is often differentiated from redevelopment of substandard settlements (*chaegaebal*). Targeting previously constructed mid- or high-rise apartment complexes, this reconstruction project transforms them into higher-density complexes (H. Shin and Kim 2016). Popular construction companies such as Hyundai, Samsung, and LG often take over the reconstruction companies, and their brand names keep up the property values.

23. Unlike other countries, Korea has a unique rental system called *chŏnse*. *Chŏnse* is a lease system in which a tenant pays a large lump-sum deposit, typically for a two-year rental period. This system is commonly believed to be a win-win strategy for both landlords and tenants. Owners are able to use the *chŏnse* deposits to invest in their businesses or to provide further leverage for the purchase of other apartments; in previous decades they could deposit the money in bank accounts that offered stable, double-digit returns. Tenants, on the other hand, are able to buy time by saving some of their wages while living in *chŏnse* apartments, in the hopes of buying a house in the near future with their savings and recoverable *chŏnse* deposits. However, recently the *chŏnse* system has lost its popularity among landlords because of the low interest typically charged, and owners have mostly shifted to a monthly rent system.

24. It is conventional in Korea for middle- or upper-class parents to spend a lump sum of money when their children get married. Many believe that grooms are responsible for obtaining a home, while brides should purchase household goods.

25. These educational equalization measures (*p'yŏngjunhwa*) produced an unintended consequence: since middle-class families could not hire private tutors or send their children to expensive cram schools, many moved to look for better public schools, particularly in Gangnam. As noted in chapter 2, this was why the massive migration to Gangnam by middle-class families accelerated in the 1980s.

26. The term "private education" as used here means after-school education such as taking extra classes in cram schools and getting private tutoring in addition to regular schooling in either a public or private school. Statistics on the size of the private education

industry count only the money spent for preschool through high school. If expenditures for college students and adults learning English or preparing for the bar or civil servant exams are included, the figure would be much higher, around $30 billion a year.

27. This expenditure is the average value of *all* households in the survey. If we calculate the average expenditure per household whose children actually get private education, the average value becomes higher.

28. Children's education is usually believed to be mainly the responsibility of mothers, because mothers spend much more time than fathers with their children and are more informed about academic matters. It is commonly believed that fathers should not intervene in their children's education and should simply accept their wives' decisions.

29. "English kindergarten" (*yŏngŏ yuch'iwŏn*) is a particular type of kindergarten that focuses on English education. These schools hire native English speakers as teachers and teach children mostly in English. This type of institution is attractive to many parents because their children can be naturally exposed to an environment where English is spoken and can learn English from very early on. English kindergarten is much more expensive than general kindergarten, and lower-income families cannot afford to send their children there.

30. The income inequality (Gini) index remains fairly moderate, the average level of OECD countries. Yet, as mentioned before, the Gini index measures only income and does not include real estate or other assets, and therefore does not reflect an accurate picture of social inequality. The economist Nak-nyun Kim notes that those who earn more than 200 million won annually are often omitted from sampling of household surveys in Korea, and the Gini index tends to underestimate income inequality (N. Kim 2015, 139).

31. The path to the power elite usually lies in becoming a high-level state official, judge, or prosecutor. One can obtain these positions after passing extremely competitive, meritocratic bar or civil service exams. Passing these exams is often seen as guaranteeing success and privilege for life. Many professional matchmakers approach successful single applicants (mostly from nonprivileged backgrounds) and try to match them with potential spouses from rich but nonprestigious families. For further details, see Kendall 1996.

32. *Op'isŭt'el* is a Korean term indicating an office and a hotel, usually a small space for living and working. Many singletons live in this type of housing because it is more affordable than an apartment.

33. Beginning in the early 1990s, some major chaebol, such as Samsung, Lotte, and Shinsegae, entered the retail industry and started opening big supermarkets, or hypermarkets, in local neighborhoods (Y.-K. Kang 2013). In the past twenty years, chaebol have opened almost 400 stores throughout the nation. Their access to capital provided better shopping experiences for consumers—neat, organized displays, diverse choices, lower prices, and quick service. With their small-scale businesses and limited capabilities, local mom-and-pop stores find it difficult to compete with big businesses. With the rise of these large supermarkets, traditional outdoor markets and small shops rapidly dwindled. The number of traditional markets decreased from 1,702 to 1,347 between 2004 and 2012 (ibid.).

Conclusion

1. Chosun was a Korean dynasty that was founded in 1392 and existed until 1897, when the country was officially renamed the Korean Empire (until it was annexed by Japan in 1910). The use of "Hell Chosun" instead of "Hell Korea" seems to reflect a wish to emphasize the feudal characteristics—the rigid social hierarchy and lack of class mobility—of contemporary Korean society.

2. OECD 2016, hours worked (indicator).

3. The *danwei* is the basic unit of urban life under Chinese socialism. In China the *danwei* provides members of society with economic rewards for their work; in addition, through the provision of housing, free medical care, child care centers, kindergartens, dining halls, bathing houses, service companies, and collective enterprises to employ the children of staff, the *danwei* provides its members with a complete social guarantee (Bray 2005, 3–4). For further details, see Bray 2005 and Walder 1986.

REFERENCES

Abelmann, Nancy. 1996. *Echoes of the Past, Epics of Dissent: A South Korean Social Movement*. Berkeley: University of California Press.

———. 2003. *The Melodrama of Mobility: Women, Talk, and Class in Contemporary South Korea*. Honolulu: University of Hawai'i Press.

Abercrombie, Nicholas, and John Urry. 1983. *Capital, Labour, and the Middle Classes*. London: G. Allen and Unwin.

Administration of Labor Affairs. 1972–1982. *Nodong t'onggye yŏn'gam* [The yearbook of labor statistics]. Seoul: Administration of Labor Affairs.

Alison, Anne. 2013. *Precarious Japan*. Durham, NC: Duke University Press.

Althusser, Louis. 1971. *Lenin and Philosophy, and Other Essays*. New York: Monthly Review Press.

Amsden, Alice. 1989. *Asia's Next Giant: South Korea and Late Industrialization*. New York: Oxford University Press.

Anagnost, Ann. 1997. *National Past-Times: Narrative, Representation, and Power in Modern China*. Durham, NC: Duke University Press.

———. 2004. "The Corporeal Politics of Quality (Suzhi)." *Public Culture* 16: 189–208.

"An toel kŏya ama, ibŏn saengae nŭn" [Nothing will probably work out, in this life]. *Hankyoreh 21*, 9/28/2015.

Asian Coalition for Housing Rights. 1989. "Evictions in Seoul, South Korea." *Environment and Urbanization* 1, no. 1: 89–94.

Baek, Jihye. 2004. "1970-nyŏndae sosŏl e nat'anan chungsanch'ŭng ŭi mosŭp koch'al" [Studying the middle class in Korean novels of the 1970s]. *Hansŏngŏ Munhak* 23: 215–41.

———. 2005. *Sŭwit'ŭ hom ŭi kiwŏn* [The origins of the sweet home]. Seoul: Salim.

Baviskar, Amita, and Raka Ray, eds. 2011. *Elite and Everyman: The Cultural Politics of the Indian Middle Classes*. London: Routledge.

Becker, Gary S. 1971. *Human Capital: A Theoretical and Empirical Analysis with Special Reference to Education*. 2nd ed. New York: Columbia University Press.

Bellin, Eva R. 2012. "The Robustness of Authoritarianism Reconsidered: Lessons of the Arab Spring." *Comparative Politics* 44, no. 2: 127–49.

Berezin, Mabel. 2009. *Illiberal Politics in Neoliberal Times: Culture, Security and Populism in the New Europe*. Cambridge: Cambridge University Press.

Bian, Yanjie. 1994. *Work and Inequality in Urban China*. Albany: State University of New York Press.

Blee, Kathleen M., and Kimberly A. Creasap. 2010. "Conservative and Right-Wing Movement." *Annual Review of Sociology* 36: 269–86.

Bourdieu, Pierre. 1984. *Distinction: A Social Critique of the Judgment of Taste*. Translated by Richard Nice. Cambridge, MA: Harvard University Press.

———. 1989. "Social Space and Symbolic Power." *Sociological Theory* 7, no. 1: 14–25.

Bray, David. 2005. *Social Space and Governance in Urban China: The Danwei System from Origins to Reform*. Stanford, CA: Stanford University Press.

Burris, Val. 1992. "Late Industrialization and Class Formation in East Asia in Research in Political Economy." In *Research in Political Economy*, vol. 13, ed. Paul Zarembka, 245–83. Greenwich, CT: JAI Press.

Caldeira, Teresa. 2000. *City of Walls: Crime, Segregation, and Citizenship in Sao Paulo*. Berkeley: University of California Press.

Campos, Jose Edgardo, and Hilton L. Root. 1996. *The Key to the Asian Miracle: Making Shared Growth Credible*. Washington, DC: Brookings Institution.

Castells, Manuel. 1996. *Rise of the Network Society: The Information Age; Economy, Society, and Culture*. Cambridge, MA: Blackwell Publishers.

———. 2004. *The Power of Identity*. 2nd ed. Malden, MA: Blackwell Publishers.

Castells, Manuel, Lee Goh, Reginald Y. W. Kwok, and Toh Lap Kee. 1988. *Economic Development and Housing Policy in the Asian Pacific Rim: A Comparative Study of Hong Kong, Singapore, and Shenzhen Special Economic Zone*. Berkeley: Institute of Urban and Regional Development, University of California.

Cha, Gi-Byug. [1965] 1998. "Oyongdoen minjokchuŭi: Minjokchuŭi nŭn kyŏlk'o sŏn'gŏ kuho e kŭch'il su ŏptta" [Abused nationalism: Nationalism is not only a political campaign slogan]. In *Sasanggye Nonmunjip* 16 [A collection of articles in *Sasanggye*], 269–75. Seoul: Sejongmunhwawon.

Chang, Jiwoong. 1978. "Pudongsan t'ugi ŭi anp'ak" [Everything about real estate speculation]. *Sin Donga* (April): 104–12.

Chang, Kang-Myung. 2015. *Han'guk i sirŏsŏ* [Because I hate Korea]. Seoul: Minumsa.

Chang, Kyung-Sup. 1999. "Compressed Modernity and Its Discontents: South Korean Society in Transition." *Economy and Society* 28, no. 1: 30–55.

Chang, Sang-Hwan. 2004. "Haebang hu Han'guk chabonjuŭi paljŏn kwa pudongsan t'ugi" [The development of Korean capitalism and real estate speculation since liberation]. *Yŏksa Pip'yŏng* (Spring): 55–78.

Chang, Sung-Su, and Jin-Kyun Kim. 1994. "Ap'at'ŭ kŏjumin ŭi sahoe kyech'ŭngjŏk sŏnggyŏk e kwanhan yŏn'gu" [A study on the social classes of apartment residents in Korea]. *Taehan Kŏnch'uk Hakhoe Nonmunjip* [Korean Journal of Architecture] 10, no. 12: 45–53.

Chibber, Vivek. 2003. *Locked in Place: State-Building and Late Industrialization in India.* Princeton, NJ: Princeton University Press.

Cho, Don-Moon. 1994. "Han'guk sahoe kyegŭp kujo ŭi pyŏnhwa, 1960–1990" [Changes in class structure in South Korea, 1960–1990]. *Han'guk Sahoehak* (Spring): 17–50.

Cho, Eunjin. 2007. "Sangnyuch'ŭng chugŏji esŏ nat'ananŭn saeroun paeje ŭi pangsik: Kangnam T'awŏ P'aellisŭ chugŏ konggan mit konggan kyŏnghŏm punsŏk" [Tower Palace, a space of dualistic representation: A study on spatial analysis of the residential complex and the significance of people's experience]. *Kyŏngje wa Sahoe* (December): 122–63.

Cho, Hae-joang. 2002. "Living with Conflicting Subjectivities: Mother, Motherly Wife, and Sexy Woman in the Transition from Colonial-Modern to Postmodern Korea." In *Under Construction: The Gendering of Modernity, Class and Consumption in the Republic of Korea*, ed. Laurel Kendall, 165–95. Honolulu: University of Hawai'i Press.

———. 2015. "The Spec Generation Who Can't Say 'No': Overeducated and Underemployed Youth in Contemporary South Korea." *Positions: Asia Critique* 23, no. 3: 437–62.

Cho, Hee-Yeon. 1998. *Han'guk ŭi kukka, minjujuŭi, chŏngch'i pyŏndong* [The state, democracy, and political changes in South Korea]. Seoul: Dangdae.

Cho, Myung-Rae. 2004. "Sin sangnyuch'ŭng ŭi pangjurosŏ ŭi Kangnam" [Gangnam, haven of the nouveau riche]. *Hwanghae Munhwa* 42, no. 3: 25–40.

Cho, Se-Hee. 1978. *Nanjangi ka ssoa ollin chagŭn kong* [A little ball launched by a dwarf]. Seoul: Munhak kua Chisŏngsa.

Cho, Suk-Gon, and Yu-Suk Oh. 2003. "Apch'uk sŏngjang ŭl wihan chŏnje chokŏn ŭi hyŏngsŏng: 1950-nyŏndae Han'guk chabonjuŭi ch'ukchŏk ch'eje ŭi chŏngbi rŭl chungsim ŭro" [The formation of conditions for compressed development: Addressing the accumulation regime of Korean capitalism in the 1950s]. *Tonghyang kwa Chŏnmang* (December): 258–302.

Cho, Uhn. 2005. "The Encroachment of Globalization into Intimate Life: The Flexible Korean Family in 'Economic Crisis.'" *Korea Journal* 45, no. 3: 8–35.

Cho, Ŭn, and Hagen Koo. 1983. "Capital Accumulation, Women's Work, and Informal Economies in Korea." Working paper, Michigan State University, Office of Women in International Development.

Choi, In-Ho. 1977. "Ŏjjŏja nŭn kŏsin ka: Mujut'aekcha ŭi kkum chitpal nŭn anakne t'ugi" [What can be done about female speculators who trample on the dreams of non-homeowners?]. *Kyunghyang Shinmun*, June 25: 3.

Choi, Jang-Jip. [1986] 1993. "Political Cleavages and Transition in a Military Authoritarian Regime: Institutionalization, Opposition, and Process in South Korea: 1972–1986." Unpublished paper.

———. 1993. "Political Cleavages in South Korea." In *State and Society in Contemporary Korea*, ed. Hagen Koo, 13–50. Ithaca, NY: Cornell University Press.

———. 1996. *Han'guk minjujuŭi chogŏn kwa chŏnmang* [The conditions and prospects of Korean democracy]. Seoul: Nanam.

———. 1997. *Han'guk nodong undong kwa kukka* [The labor movement and the state in Korea]. Seoul: Nanam.

———. 2002. *Minjuhwa ihu ŭi minjujuŭi: Han'guk minjujuŭi posujŏk kiwon kwa wigi* [Democracy after democratization: The conservative origins of Korean democracy and its crisis]. Seoul: Humanitas.

Choi, Minsup, Youngwoo Nam, Eunyoung Choi, Minsuk Kang, Hyunsook Cheon, and Taesup Kim. 2010. *Chugŏ sinbun sahoe: T'awŏ P'aellisŭ esŏ konggong imdae chut'aek kkaji* [Residence class society: From Tower Palace to public housing]. Seoul: Ch'angbi.

Chun, In-Kwon. 2006. *Park Chung Hee p'yŏngjŏn: Park Chung Hee ŭi chŏngch'isasang kwa haengdong e kwanhan chŏn'gijŏk yŏn'gu* [Biography of Park Chung Hee: A biographical study of Park Chung Hee's political thoughts and behaviors]. Seoul: Yihaksa.

Chun, Namil, Sehwa Yang, and Hyoung-Ok Hong. 2009. *Han'guk chugŏ ŭi misisa* [Microhistory of Korean residences]. Seoul: Tolbegae.

Chun, Sang-In. 2009. *Ap'at'ŭ e mich'ida: Hyŏndae Han'guk ŭi chugŏ sahoehak* [Crazy for apartments: Residential sociology of modern Korea]. Seoul: Yisup.

Chun, Soonok. 2003. *They Are Not Machines: Korean Women Workers and Their Fight for Democratic Trade Unionism in the 1970s*. Burlington, VT: Ashgate.

Chung, Eulbyung. 1978. "Pokpuindŭl" [Mrs. Realtor]. *Wŏlgan JoongAng* (June): 292–98.

Chung, Tae-Sung. 1978. "Nugu wihan ap'atŭ kŏnsŏl in'ga" [For whom are apartments built?]. *Wŏlgan JoongAng* (May): 120–38.

Clifford, Mark L. 1998. *Troubled Tiger: Businessmen, Bureaucrats, and Generals in South Korea*. New York: M. E. Sharpe.

Cohen, Lizabeth. 2006. "The Consumers' Republic: An American Model for the World?" In *The Ambivalent Consumer: Questioning Consumption in East Asia and the West*, ed. Sheldon Garon and Patricia L. Maclachlan, 45–62. Ithaca, NY: Cornell University Press.

Cooper, Marianne. 2014. *Cut Adrift: Families in Insecure Times*. Berkeley: University of California Press.

Cumings, Bruce. 1997. *Korea's Place in the Sun: A Modern History: Increases on the Margins*. New York: W. W. Norton.

Davis, Deborah S. 1992. "Job Mobility in Post-Mao China." *China Quarterly* 132: 1062–85.

———. 2000. "Introduction: A Revolution in Consumption." In *The Consumer Revolution in Urban China*, ed. Deborah S. Davis, 1–22. Berkeley: University of California Press.

Davis, Diane E. 2004. *Discipline and Development: Middle Classes and Prosperity in East Asia and Latin America*. Cambridge: Cambridge University Press.

———. 2010. "The Sociospatial Reconfiguration of Middle Classes and Their Impact on Politics and Development in the Global South: Preliminary Ideas for Future Research." *Political Power and Social Theory* 21: 241–67.

Deyo, Frederic C. 1989. *Beneath the Miracle: Labor Subordination in the New Asian Industrialism*. Berkeley: University of California Press.

Doner, Richard F., Bryan K. Ritchie, and Dan Slater. 2005. "Systemic Vulnerability and the Origins of Developmental States: Northeast and Southeast Asia in Comparative Perspective." *International Organization* 59, no. 2: 327–61.

Economically Active Population Survey. 2013–2016. Korean Statistical Information Service.

Ehrenreich, Barbara. 1989. *Fear of Falling: The Inner Life of the Middle Class*. New York: Pantheon Books.

England, Paula. 1992. *Comparable Worth: Theories and Evidence*. Hawthorne, NY: Aldine de Gruyter.

England, Paula, and Steven McLaughlin. 1979. "Sex Segregation of Job and Male-Female Income Differentials." In *Discrimination in Organization*, ed. R. Alvarez, K. Letterman, and associates, 189–213. San Francisco: Jossey-Bass.

Evans, Peter. 1995. *Embedded Autonomy: States and Industrial Transformation*. Princeton, NJ: Princeton University Press.

Fainstein, Susan S. 1994. *City Builders: Property, Politics, and Planning in London and New York*. Oxford: Blackwell.

Fernandes, Leela. 2006. *India's New Middle Class: Democratic Politics in an Era of Economic Reform*. Minneapolis: University of Minnesota Press.

Fernandes, Leela, and Patrick Heller. 2006. "Hegemonic Aspirations: New Middle Class Politics and India's Democracy in Comparative Perspective." *Critical Asian Studies* 38, no. 4: 495–522.

Finch, John, and Seung-kyung Kim. 2012. "Globalization, Transnational Migration and Education in South Korean Kirogi Families." *Journal of Ethnic and Migration Studies* 38, no. 3: 485–506.

Foucault, Michel. 1977. *Discipline and Punish: The Birth of the Prison*. Translated by Alan Sheridan. New York: Random House.

Frank, Robert H. 2007. *Falling Behind: How Rising Inequality Harms the Middle Class*. Berkeley: University of California Press.

Freeman, Carla. 2014. *Entrepreneurial Selves: Neoliberal Respectability and the Making of a Caribbean Middle Class*. Durham, NC: Duke University Press.

Gangnam-gu. 2014. *2013 Kangnam ŭi sahoe chip'yo* [2013 social indicators of Gangnam]. Seoul: Gangnam-gu.

Garon, Sheldon. 2006. "The Transnational Promotion of Saving in Asia: 'Asian Values' or the 'Japanese Model'?" In *The Ambivalent Consumer: Questioning Consumption in East Asia and the West*, ed. Sheldon Garon and Patricia L. Maclachlan, 163–87. Ithaca, NY: Cornell University Press.

Gelézeau, Valérie. 2007. *Ap'at'ŭ konghwaguk*. Translated by Hyeyeon Gil as *The Republic of Apartments*. Seoul: Humanitas.

Giddens, Anthony. 1973. *The Class Structure of the Advanced Societies*. New York: Harper and Row.

"Gini out of the Bottle." 2013. *Economist*, January 26. http://www.economist.com/news/china/21570749-gini-out-bottle.

Go, Youngbok. 1966. "Han'guk minjokchuŭi chudogwŏn kwa lidŏsip" [The initiatives and leadership of Korean nationalism]. *Sin Donga* (December): 128–34.

Goldthorpe, John. 2008. "Two Oppositions in Studies of Class." In *Social Class: How Does It Work?*, ed. Annette Lareau and Dalton Conley, 350–53. New York: Russell Sage Foundation.

Gong, Je-Wook. 1989. "1950-nyŏndae Han'guk sahoe ŭi kyegŭp kusŏng" [Class structures in 1950s Korea]. *Kyŏngje wa Sahoe* 3: 227–63.

Goodman, David S. G., ed. 2008. *The New Rich in China: Future Rulers, Present Lives*. London: Routledge.

Gorski, Philip S. 1993. "The Protestant Ethic Revisited: Disciplinary Revolution and State Formation in Holland and Prussia." *American Journal of Sociology* 99, no. 2: 265–316.

———. 2003. *The Disciplinary Revolution: Calvinism and the Rise of the State in Early Modern Europe*. Chicago: University of Chicago Press.

Haggard, Stephan, and Chung-in Moon. 1993. "The State, Politics, and Economic Development in Postwar South Korea." In *State and Society in Contemporary Korea*, ed. Hagen Koo, 51–93. Ithaca, NY: Cornell University Press.

Han, Soo-san. 1982. "Mun" [Door]. *Hyŏndae Munhak* 28, no. 6: 84–99.

Han, Wansang, Taehwan Kwon, and Dooseung Hong. 1987. *Han'guk ŭi chungsanch'ŭng: Chŏnhwan'gi ŭi Han'guk sahoe chosa charyojip* [Korea's middle class: A survey of its transitional period in Korean society]. Seoul: Hankook Ilbosa.

Harvey, David. 1985. *The Urbanization of Capital*. Baltimore, MD: Johns Hopkins University Press.

He, Qinglian. 2003. "A Volcanic Stability." *Journal of Democracy* 14: 66–72.

Heiman, Rachel, Carla Freeman, and Mark Liechty, eds. 2012. *The Global Middle Classes: Theorizing through Ethnography*. Santa Fe, NM: School for Advanced Research Press.

Heiman, Rachel, Carla Freeman, and Mark Liechty. 2012. "Introduction: Charting an Anthropology of the Middle Classes." In *The Global Middle Classes: Theorizing through Ethnography*, ed. Rachel Heiman, Carla Freeman, and Mark Liechty, 3–29. Santa Fe, NM: School for Advanced Research Press.

Heo, Eun. 2007. "1960-nyŏndae huban 'choguk kŭndaehwa' ideollogi chujo wa tamdang chisigin ŭi insik" [The production of ideology of "Modernization of the Fatherland" and recognition of the intellectuals in the late 1960s]. *Yŏksa Yŏn'gu* 86: 247–91.

Hirschman, Albert. 1970. *Exit, Voice, and Loyalty: Responses to Decline in Firms, Organizations, and States*. Cambridge, MA: Harvard University Press.

Hochschild, Arlie R. 2016. *Strangers in Their Own Land: Anger and Mourning on the American Right*. New York: New Press.

Hong, Doo-Seung. 1983. "Chigŏp punsŏk ŭl t'onghan kyech'ŭng yŏn'gu: Han'guk p'yojun chigŏp pullyu rŭl chungsim ŭro" [Studying social classes through an occupational analysis]. *Sahoe Kwahak kwa Chŏngch'aek Yŏn'gu* 5, no. 3: 69–87.

———. 2005. *Han'guk ŭi chungsanch'ŭng* [The Korean middle class]. Seoul: SNU Press.

Hsiao, Hsin-Huang M. 2006. "Prioritizing the Middle Classes: Research in Asia-Pacific." In *The Changing Faces of the Middle Classes in Asia-Pacific*, ed. Hsin-Huang M. Hsiao, 3–8. Taipei: Center for Asia-Pacific Area Studies.

Hsiao, Hsin-Huang Michael, ed. 1993. *Discovery of the Middle Classes in East Asia*. Taipei: Academia Sinica.

Huntington, Samuel P. 1968. *Political Order in Changing Societies*. New Haven, CT: Yale University Press.

Hyun, Youngjin. 1978. "Ap'at'ŭ rŭl wŏn'ga kyesan handa" [Calculating the production costs of apartments]. *Wŏlgan JoongAng* (May): 140–48.

Hyundai Research Institute. 2007. "Sagyoyuk, nohu puran ŭi chudoen yoin" [Private education, the major cause of anxious old age: Survey on private education and estimation of the private education market]. *Weekly Economic Review* 246: 1–16. Seoul: Hyundai Research Institute.

———. 2011. "Han'guk chungsanch'ŭng ŭi kujojŏk pyŏnhwa: 1990-nyŏn ihu sodŭk mit sobi kujo ŭi pyŏnhwa" [The structural changes in the Korean middle class: The changes in income and consumption from 1990]. *Weekly Economic Review* 457: 1–19. Seoul: Hyundai Research Institute.

Jaffrelot, Christophe, and Peter van der Veer. 2008. *Patterns of Middle Class Consumption in India and China*. Thousand Oaks, CA: Sage Publications.

Jung, Hee-nam. 1998. "Land Prices and Land Market in Korea, 1963–1996: Explanations from Political Economy Perspectives." *Korean Spatial Planning Review* 27: 127–46.

Jung, Jae-Young. 1988. "Taehan Min'guk kyoyuk t'ŭkku Sŏul 8-hakkun" [The privileged educational district in Korea: District Eight in Seoul]. *Sin Donga* (March): 542–55.

Jung, Minwoo. 2017. "Precarious Seoul: Urban Inequality and Belonging of Young Adults in South Korea." *Positions: Asia Critique* 25, no. 4.

Kalleberg, Arne L. 2009. "Precarious Work, Insecure Workers: Employment Relations in Transition." *American Sociological Review* 74, no. 1: 1–22.

Kang, David C. 2002. *Crony Capitalism: Corruption and Development in South Korea and the Philippines*. Cambridge: Cambridge University Press.

Kang, Junman. 2006. *Kangnam, natsŏn Taehan Min'guk ŭi chahwasang* [Gangnam, an unfamiliar self-portrait of Korea]. Seoul: Inmul kwa Sasangsa.

Kang, Naehui. 2004. "Kangnam ŭi kyegŭp kwa munhwa" [Social Class and Culture in Gangnam]. *Hwanghae Munhwa* 42, no. 3: 62–84.

Kang, Yoon-Kyung. 2013. "Taehyŏngmat'ŭ 20 nyŏn pit kwa kŭrimja" [Twenty years of super hypermarkets: Light and shadow]. *Wŏlgan Maidas* (December). http://www.yonhapmidas.com/print/131214142648_903846.

Katznelson, Ira. 1986. "Working-Class Formation: Constructing Cases and Comparisons." In *Working-Class Formation: Nineteenth-Century Patterns in Western Europe and the United States*, ed. Ira Katznelson and Aristide R. Zolberg, 3–41. Princeton, NJ: Princeton University Press.

KB Research Institute. 2012. "Kaein saŏpcha ch'angp'yeŏp t'ŭksŏng mit hyŏnhwang punsŏk" [An analysis of opening and closure of small businesses]. *KB Kyŏngyŏng Chŏngbo Report* 12. Seoul: KB Research Institute.

Kendall, Laurel. 1996. *Getting Married in Korea: Of Gender, Morality, and Modernity.* Berkeley: University of California Press.

Kim, Bohyun. 2006. *Park Chung Hee chŏnggwŏn'gi kyŏngje kaebal: Minjokchuŭi wa paljŏn* [Economic Development during the Park Chung Hee Regime: Nationalism and Development]. Seoul: Kalmuri.

Kim, Chaeyoon. 1966. "Kŭndaehwa wa chungsanch'ŭng: Sahoehakchŏk koch'al" [Modernization and the middle class: The sociological perspective]. *Chosun Ilbo,* January 28.

Kim, Dae Jung. 1971 [1986]. *Taejung kyŏngjeron* [Theory of Popular Economy]. Seoul: Chungsa.

Kim, Eunmee. 1997. *Big Business, Strong State: Collusion and Conflict in South Korean Development, 1960–1990.* Albany: State University of New York Press.

Kim, GiSeung, and Joonmo Cho. 2009. "Entry Dynamics of Self-Employment in South Korea." *Entrepreneurship and Regional Development* 21, no. 3: 303–23.

Kim, Hyun. 1978. "Algoboni ap'at'ŭ nŭn saldega anidŏra" [An apartment is not a livable place]. *Ppuri Kip'ŭn Namu* (September): 54–59.

Kim, Hyung-A. 2004. *Korea's Development under Park Chung Hee: Rapid Industrialization, 1961–1979.* London: RoutledgeCurzon.

Kim, Hyung-Guk. 1989. *Tosi sidae ŭi Han'guk munhwa* [Korean culture of the urban era]. Seoul: Nanam.

———. 2004. "Kangnam ŭi t'ansaeng" [The birth of Gangnam]. *Hwanghae Munhwa* 42, no. 3: 10–24.

Kim, Jinman. 1963. "Ap'at'ŭmŏnt'ŭ wa tip'at'ŭmŏnt'ŭ" [Apartments and departments]. *Sedae* (September): 58–63.

Kim, Joo-Chul, and Sang-Chuel Choe. 1997. *Seoul: The Making of a Metropolis.* New York: John Wiley and Sons.

Kim, Kyong-Dong. 1993. "Studies on the Middle Class in Korea: Some Theoretical and Methodological Considerations." In *Discovery of the Middle Classes in East Asia,* ed. Hsin-Shuang Michael Hsiao, 23–54. Taipei: Academia Sinica.

Kim, Nak-nyun. 2015. "Han'guk ŭi sodŭk pulp'yŏngdŭng" [Income inequality in Korea]. In *Pulp'yŏngdŭng Han'guk, pokchigukka rŭl kkumgguda* [Unequal Korea, hoping for a welfare state], ed. Jung-Woo Lee and Chang-Gon Lee, 137–48. Seoul: Humanitas.

Kim, Ok-Seok. 1967. "Ap'at'ŭ saenghwal i ŏddŏseyo" [What is living in apartments like?]. *Sedae* (November): 238–43.

Kim, Seung-Kyung. 1997. *Class Struggle or Family Struggle? Lives of Women Factory Workers in South Korea.* Cambridge: Cambridge University Press.

Kim, To-Il. 2014. "Peibibum sedae, chayŏngŏp ttuiŏ dŭrŏddaga pit tŏmi" [Baby-boomers saddled with huge debts after self-employment]. *Yonhap News.* May 26. http://www.yonhapnews.co.kr/bulletin/2014/05/24/0200000000AKR20140524038200002.HTML.

Kim, Yerim. 2007. "1960-nyŏndae chunghuban kaebal naesyonallijŭm kwa chungsanch'ŭng kajŏng p'ant'aji ŭi munhwa chŏngch'ihak" [The cultural politics of developmental nationalism and fantasy of middle-class families in the mid- and late 1960s]. *Hyŏndae Munhak ŭi Yŏn'gu* 32: 339–75.

Kim, Young-Mi. 2009. *Kŭdŭl ŭi Saemaŭlundong: Han maŭl kwa han nongch'onundong'ga rŭl t'onghae pon minjungdŭl ŭi Saemaŭlundong iyagi* [Their New Village Movement:

A story of people's New Village Movement through one village and one rural activist]. Seoul: P'urŭn Yŏksa.

Kim, Yu-Sun. 2004. *Nodong sijang yuyŏnhwa wa pijŏngkyujik koyong* [Flexibilization of the labor market and the employment of irregular workers]. Seoul: Han'guk Nodong Sahoe Yŏn'guso.

———. 2015. "Han'guk ŭi imgŭm pulp'yŏngdŭng" [Income inequality in Korea]. In *Pulp'yŏngdŭng Han'guk, pokchi kukka rŭl kkumgguda* [Unequal Korea, hoping for a welfare state], ed. Jeong-Woo Lee and Changgon Lee, 149–62. Seoul: Humanitas.

Kohli, Atul. 2004. *State-Directed Development: Political Power and Industrialization in the Global Periphery*. Cambridge: Cambridge University Press.

———. 2009. "Nationalist versus Dependent Capitalist Development: Alternate Pathways of Asia and Latin America in a Globalized World." *Studies in Comparative International Development* 44, no. 4: 386–410.

Koo, Hagen. 1991. "Middle Classes, Democratization, and Class Formation: The Case of South Korea." *Theory and Society* 20, no. 4: 485–509.

———. 1993. "The State, *Minjung*, and the Working Class in South Korea." In *State and Society in Contemporary Korea*, ed. Hagen Koo, 131–62. Ithaca, NY: Cornell University Press.

———. 2001. *Korean Workers: The Culture and Politics of Class Formation*. Ithaca, NY: Cornell University Press.

———. 2007. "The Changing Faces of Inequality in South Korea in the Age of Globalization." *Korean Studies* 31: 1–18.

———. 2012. "Han'guk ŭi chungsanch'ŭng ŭl tasi saenggak handa" [Reconsidering the Korean middle class]. *Ch'angjak kwa Pip'yŏng* [Creation and Criticism] 40, no. 1: 403–21.

———. 2016. "The Global Middle Class: How Is It Made, What Does It Represent?" *Globalizations* 13, no. 4: 440–53.

Korean Housing Corporation. 1992. *Taehan Chut'aek Kongsa 30-nyŏnsa* [Thirty years of history of the Korean Housing Corporation]. Seoul: Korean Housing Corporation.

Korean National Statistics Office. 1993, 1995. *T'onggyero pon Han'guk ŭi paljach'wi* [Looking at Korea's changes through statistical numbers]. Daejon: Korean Statistical Office.

———. 1998. *T'onggyero pon Taehan Min'guk 50nyŏn ŭi kyŏngjesahoesang pyŏnhwa* [The socioeconomic changes during the fifty years of Korea through statistical numbers]. Daejon: Korean National Statistics Office.

———. 2011–2014. *2011–2014 sahoe chosa* [2011–2014 social survey]. Daejon: Korean National Statistics Office.

———. 2015. *2014 Sagyoyukpi chosa kyŏlgwa* [2014 survey results of spending on private education]. Daejon: Korean National Statistics Office.

Kum, Jae-Ho, Gi-Seung Kim, Dong-Hoon Cho, and Jun-Mo Cho. 2009. *Chayŏngŏp nodongsijang yŏn'gu: Chayŏngŏp ŭi pyŏnhwa ch'ui wa t'ŭksŏng* [A Study of the Self-Employed Labor Market: Trends in Changes and Characteristics of Self-Employment]. Seoul: Korea Labor Institute.

Kyŏngje Kihoegwŏn. 1970–1985. *Ch'ong in'gu mit chut'aek chosa pogo* [Korean population and housing census report]. Seoul: Kyŏngje Kihoegwŏn.

Lee, Ching Kwan. 2007. *Against the Law: Labor Protests in China's Rustbelt and Sunbelt*. Berkeley: University of California Press.

Lee, Jeong-Woo. 2015. "Han'guk ŭn wae salgi ŏryŏun nara in'ga?" [Why is it so difficult to live in Korea?]. In *Pulp'yŏngdŭng Han'guk, pokchi kukka rŭl kkumgguda* [Unequal Korea, hoping for a welfare state], ed. Jeong-Woo Lee and Chang-Gon Lee, 39–54. Seoul: Humanitas.

Lee, Jongsu. 1967. "Hyŏndae samsin'gi ŭi yongmang" [Desires for three modern sacred treasures]. *Sedae* (July): 129–31.

Lee, Moon-Jae, and Min-Soo Oh. 1992. "Yongmang ŭi 'haebang'gu' Apkujŏng" [Haven for desires, Apgujeong]. *Sisa Journal* (January 16): 22–25.

Lee, Namhee. 2007. *The Making of Minjung: Democracy and the Politics of Representation in South Korea*. Ithaca, NY: Cornell University Press.

Lee, Taesu. 2015. "Pokchi nŭn wae pulp'yŏngdŭng wanhwa e kiyŏhaji mot'aenna" [Why welfare did not contribute to reducing social inequality]. In *Pulp'yŏngdŭng Han'guk, pokchi kukka rŭl kkumgguda* [Unequal Korea, hoping for a welfare state], ed. Jeong-Woo Lee and Chang-Gon Lee, 39–54. Seoul: Humanitas.

Lee, Yean-Ju, and Hagen Koo. 2006. "'Wild Geese Fathers' and a Globalised Family Strategy for Education in Korea." *International Review of Development and Planning* 28, no. 4: 533–53.

Lee, Yoonkyung. 2015. "Labor after Neoliberalism: The Birth of the Insecure Class in South Korea." *Globalizations* 12, no. 2: 184–202.

Lefebvre, Henri. [1970] 2003. *The Urban Revolution*. Translated by Robert Bononno. Minneapolis: University of Minnesota Press.

———. 1991. *The Production of Space*. Translated by Donald Nicholson-Smith. Malden, MA: Blackwell.

Lett, Denise Potrzeba. 1998. *In Pursuit of Status: The Making of South Korea's "New" Urban Middle Class*. Cambridge, MA: Harvard University Asia Center.

Li, Cheng, ed. 2010. *China's Emerging Middle Class: Beyond Economic Transformation*. Washington, DC: Brookings Institution Press.

Lie, John. 1998. *Han Unbound: The Political Economy of South Korea*. Stanford, CA: Stanford University Press.

Liechty, Mark. 2003. *Suitably Modern: Making Middle-Class Culture in a New Consumer Society*. Princeton, NJ: Princeton University Press.

Lim, Banghyun. 1973. *Kŭndaehwa wa chisigin* [Modernization and intellectuals]. Seoul: Chisik Sanŏpsa.

Lim, Bonggil. 1992. "Tosi chungsanch'ŭng ŭi saenghwal yuhyŏng kwa chŏngch'i ŭisik" [Lifestyles and political consciousness of the urban middle class]. In *Tosi chungsanch'ŭng ŭi saenghwal munhwa* [Urban middle class lifestyles], ed. Okpyo Mun, 105–41. Seongnam: Academy of Korean Studies.

Lim, Dong-Geun, and Jong-Bae Kim. 2015. *Met'ŭrop'ollisŭ Sŏul ŭi t'ansaeng* [The birth of metropolis Seoul]. Seoul: Panbi.

Lipset, Seymour Martin. 1959. "Some Social Requisites of Democracy: Economic Development and Political Legitimacy." *American Political Science Review* 53, no. 1: 69–105.

López, A. Ricardo, and Barbara Weinstein, eds. 2012. *The Making of the Middle Class: Toward a Transnational History*. Durham, NC: Duke University Press.

Luebbert, Gregory. 1991. *Liberalism, Fascism, or Social Democracy: Social Classes and the Political Origins of Regimes in Interwar Europe*. New York: Oxford University Press.

Lust, Ellen. 2011. "Why Now? Micro Transitions and the Arab Uprisings." *Comparative Democratization* 9, no. 3: 1–8.

Madden, David, and Peter Marcuse. 2016. *In Defense of Housing: The Politics of Crisis*. London: Verso.

Marx, Karl. 1978. "Manifesto of the Communist Party." In *The Marx-Engels Reader*, ed. Robert C. Tucker, 469–500. New York: W. W. Norton.

Massey, Douglas S., and Nancy A. Denton. 1993. *American Apartheid: Segregation and the Making of the Underclass*. Cambridge, MA: Harvard University Press.

Mazzarella, William. 2004. "Middle Class." https://www.soas.ac.uk/south-asia-institute /keywords/file24808.pdf.

Minju Konghwadang. 1978. *1986 sŏnjin Han'guk* [1986 advanced Korea]. Seoul: Minju Konghwadang Committee of Policy Making.

Moon, Okpyo. 1990. "Urban Middle Class Wives in Contemporary Korea: Their Roles, Responsibilities and Dilemma." *Korea Journal* 30: 30–43.

———, ed. 1992. *Tosi chungsanch'ŭng ŭi saenghwal munhwa* [Urban middle-class lifestyles]. Seongnam: Academy of Korean Studies.

Moon, Seungsook. 2005. *Militarized Modernity and Gendered Citizenship in South Korea*. Durham, NC: Duke University Press.

Moon, Sukjae. 2000. *Han'guk chungsanch'ŭng ŭi saenghwal munhwa* [The Korean middle-class lifestyles]. Seoul: Jimmundang.

Mudde, Cas. 2007. *Populist Radical Right Parties in Europe*. Cambridge: Cambridge University Press.

Neitzel, Laura. 2016. *"The Life We Longed For": Danchi Housing and the Middle Class Dream in Postwar Japan*. Portland, ME: Merwinasia.

Nelson, Laura C. 2000. *Measured Excess: Status, Gender, and Consumer Nationalism in South Korea*. New York: Columbia University Press.

Newman, Katherine S. [1988] 1999. *Fall from Grace: Downward Mobility in the Age of Affluence*. Berkeley: University of California Press.

———. 2012. *The Accordion Family: Boomerang Kids, Anxious Parents, and the Private Toll of Global Competition*. Boston: Beacon Press.

Ngai, Pun, and Chris King-Chi Chan. 2008. "The Subsumption of Class Discourse in China." *Boundary* 35, no. 2: 75–91.

Nijman, Jan. 2000. "Mumbai's Real Estate Market in the 1990s: Deregulation, Global Money and Casino Capitalism." *Economic and Political Weekly* 35, no. 7: 575–82.

OECD. 2011. *Divided We Stand: Why Inequality Keeps Rising*. OECD Publishing. http://www.oecd.org/els/soc/49564983.pdf.

———. 2016. "Self-Employment Rate (Indicator)." https://data.oecd.org/emp/self -employment-rate.htm.

Oh, Woncheol. 1999. *Han'gukhyŏng kyŏngje kŏnsŏl: Enjiniŏring ŏp'ŭroch'i* [A Korean way of economy building: An engineering approach]. Vol. 7. Seoul: Han'gukhyŏng Kyŏngje Kŏnsŏl Yŏn'guso.

Ong, Aihwa, and Li Zhang. 2008. "Introduction: Privatizing China; Powers of the Self, Socialism from Afar." In *Privatizing China: Socialism from Afar*, ed. Li Zhang and Aihwa Ong, 1–19. Ithaca, NY: Cornell University Press.

Parish, William L. 1984. "Destratification in China." In *Class and Social Stratification in Post-Revolution China*, ed. James L. Watson, 84–120. Cambridge: Cambridge University Press.

Park, Bae Gyoon. 1998. "Where Do Tigers Sleep at Night? The State's Role in Housing Policy in South Korea and Singapore." *Economic Geography* 74, no. 3: 272–88.

Park, Chul-Soo. 2006. *Ap'at'ŭ munhwasa* [A cultural history of apartments]. Seoul: Salim.

Park, Chung Hee. [1962] 1970. *The Country, the Revolution and I*. Seoul: Hallym.

———. 1973a. *Pak Chung Hi taet'ongnyŏng yŏnsŏl munjip* 2 [President Park Chung Hee's speeches. Vol. 2]. Seoul: Office of the Presidential Secretary.

———. 1973b. *Pak Chung Hi taet'ongnyŏng yŏnsŏl munjip* 3 [President Park Chung Hee's speeches. Vol. 3]. Seoul: Office of the Presidential Secretary.

Park, Hae-Chun. 2013. *Ap'at'ŭ keim: Kŭdŭl i chungsanch'ŭng i toel su issŏddŏn iyu* [Apartment game: The reason they could be middle class]. Seoul: Humanist.

Park, So-Jin. 2009. "'Chagi kwalli wa 'kajok kyŏngyŏng' sidae ŭi puranhan sam: Sinjayujuŭi wa sinjayujuŭijŏk chuch'e" [Anxious lives in the period of "self-management" and "family management": Neoliberalism and neoliberal subjectivity]. *Kyŏngje wa Sahoe* 84 (Winter): 12–39.

Park, So-Jin, and Nancy Abelmann. 2004. "Class and Cosmopolitan Striving: Mothers' Management of English Education in South Korea." *Anthropological Quarterly* 77, no. 4: 645–72.

Park, Wan-Seo. 1989. *Sŏul saramdŭl* [Seoulites]. In *Kŭdae ajikto kkumkkugo innŭn'ga* [Are you still dreaming?], 169–264. Seoul: Samjin.

Parkin, Frank. 1971. *Class Inequality and Political Order*. New York: Praeger.

Piketty, Thomas. 2014. *Capital in the Twenty-First Century*. Translated by Arthur Goldhammer. Cambridge, MA: Belknap Press of Harvard University Press.

Polanyi, Karl. [1944] 1957. *The Great Transformation: The Political and Economic Origins of Our Time*. Boston: Beacon Press.

Portes, Alejandro, and Kelly Hoffman. 2003. "Latin American Class Structures: Their Composition and Change during the Neoliberal Era." *Latin American Research Review* 38, no. 1: 41–82.

Pow, Choon-Piew. 2007. "Securing the 'Civilized' Enclaves: Gated Communities and the Moral Geographies of Exclusion in (Post-)Socialist Shanghai." *Urban Studies* 44, no. 8: 1539–58.

Radhakrishnan, Smitha. 2007. "Rethinking 'Knowledge for Development': 'Global' Indian Knowledge Workers and the 'New' India." *Theory and Society* 36, no. 2: 141–60.

Ren, Hai. 2013. *The Middle Class in Neoliberal China: Governing Risk, Life-Building, and Themed Spaces*. London: Routledge.

Robison, Richard, and David S. G. Goodman. 1996. "The New Rich in Asia: Economic Development, Social Status, and Political Consciousness." In *The New Rich in Asia: Mobile Phones, McDonald's, and Middle-Class Revolution*, ed. David S. G. Goodman and Richard Robison, 1–18. London: Routledge.

Rostow, Walt W. 1960. *The Stages of Economic Growth: A Non-Communist Manifesto.* Cambridge, MA: Cambridge University Press.

Rueschemeyer, Dietrich, Evelyne H. Stephens, and John D. Stephens. 1992. *Capitalist Development and Democracy.* Chicago: University of Chicago Press.

Rydgren, Jens. 2007. "The Sociology of the Radical Right." *Annual Review of Sociology* 33: 241–62.

"Saenghwalmunhwa ŏmnŭn Han'guk: Munhwajŏk hyŏnsil kwa chŏngch'ijŏk hyŏnsil" [Korea without living culture: realities in culture and politics]. *Sasanggye* (May 1965): 194–215.

Savage, Mike, James Barlow, Peter Dickens, and Tony Fielding. 1992. *Property, Bureaucracy and Culture: Middle-Class Formation in Contemporary Britain.* London: Routledge.

Seoul Metropolitan Office. 1983. *Housing Construction of Seoul.* Seoul: Seoul Metropolitan Office.

———. 1996. *Sŏul yukpaengnyŏnsa 6: 1961–1979* [Six hundred years of the history of Seoul]. Seoul: Seoul Metropolitan Office.

———. 2012. *Sadaemun an hakkyo dŭl Kangnam ŭro kada* [Schools within the Four Big Gates Have Moved to Gangnam]. Seoul: Seoul Metropolitan Office.

Seoul Museum of History. 2011. *Kangnam sasimnyŏn 1, Yŏngdong eso* [Forty Years of Gangnam: From Yeongdong]. Seoul: Seoul Museum of History.

Shatkin, Gavin. 2014. "Reinterpreting the Meaning of the 'Singapore Model': State Capitalism and Urban Planning." *International Journal of Urban and Regional Research* 38, no. 1: 116–37.

Shin, Bum Shik. 1970. *Major Speeches by Korea's Park Chung Hee.* Seoul: Hallym.

Shin, Hyun Bang, and Soo-Hyun Kim. 2016. "The Developmental State, Speculative Urbanisation and the Politics of Displacement in Gentrifying Seoul." *Urban Studies* 53, no. 3: 540–59.

Shin, Jong-Su. 1976. "Sinhŭng 'ap'at'ŭ' chaebŏl" [New Apartment Chaebols]. *Wŏlgan JoongAng* (July): 226–37.

Shin, Kwang-Yeong. 2004. *Han'guk ŭi kyegŭp kwa pulp'yŏngdŭng* [Social Classes and Inequality in Korea]. Seoul: Ŭlyu Munhwasa.

———. 2013. "Economic Crisis, Neoliberal Reforms, and the Rise of Precarious Work in South Korea." *American Behavioral Scientist* 57, no. 3: 335–53.

———. 2015. "Chungsanch'ŭng wigi" [The Middle Class in Crisis]. In *Pulp'yŏndŭng Han'guk, pokchi kukka rŭl kkumgguda* [Unequal Korea, Hoping for a Welfare State], ed. Jeong-Woo Lee and Chang-Gon Lee, 55–68. Seoul: Humanitas.

Small and Medium Business Administration and Small Enterprise Development Agency. 2013. *2013 nyŏn chŏn'guk sosanggong'in silt'ae chosa pogosŏ* [2013 Survey of Conditions of Small Enterprises in Korea]. Daejun: Small Enterprise Development Agency.

Smith, Neil. 2002. "New Globalism, New Urbanism: Gentrification as Global Urban Strategy." *Antipode: A Radical Journal of Geography* 34, no. 3: 427–50.

So, Hyunsuk. 2006. "'Kŭndae' ŭi yŏlmang kwa ilsang saenghwal ŭi singminhwa" [Aspirations to Modernity and Colonization of Everyday Life]. In *Ilsangsa ro ponŭn Han'guk kŭn-hyŏndaesa: Han'guk kwa Togil ilsangsa ŭi saeroun mannam* [Modern Korean History through Everyday Life: The New Encounter between Korean and German Micro-Histories], ed. Sangrok Lee and Woojae Lee, 120–73. Seoul: Ch'aek kwa Hamgge.

Son, Jung-Mok. 2003. "Namgigo sip'ŭn iyagi tŭl: Han'gang kaebal kyehoek" [The stories that I want to remember: Development plans for the Han River]. *JoongAng Ilbo*. September 22.

———. 2005. *Han'guk tosi 60-nyŏn ŭi iyagi* [Sixty years of Korean cities]. Seoul: Hanul.

Son, Nak-Gu. 2008. *Pudongsan kyegŭp sahoe* [Real Estate Class Society]. Seoul: Humanitas.

Song, Ho-Keun, and Kyung-Zoon Hong. 2008. "Globalization and Social Policy in South Korea." In *Globalization and the Future of the Welfare State*, ed. M. Glatzer and D. Rueschemeyer, 179–202. Pittsburgh: University of Pittsburgh Press.

Standing, Guy. 2011. *The Precariat: The New Dangerous Class*. London: Bloomsbury Academic.

Suh, Byung-Wook. 1983. "Ap'at'ŭ nŭn t'ugijangt'ŏ in'ga" [Is an apartment a site of speculation?]. *Wŏlgan Chosun* (March): 340–63.

Suh, Kwanmo. 1987. "Han'guk sahoe kyegŭp kusŏng ŭi yŏn'gu" [A Study of Class Structure in Korea]. PhD diss., Seoul National University.

Sullivan, Teresa A., Elizabeth Warren, and Jay Lawrence Westbrook. 2000. *The Fragile Middle Class: Americans in Debt*. New Haven, CT: Yale University Press.

Supreme Council for National Reconstruction. 1961. *Military Revolution in Korea*. Seoul: Supreme Council for National Reconstruction.

Teichman, Judith A. 2012. *Social Forces and States: Poverty and Distributional Outcomes in South Korea, Chile, and Mexico*. Stanford, CA: Stanford University Press.

Therborn, Göran. 2012. "Class in the 21st Century." *New Left Review* 78 (November–December): 5–29.

Thompson, E. P. 1966a. *The Making of the English Working Class*. New York: Vantage Books.

———. 1966b. "The Peculiarities of the English." In *Socialist Register 1965*, ed. Ralph Miliband and John Saville, 311–62. London: Merlin Press.

Tilly, Charles. 1998. *Durable Inequality*. Cambridge: Cambridge University Press.

Tomba, Luigi. 2004. "Creating an Urban Middle Class: Social Engineering in Beijing." *China Journal* 51: 1–26.

———. 2009. "Of Quality, Harmony, and Community: Civilization and the Middle Class in Urban China." *Positions: Asia Critique* 17, no. 3: 591–616.

United Nations, Department of Economic and Social Affairs. 1962. "Industrialization for Economic Development in the Under-Developed Countries." In *World Economic Survey 1961*. New York: United Nations.

Villegas, Celso, and Myungji Yang. 2013. "Making Narratives of Revolution: Democratic Transition and the Language of Middle-Class Identity in the Philippines and South Korea, 1970s–1987." *Critical Asian Studies* 45, no. 3: 335–64.

Vogel, Ezra F. 1963. *Japan's New Middle Class: The Salary Man and His Family in a Tokyo Suburb*. Berkeley: University of California Press.

Wacquant, Loïc J. D. 1991. "Making Class: The Middle Class(es) in Social Theory and Social Structure." In *Bringing Class Back In: Contemporary and Historical Perspectives*, ed. Scott G. McNall, Rhonda F. Levine, and Rick Fantasia, 39–64. Boulder, CO: Westview Press.

Walder, Andrew. 1986. *Communist Neo-Traditionalism: Work and Authority in Chinese Industry.* Berkeley: University of California Press.

Waldner, David. 1999. *State Building and Late Development.* Ithaca, NY: Cornell University Press.

Weber, Max. [1930] 2001. *The Protestant Ethic and the Spirit of Capitalism.* London: Taylor and Francis.

Weeden, Kim A., and David B. Grusky. 2005. "The Case for a New Class Map." *American Journal of Sociology* 111, no. 1: 141–212.

Williams, Raymond. 1983. *Keywords: A Vocabulary of Culture and Society.* New York: Oxford University Press.

Won, Jaeyoun. 2005. "The Making of Post-Proletariat in China." *Development and Society* 34, no. 2: 191–216.

Woo, Sukhoon, and Park Kwon-il. 2007. *P'alsip p'al-manwŏn sidae: Chŏlmang ŭi sidae e ssŭnŭn hŭimang ŭi kyŏngjehak* [The 880,000 Won Generation: Hopeful Economics in the Era of Despair]. Seoul: Redian Media.

Woo-Cumings, Meredith, ed. 1999. *The Developmental State.* Ithaca, NY: Cornell University Press.

World Development Indicators. 1980–1989. The World Bank

Wright, Erik Olin. 1985. *Classes.* London: Verso.

———. 2008. "Logics of Class Analysis." In *Social Class: How Does It Work?*, ed. Annette Lareau and Dalton Conley, 329–49. New York: Russell Sage Foundation.

Yang, Myungji. 2012. "The Making of the Urban Middle Class in South Korea: Nation-Building, Discipline, and the Birth of Ideal National Subjects." *Sociological Inquiry* 82, no. 3: 424–45.

Yates, Alexia. 2012. "Selling Paris: The Real Estate Market and Commercial Culture in the Fin-de-siècle Capital." *Enterprise and Society* 13, no. 4: 773–89.

Yoshimi, Shunya. 2006. "Consuming America, Producing Japan." In *The Ambivalent Consumer: Questioning Consumption in East Asia and the West*, ed. Sheldon Garon and Patricia L. Maclachlan, 63–84. Ithaca, NY: Cornell University Press.

Young, Louise. 1999. "Marketing the Modern: Department Stores, Consumer Culture, and the New Middle Class in Interwar Japan." *International Labor and Working-Class History* 55: 52–70.

Yu, Ha. 1991. *Param punŭn nal imyŏn Apkujŏng-dong e kaya handa: Yu Ha sijip* [We have to go to Apgujeong-dong when it is a windy day]. Seoul: Munhak kwa Chisŏngsa.

Yuen, Belinda. 2009. "Reinventing Highrise Housing in Singapore." *Cityscape: A Journal of Policy Development and Research* 11, no. 1: 3–18.

Yun, Ji-Whan. 2011. "Unbalanced Development: The Origin of Korea's Self-Employment Problem from a Comparative Perspective." *Journal of Development Studies* 47, no. 5: 786–803.

Zhang, Li. 2010. *In Search of Paradise: Middle-Class Living in a Chinese Metropolis.* Ithaca, NY: Cornell University Press.

Zunz, Oliver, Leonard Schoppa, and Nobuhiro Hiwatari, eds. 2002. *Social Contracts under Stress: The Middle Classes of America, Europe, and Japan at the Turn of the Century.* New York: Russell Sage Foundation.

Index

CPSIA information can be obtained
at www.ICGtesting.com
Printed in the USA
LVHW091542310721
694233LV00010B/338/J

9 781501 710735